STUDY GUIDE FOR

A Biography ★ of AMERICA

Produced by  Boston

Funded by  Annenberg/CPB

HOUGHTON MIFFLIN

Sponsoring Editor: Jeffrey Greene
Associate Editor: Leah Strauss
Contributing Editor: Margaret Manos
Senior Manufacturing Coordinator: Sally Culler
Senior Marketing Manager: Sandra McGuire

This guide was written for use with *A Biography of America*, a college-level American history series and telecourse. The telecourse consists of 26 half-hour video programs, a textbook, a study guide, a faculty guide, a high school guide, and a Web site.

A Biography of America is a production of WGBH Boston, in cooperation with the Library of Congress, the National Archives and Records Administration, and the National Council for Social Studies. Selected images from the American History CD-ROM by Instructional Resource Corporation (http://www.historypictures.com).

Funding for *A Biography of America* is provided by Annenberg/CPB. Annenberg/CPB, a partnership between the Annenberg Foundation and the Corporation for Public Broadcasting, uses media and telecommunications to advance excellent teaching in American schools. Annenberg/CPB funds educational series and teacher professional development workshops for the Annenberg/CPB Channel. The Channel is distributed free by satellite to schools and to other educational and community organizations nationwide.

The notable series, workshops and activities of Annenberg/CPB include A Biography of America, Destinos, Exploring the World of Music, French in Action, Journey North, The Mechanical Universe, The Private Universe Project, the Teaching Math Libraries, and The Western Tradition.

For more information about *A Biography of America*, call 1-800-LEARNER or visit www.learner.org.

Printed in the U. S. A.

ISBN: 0-618-114904

123456789-B+B-04 03 02 01 00

STUDY GUIDE

A Biography of America

Volume 2

Rick Moniz
Chabot College

This guide was written for use with *A Biography of America*, a college-level American history telecourse that includes the textbook *A People and a Nation*, Sixth Edition by Norton, et al., published by Houghton Mifflin Company.

A Biography of America is a production of WGBH Boston, in cooperation with the Library of Congress, the National Archives and Records Administration, and the National Council for Social Studies.

Funding for *A Biography of America* is provided by the Annenberg/CPB.

Contents

Course Overview

A Biography of America, a telecourse and video series produced by WGBH Boston and funded by Annenberg/CPB, presents history not as simply a series of irrefutable facts for students to memorize, but as a living narrative. In this 26-part series, prominent historians present America's story as something that must be presented and debated from a variety of perspectives in order to be truly understood. Their thought-provoking debates and lectures—using first-person narratives, photos, film footage, and documents—will pique students' interest and encourage them to think critically about the forces that have shaped America. Students will see the human side of American history—how historical figures affected events and the impact of these events on citizens' lives.

An extensive array of visual images and footage from WGBH Boston, the National Archives, and the Library of Congress enhances the biographical and narrative approach of the series, allowing students to get an intimate look at the people and places they are studying. Featuring a master teacher as the pedagogical focus, the format presents a single lead scholar delivering a narrative lecture that is illustrated with appropriate and compelling visuals. Special "footnote" sections focus on the analysis of visual material as important historical evidence. This material comes from many sources, including the Library of Congress and the National Archives.

To reinforce the central notion that history is a dynamic process and not simply a collection of facts, this series will capture the discussion, debate, and sense of discovery that is increasingly seen as essential to the study of American history. Round-table discussions, interviews, and behind-the-scenes segments afford a glimpse into the process of research and the controversies of American history.

The narrative of the lectures is complemented by the analysis offered in the textbook that accompanies the series. *A People and a Nation*, Sixth Edition, published by Houghton Mifflin Company, is an integral part of the telecourse and provides students with the historical context required to get the most from the lectures presented in the video programs. Students are expected to read the appropriate sections of the text prior to viewing the programs as well as the appropriate unit in the study guide that was written specifically for *A Biography of America*. The study guide is the link between the textbook and the programs and prepares the student to be an efficient and informed viewer and reader. Additional resources for students and instructors can be found on the Web site that WGBH has developed to accompany this series. For more information about the Web site, please visit http://www.learner.org.

The video programs, the textbook, the study guide, and the companion web site offer a complete educational package that presents a new and exciting approach to learning about U. S. history.

Scholar Team

Professor Donald L. Miller, Professor of History, Lafayette College
and
Professor Pauline Maier, Massachusetts Institute of Technology
Professor Louis P. Masur, City College of New York
Professor Waldo E. Martin, Jr., University of California—Berkeley
Professor Douglas Brinkley, University of New Orleans
Professor Virginia Scharff, University of New Mexico
and
Raymond Smock, Senior Historical Consultant and former Historian of the U. S. House of
    Representatives

Course Components

The study guide is the link between the textbook and the programs and prepares you to be an efficient and informed viewer and reader. This study guide offers an overview of the programs, exercises, and resources that help integrate the video programs with the textbook. These study guides are designed to be used with the textbook *A People and a Nation*, Sixth Edition, also published by Houghton Mifflin Company. You should read the appropriate sections of the textbook prior to viewing the programs as well as the appropriate unit in the study guide that was written specifically for *A Biography of America*.

Each unit corresponds to one of the 26 programs and includes the following sections:

Unit Summary: provides a brief summary of the unit topic.

Assignment: assigns the corresponding chapters in the textbook *A People and a Nation* and the study guide unit that should be read before viewing the video program.

Learning Objectives: describes the objectives that you should be able to achieve after completing the assignment.

Program Guide: describes the video program and highlights its themes.

Historical Overview: provides the historical context and describes the major events and actors of the time period that is featured in the video program.

Map Exercises: poses several questions for you to answer using the maps in the corresponding chapters in *A People and a Nation*.

People, Events, and Concepts: lists names of people, events, and concepts for you to identify.

Essay Questions: poses questions to be answered in essay form, based on what you have learned from the textbook and the video program.

Multiple Choice Questions: poses questions to test your knowledge of certain facts, based on what you have learned from the textbook and the video program.

Primary Source Documents: provides you with a sampling of important historical documents from the given time period, including an introductory headnote and questions to consider.

If you follow these steps, you should find that you understand thoroughly the curriculum of *A Biography of America*.

1. Read the Unit Summary and Learning Objectives sections in the appropriate unit of the Study Guide.

2. Read the text assignment chapter(s).

3. Read the Program Guide and Historical Overview sections in the appropriate unit of the Study Guide.

4. View the video program.

5. Complete the exercises in the following sections of the study guide unit: map exercises; multiple-choice questions; people, events, and concepts (identification terms).

6. Read the primary source documents.

7. Visit the Web site <http://www.learner.org/biographyofamerica>. Explore the exercises for the given unit.

The study guide for Volume I covers programs 1–13, and the Volume II study guide covers programs 14–26, with the Units for programs 12 and 13 reprinted in the beginning of Volume II for those who are taking the second half of the course that begins with coverage of the Reconstruction period.

The Video Programs

12. Reconstruction
Professor Miller begins the program by evoking in word and picture the battlefield after the Battle of Gettysburg. With the assassination of President Lincoln, one sad chapter of American history comes to a close. In the fatigue and cynicism of the Civil War's aftermath, Reconstruction becomes a promise unfulfilled.

13. America at its Centennial
As America celebrates its centennial, five million people descend on Philadelphia to celebrate America's technological achievements, but some of the early principles of the Republic remain unrealized. Professor Miller and his team of historians examine where America is in 1876 and discuss the question of race in America.

14. Industrial Supremacy
Steel and stockyards are featured in this program as the mighty engine of industrialism thunders forward at the end of the 19th century. Professor Miller continues the story of the American Industrial Revolution in New York and Chicago, looking at the lives of Andrew Carnegie, Gustavus Swift, and the countless workers on the packinghouse and factory floor.

15. The New City
Professor Miller explores the tension between the messy vitality of cities that grow on their own and those where orderly growth is planned. Chicago—with Hull House, the World's Columbian Exposition, the new female workforce, the skyscraper, the department store, and unfettered capitalism—is the place to watch a new world in the making at the turn of the century.

16. The West
Professor Scharff continues the story of Jefferson's Empire of Liberty. Railroads and ranchers, rabble-rousers and racists populate America's distant frontiers, and Native Americans are displaced from their homelands. Feminists gain a foothold in their fight for the right to vote, while farmers organize and the Populist Party appears on the American political landscape.

17. Capital and Labor
The making of money pits laborers against the forces of capital as the 20th century opens. Professor Miller introduces the miner as the quintessential laborer of the period—working under grinding conditions, organizing into unions, and making a stand against the reigning money man of the day, J. Pierpont Morgan.

18. Theodore Roosevelt and Woodrow Wilson
Professor Brinkley compares the presidencies of Theodore Roosevelt and Woodrow Wilson—the Warrior and the Minister—in the first decades of the 20th century. Professor Miller discusses American socialism, Eugene Debs, international communism, and the roots of the Cold War with Professor Brinkley.

19. A Vital Progressivism
Professor Martin offers a fresh perspective on Progressivism, arguing that its spirit can be best seen in the daily struggle of ordinary people. In a discussion with Professors Scharff and Miller, the struggles

of Native Americans, Asian Americans, and blacks are placed in the context of the traditional white Progressive movement.

20. The Twenties
The Roaring Twenties take to the road in Henry Ford's landscape-altering invention—the Model T. Ford's moving assembly line, the emergence of a consumer culture, and the culmination of forces let loose by these entities in Los Angeles are all explored by Professor Miller.

21. FDR and the Depression
Professor Brinkley continues his story of 20th-century presidents with a profile of Franklin Delano Roosevelt. Brinkley paints a picture of America during the Depression and chronicles some of Roosevelt's programmatic and personal efforts to help the country through its worst economic crisis. First Lady Eleanor Roosevelt is at FDR's side and, in many respects, ahead of him as the decade unfolds.

22. World War II
America is enveloped in total war, from mobilization on the home front to a scorching air war in Europe. Professor Miller's view of World War II is a personal essay on the morality of total war, and its effects on those who fought, died, and survived it, including members of his own family.

23. The Fifties: From War to Normalcy
World War II is fought to its bitter end in the Pacific and the world lives with the legacy of its final moment: the atomic bomb. Professor Miller continues the story as veterans return from the war and create new lives for themselves in the '50s. The GI Bill, Levittown, civil rights, the Cold War, and rock 'n' roll are discussed.

24. The Sixties
Professor Scharff weaves the story of the Civil Rights movement with the stories of the Vietnam War and Watergate to create a portrait of a decade. Lyndon Johnson emerges as a pivotal character, along with Stokely Carmichael, Fannie Lou Hamer, and other luminaries of the era.

25. Contemporary History
The entire team of historians joins Professor Miller in examining the last quarter of the 20th century. A montage of events opens the program and sets the stage for a discussion of the period—and of the difficulty of examining contemporary history with true historical perspective. Television critic John Leonard offers a footnote on the impact of television on the way we experience recent events.

26. The Redemptive Imagination
Storytelling is a relentless human urge and its power forges with memory to become the foundation of history. Novelists Charles Johnson (Middle Passage), Arthur Golden (Memoirs of a Geisha), and Esmeralda Santiago (America's Dream) join Professor Miller in discussing the intersection of history and story. Kurt Vonnegut, Jr. closes the series with a reflection on the power of the human imagination.

The Textbook

The sixth edition of *A People and a Nation*, written by Mary Beth Norton, David M. Katzman, David W. Blight, Howard P. Chudacoff, Thomas G. Paterson, and William M. Tuttle, Jr., is published by Houghton Mifflin Company. The text, which has been one of the leading books for American history since it was first published in 1982, is a spirited narrative that challenges students to think critically about the meaning of American history. The thoughtful inclusion of everyday people, cultural diversity, work, and popular culture brings history to life.

UNIT 12
Reconstruction

UNIT SUMMARY

In Unit 12 we look at the end of the Civil War, from Gettysburg to Appomattox Courthouse. Then we focus on Reconstruction: the effort to restore the defeated Confederate states to the Union, to help African Americans make the transition to freedom, and to deal with the social and political changes that defeat and emancipation brought to the South.

ASSIGNMENT

1.   Before viewing Program 12, read this unit, and in *A People and a Nation* read Chapter 15, pages 411–424, and Chapter 16.

2.   View Program 12, "Reconstruction."

3.   Visit the Web site <http://www.learner.org/biographyofamerica>.
     Explore the exercises for Program 12.

LEARNING OBJECTIVES

Upon completing this unit, students should be able to:

1.   Summarize General Grant's strategy for conquering the Confederacy and ending the war.

2.   Compare and contrast President Lincoln's and President Johnson's ideas about Reconstruction.

3.   Compare and contrast presidential and congressional ideas about Reconstruction.

4.   Account for the failure of Reconstruction.

5.   Describe how the failure of Reconstruction affected freed men and women.

PROGRAM GUIDE

Professor Miller begins the program by evoking in word and picture the battlefield after the Battle of Gettysburg. Less than two years later, with the assassination of President Lincoln, one sad chapter of American history comes to a close and another opens. In the fatigue and cynicism of the Civil War's aftermath, Reconstruction becomes a promise unfulfilled.

On July 4, 1863, the Battle of Gettysburg ends with a Union victory. On the same day, General Sherman takes Vicksburg. By March 1864, President Lincoln has promoted Grant to general-in-chief of the Union armies. Grant is willing to do whatever is necessary to defeat the Confederacy.

On April 9, 1865, Grant accepts Lee's surrender at the courthouse in Appomattox, Virginia. Grant's tenacity in a series of battles around Richmond, Sherman's destructive march from

Chattanooga to Savannah and then into the Carolinas, and General Philip Sheridan's torching of the Shenandoah Valley in Virginia have brought the fighting to an end.

Less than a week after Lee's surrender, President Lincoln is shot and dies. The vice president, Andrew Johnson, from Tennessee, becomes president.

President Johnson and Radical Republicans in Congress have different ideas about the appropriate federal treatment of the defeated southern states and of the millions of newly free African Americans. The president wants to show leniency to the southern states and preserve white supremacy. The Radical Republicans want to punish the southern states and secure equal civil and political rights for the former slaves. In 1866 Congress wrests control of Reconstruction from the president, places the South under military occupation, and makes acceptance of the Fourteenth Amendment the price of readmission to the Union.

In 1868 Grant is elected president. Throughout the South blacks are the victims of racial violence. In a few instances, Grant calls out federal troops to halt the violence. Then, during his second term of office, Grant and Republicans in Congress become increasingly reluctant to do anything to offend white southerners or northern business interests. Looking ahead to the 1876 presidential election, Grant wants to do nothing to preclude a Republican victory, even if that means the undoing of gains made by African Americans in the preceding ten years.

HISTORICAL OVERVIEW

In May 1863, while General Grant was struggling to take Vicksburg in the West, General Lee, at Chancellorsville, north of Richmond, was repulsing Union armies trying again to take the Confederate capital. Lee's pleasure in his victory was considerably lessened by the death of Stonewall Jackson, accidentally shot by his own troops.

After Chancellorsville, Lee again wanted to invade the North, and Confederate president Davis agreed. On July 1–3 a bloody battle raged at Gettysburg, Pennsylvania. Then on the Fourth of July, Lee and what remained of his forces began a slow retreat to Virginia. General George Meade, the Union commander, did not pursue Lee and the Confederates. Like General McClellan at Antietam, he let them go, much to President Lincoln's displeasure.

Grant's victory at Vicksburg and successes later that fall in Tennessee convinced President Lincoln first to put Grant in charge of Union armies in the West and then, early in 1864, to promote Grant to general-in-chief—commander of all Union armies. Unlike his predecessors in that position—McClellan was one—Grant had no qualms about doing whatever was necessary to win.

He planned a three-part offensive: (1) A Union army commanded by General Sherman, would march southeast from Chattanooga, Tennessee, to Atlanta to destroy rail lines and anything else that couldn't be eaten or carried away. (2) Union cavalry, commanded by Philip Sheridan, would clear enemy forces out of the fertile Shenandoah Valley of Virginia and destroy the valley by fire so no crops could be grown there. (3) A Union army commanded by Grant himself would again go after General Lee and Richmond.

By the first week of April 1865, Sheridan had laid waste to the Shenandoah Valley, Sherman had cut a wide path of destruction not only to Atlanta but east to Savannah and then north into the Carolinas, and Grant had taken Richmond. On April 9, Lee (without Jefferson Davis's approval) surrendered to Grant at the courthouse in Appomattox, Virginia. Confederate general Joseph Johnston, whom Sherman had been pursuing, surrendered nine days later in North Carolina. The war was over. In May, Jefferson Davis, who with his cabinet had fled Richmond, was captured in Georgia and imprisoned for two years at Fort Monroe, Virginia.

Five days after Lee's surrender, President Lincoln was shot while attending the theater in Washington. On April 15 he died and his vice president, Andrew Johnson, succeeded him as president.

Even before the end of the war, President Lincoln and members of Congress were giving serious thought to the Reconstruction of the Union if the Confederacy was defeated. There were several issues: (1) how to bring the South back into the Union; (2) the status of high-ranking Confederates, given their treasonous behavior; and (3) the status of the freedmen.

In December 1863 the president issued a "proclamation of amnesty and reconstruction" to readmit any southern state in which voters (except for high-ranking Confederate civilian and military leaders) equal in number to 10 percent of the number of voters in that state in the 1860 presidential election swore to support the Union and the Constitution and accept the abolition of slavery. Thaddeus Stevens, Charles Sumner, and other Radical Republicans strongly opposed Lincoln's lenient, forgiving approach. They preferred Reconstruction to be a long, harsh process and in July 1864 presented the Wade-Davis bill, passed by both houses of Congress, to the president for his signature.

The Wade-Davis bill required 50 percent of the white men in a state to swear an "iron-clad" oath of loyalty to the Union and swear that they had never supported the Confederacy. In addition, it disfranchised all Confederate officers above the rank of lieutenant and anyone who had served the Confederacy as a civil official. Lincoln pocket-vetoed the bill.

Congress was not in session when Andrew Johnson became president, and he quickly implemented his own plan for Reconstruction. Using his power to issue pardons and grant amnesty, he restored state governments in the South. Under Johnson's plan, to be restored to the Union, states had to write and ratify new state constitutions that accepted the Thirteenth Amendment (which ended slavery) and repealed ordinances of secession; then they had to elect new state and national officials. Voting in these elections was limited to southerners who swore an oath of allegiance to the United States and had been eligible to vote when the state seceded. The president was not interested in granting equal civil rights to blacks or in disqualifying high-ranking former Confederates from voting and holding office.

When Congress reconvened in December 1865, Republicans denounced Johnson's plan because they found it too lenient toward the South, unacceptable for its slighting of African Americans, and unwarranted in its assumption that the president, not Congress, could dictate the terms of Reconstruction. Newly elected southern congressional representatives arriving in Washington were denied admission to the House and Senate.

Racial justice and full citizenship for the former slaves stood at the center of the controversy between the president and Congress. Compromise proved illusive. Many northerners were skeptical of the notion of racial equality. Former Confederate leaders preferred a return to paternalism, segregation, and some form of de facto slavery. The nation was badly divided and also preoccupied with other issues, such as industrialization, Indian hostilities, westward migration, and immigration. African Americans, however, had an important congressional ally in the small group of very powerful Radical Republicans, who favored guarantees and protection for the freedmen.

In 1866 Radical Republicans in Congress won control of Reconstruction. Their alternative to President Johnson's plan was embodied in the Fourteenth Amendment, and accepting that amendment was a precondition for readmission.

The president asked the southern states not to accept the Fourteenth Amendment. Johnson's home state, Tennessee, accepted it and was the first southern state readmitted to the Union. The other ten states of the former Confederacy refused to accept the amendment. Congress then split those states into five military districts, each one under a federal commander with power over police, judicial, and civil functions within his district. When the president resisted and spoke out against what he viewed as congressional infringement of presidential authority, Radical Republicans, led by Thaddeus Stevens, tried to remove him from office. He escaped impeachment by one vote in May 1868.

Congress imposed the terms by which southern states could return to the Union. While Union troops continued their occupation of the south, black and white delegates to a new round of state conventions drafted new state constitutions that mandated democratic rule, universal public education, and a host of other democratic reforms. These provisions along with federal guarantees—the Fourteenth and Fifteenth Amendments—marked a bold step forward toward securing racial justice. Unfortunately, the vision to secure full equality met with stiff resistance.

In 1868 Ulysses S. Grant, running as a Republican committed to national reconciliation, was elected to the first of his two terms as president. As he campaigned, racial violence ripped the South.

For blacks, Reconstruction had begun with hope. With freedom came the opportunity to shed slave-names, to search for family members, to marry, to learn to read, to worship. Freedom also brought assertiveness and expectations for landownership, personal safety, and civil rights. It soon became clear, however, that racial prejudice loomed as an enormous obstacle to African Americans' progress.

Throughout the South, black men voted in large numbers, and they voted Republican—the party of Lincoln. Southerners who had supported the Confederacy were disqualified from voting and from holding public office in the unreconstructed southern states. This limitation opened the way for blacks' participation in politics—for example, as delegates to the conventions drafting new state constitutions, as state legislators, as justices of the peace. Coalitions of blacks and whites governed the southern states. At various times blacks served as lieutenant governor in South Carolina, Mississippi, and Louisiana; as secretary of state in South Carolina, Mississippi, Louisiana, and Florida; as superintendent of education in Mississippi, Louisiana, and Florida.

Black officeholders, their black supporters, and their white supporters—called carpetbaggers if hey were from the North, scalawags if from the South—often were the targets of intimidation and violence by southern whites. Conservative white forces organized a powerful offensive against "carpetbagging regimes." They used inflammatory language to disparage what they derisively labeled the "Africanization of the South." Images of miscegenation carried a powerful stigma. Where rhetoric failed to win the day, terrorist organizations like the Ku Klux Klan rode into action. Intent on ending Republican influence in the South and denying African Americans any chance for advancement, paramilitary groups harassed, intimidated, and murdered anyone collaborating with the carpetbaggers. As president, Grant several times called out federal troops to restore order in southern states in the wake of murder and mayhem perpetrated by the KKK and other racist groups. But within a few years "redeemer" Democrats—defiant opponents of Reconstruction—returned to power in the South.

By 1870, all the states of the former Confederacy were back in the Union, having accepted not only the Fourteenth Amendment but also the Fifteenth. Seven years later, Democrats were in control in all southern states, and the hard-won rights of African Americans were being systematically undermined or ignored. African Americans were relegated to a status little better than that of slaves. Most were disfranchised, and many returned to a sort of serfdom, working as sharecroppers in the fields of former slaveowners.

By the mid-1870s, the national Republican Party was no longer the party of radicals such as Thaddeus Stevens and Charles Sumner, with roots in abolitionism. The party was controlled by powerful northern businessmen who, like many other Americans, weren't particularly interested in the economic well-being, political rights, or personal safety of African Americans in the South now that slavery was a thing of the past. What these Republicans were concerned about was holding on to the presidency in the 1876 election, and they had good reasons for concern. A severe economic downturn had begun in 1873. The Democrats had gained control of the House of Representatives in 1874. And the Grant administration had turned out to be corrupt and dogged by scandal.

The outcome of the election—the compromise of 1877—brought another Republican to the White House (Rutherford B. Hayes), but it also brought an end to Reconstruction and left African Americans in the former Confederate states at the mercy of southern white supremacists. White southerners were freed of what they saw as unwarranted federal interference in their lives, and they received federal appointments and dollars. Republicans held on to the White House. America proceeded with the business of industrialization and westward migration. A turbulent era closed.

MAP EXERCISE

Refer to the following maps in Chapters 15 and 16 of *A People and a Nation* to answer the questions listed below.

- The War in Virginia, 1864–1865 (p. 421)
- The Reconstruction (p. 443)
- Presidential Election of 1876 and the Compromise of 1877 (p. 454)

1. In what order were the former Confederate states readmitted to the Union? When was conservative rule reestablished in each one?
2. The migrants known as Exodusters moved to which state?
3. Nineteen of the twenty disputed electoral votes in 1876 were in which states?
4. The Union general who destroyed the Shenandoah Valley became commanding general of which military district in the South?

PEOPLE, EVENTS, AND CONCEPTS

Identify and explain the historical significance of each item.

Petersburg, Virginia

Identification

Significance

Battle of Gettysburg

Identification

Significance

Gettysburg Address

Identification

Significance

Andrew Johnson

Identification

Significance

Proclamation of Amnesty and Reconstruction

Identification

Significance

Freedmen's Bureau

Identification

Significance

Radical Republicans

Identification

Significance

Wade-Davis bill

Identification

Significance

Ulysses S. Grant

Identification

Significance

Fourteenth Amendment

Identification

Significance

carpetbaggers and scalawags

Identification

Significance

Sherman's march to the sea

Identification

Significance

Fifteenth Amendment

Identification

Significance

Appomattox, Virginia

Identification

Significance

John Wilkes Booth

Identification

Significance

Civil Rights Act of 1866

Identification

Significance

Redeemers

Identification

Significance

Rutherford B. Hayes

Identification

Significance

Compromise of 1877

Identification

Significance

black codes

Identification

Significance

Thaddeus Stevens

Identification

Significance

sharecroppers

Identification

Significance

Exodusters

Identification

Significance

ESSAY QUESTIONS

1. What were the major differences in the approaches of President Johnson and Congress towards Reconstruction? Explain the specifics of their respective plans.

2. Why did Congress move to impeach President Johnson? Was the action warranted? Why or why not?

3. Discuss the successes and failures of Reconstruction from the point of view of (a) the freedpeople and (b) conservative southern planters.

MULTIPLE-CHOICE QUESTIONS

1. The goals of congressional Reconstruction included each of the following *except*
   a. abolition of slavery.
   b. limiting the political participation of high-ranking Confederates.
   c. returning seceded states to the Union.
   d. providing land for freedmen.
2. Slavery throughout the United States was abolished
   a. by the Emancipation Proclamation.
   b. when Lincoln was reelected in 1864.
   c. by the Thirteenth Amendment.
   d. by the Compromise of 1877.
3. Among the factors helping President Lincoln get reelected in 1864 was
   a. the Proclamation of Amnesty and Reconstruction.
   b. Sherman's capture of Atlanta.
   c. a vote of confidence by congressional Republicans.
   d. the abolishion of slavery by executive order.
4. Andrew Johnson's Reconstruction proposal
   a. mirrored ideas expressed by Thaddeus Stevens.
   b. called for large-scale redistribution of land.
   c. reflected his desire to secure political and civil rights for African Americans.
   d. made acceptance of the Thirteenth Amendment a precondition for readmission to the Union.
5. Black Codes were created by
   a. both Lincoln and Johnson to protect the freedmen.
   b. southerners to segregate the races.
   c. the Ku Klux Klan to intimidate blacks.
   d. Radical Republicans to embarrass southern Democrats.
6. Among the influential Radical Republicans in Congress were
   a. Davis and Lee.
   b. Grant and Sherman.
   c. Stevens and Sumner.
   d. Hayes and Tilden.
7. The Fourteenth Amendment did *not*
   a. bar Confederate leaders from holding state and federal office.
   b. guarantee freedmen the right to vote.
   c. reverse the Supreme Court's *Dred Scott* decision.
   d. prohibit payment of the Confederate war debt.
8. Reconstruction came to an end as a result of
   a. compromise following the election of 1876.
   b. the Fourteenth Amendment.
   c. Grant's reelection in 1868.
   d. military occupation of the South.

Answers

1.	d	3.	b	5.	b	7.	b
2.	c	4.	d	6.	c	8.	a

PRIMARY SOURCE DOCUMENTS

The accounts of actual participants are useful for understanding the motives and thoughts of historical characters.

1. *Slaughter-House Cases (1873)* **U.S. Supreme Court**

Officially known as *The Butchers' Benevolent Association of New Orleans v. The Crescent City Livestock Landing and Slaughter House Company,* the Slaughter-House decision is among the most complicated and far-reaching nineteenth-century Supreme Court cases. In 1869 the Louisiana legislature granted a monopoly to the Crescent City Company to maintain slaughterhouses in the New Orleans area. The legislation prohibited "all other persons from building, keeping, or having slaughter-houses" within the New Orleans region. In return the Crescent City Company would maintain fees and sanitation standards established by the state. The Butchers' Benevolent Association sued, arguing that such economic regulation violated their new Fourteenth Amendment due process rights. The Supreme Court held that the grant of a monopoly was within the police powers of the state; in other words, the state's right to establish "regulation for the health and comfort of the people." The Court also held that the Thirteenth and Fourteenth Amendments only affected "the freedom of the African race...and their protection from the oppressions of the white men who had formerly held them in slavery." Both aspects of the Slaughter-House decision would be severely altered by Court decisions over the next twenty years.

Questions to Consider

- Are there any limitations on the police powers of the state?

- What, according to the Court, is the purpose of the Thirteenth and Fourteenth Amendments?

Mr. Justice Miller...delivered the opinion of the court....

That the landing of livestock in large droves, from steamboats on the bank of the river, and from railroad trains, should, for the safety and comfort of the people and the care of the animals, be limited to proper places, and those not numerous, it needs no argument to prove. Nor can it be injurious to the general community that while the duty of making ample preparation for this is imposed upon a few men, or a corporation, they should, to enable them to do it successfully, have the exclusive right of providing such landing-places, and receiving a fair compensation for the service....

The institution of African slavery, as it existed in about half the States of the Union, and the contests pervading the public mind for many years, between those who desired its curtailment and ultimate extinction and those who desired additional safeguards for its security and perpetuation, culminated in the effort, on the part of most of the States in which slavery existed, to separate from the Federal government, and to resist its authority. This constituted the war of the rebellion, and whatever auxiliary causes may have contributed to bring about this war, undoubtedly the overshadowing and efficient cause was African slavery.

In that struggle slavery, as a legalized social relation, perished. It perished as a necessity of the bitterness and force of the conflict. When the armies of freedom found themselves upon the soil of slavery they could do nothing less than free the poor victims whose enforced servitude was the foundation of the quarrel....But the war being over, those who had succeeded in re-establishing the authority of the Federal government were not content to permit this great act of emancipation to rest on the actual results of the contest or the proclamation of the Executive, both of which might have been questioned in after times, and they determined to place this main and most valuable result in the Constitution of the restored Union as one of its fundamental articles. Hence the thirteenth article of amendment of that instrument....

The process of restoring to their proper relations with the Federal government and with the other States those which had sided with the rebellion, ...developed the fact that...the condition of the slave race would, without further protection of the Federal government, be almost as bad as it was before. Among the first acts of legislation adopted by several of the States in the legislative bodies which claimed to be in their normal relations with the Federal government, were laws which imposed upon the colored race onerous disabilities and burdens, and curtailed their rights in the pursuit of life, liberty, and property to such an extent that their freedom was of little value....

These circumstances...forced upon the statesmen who had conducted the Federal government in safety through the crisis of the rebellion...the conviction that something more was necessary in the way of constitutional protection to the unfortunate race who had suffered so much. They accordingly passed through Congress...the fourteenth amendment....

...Was it the purpose of the fourteenth amendment, by the simple declaration that no State should make or enforce any law which shall abridge the privileges and immunities of *citizens of the United States,* to transfer the security and protection of all the civil rights which we have mentioned, from the States to the Federal government?...

...[S]uch a construction...would constitute this court a perpetual censor upon all legislation of the States, on the civil rights of their own citizens, with authority to nullify such as it did not approve as consistent with those rights, as they existed at the time of the adoption of this amendment. The argument we admit is not always the most conclusive which is drawn from the consequences urged against the adoption of a particular construction of an instrument. But when, as in the case before us, these consequences are so serious, so far-reaching and pervading, so great a departure from the structure and spirit of our institutions; when the effect is to fetter and degrade the State governments by subjecting them to the control of Congress, in the exercise of powers heretofore universally conceded to them of the most ordinary and fundamental character; when in fact it radically changes the whole theory of the relations of the State and Federal governments to each other and of both these governments to the people; the argument has a force that is irresistible....

We are convinced that no such results were intended by the Congress which proposed these amendments nor by the legislatures of the States which ratified them....

SOURCE: John W. Wallace, ed., *United States Reports* 16 (1873): pp. 36–130.

2. *The Gettysburg Address (1863)* Abraham Lincoln

Justly celebrated as one of the greatest—and briefest—speeches in American history, Lincoln's Gettysburg Address was delivered at the commemoration of the battlefield cemetery. After the bloody Union triumph at Gettysburg, a special national commission sought to make a memorial of the battlefield. On November 19, 1863, Edward Everett, the prominent former governor and senator from Massachusetts, spoke for two hours on the soldiers' sacrifices and the cause of the Union. He was followed by President Lincoln, who finished his speech before many in the crowd of 15,000 were even aware that he had begun. Everett correctly perceived that his own speech would be forgotten, while Lincoln's would attain immortality.

Questions to Consider

• Why, according to Lincoln, are Americans fighting one another?

• What duty lies before those still alive?

Fourscore and seven years ago our fathers brought forth on this continent a new nation, conceived in liberty, and dedicated to the proposition that all men are created equal.

Now we are engaged in a great civil war, testing whether that nation, or any nation so conceived and so dedicated, can long endure. We are met on a great battle-field of that war. We have come to dedicate a portion of that field as a final resting-place for those who here gave their lives that that nation might live. It is altogether fitting and proper that we should do this.

But, in a larger sense, we cannot dedicate—we cannot consecrate—we cannot hallow—this ground. The brave men, living and dead, who struggled here, have consecrated it far above our poor power to add or detract. The world will little note nor long remember what we say here, but it can never forget what they did here. It is for us, the living, rather, to be dedicated here to the unfinished work which they who fought here have thus far so nobly advanced. It is rather for us to be here dedicated to the great task remaining before us—that from these honored dead we take increased devotion to that cause for which they gave the last full measure of devotion; that we here highly resolve that these dead shall not have died in vain; that this nation, under God, shall have a new birth of freedom; and that government of the people, by the people, for the people, shall not perish from the earth.

SOURCE: John G. Nicolay and John Hay, eds., *Complete Works of Abraham Lincoln* (New York, 1905), 9: pp. 209–210.

3. *A Southern View of Defeat (1866)* Alexander H. Stephens

In April 1866 the Congressional Joint Committee on Reconstruction began to determine the opinions of leading white Southerners toward their defeat. One witness was the former vice president of the Confederacy, Alexander H. Stephens of Georgia. Interestingly, Stephens had opposed secession and accepted the position of vice president reluctantly. A former Whig friend of Abraham Lincoln, Stephens had tried on several occasions to end the war, without success. Though he had always insisted that slavery was the very pillar of secession and of the Confederate States, after the war he shifted his judgment, arguing that the Southern defense of states' rights had brought on the conflict. In this testimony, Stephens tested the logic that he later developed in his magisterial *A Constitutional View of the Late War Between the States* (1870).

Questions to Consider

- Why did Stephens shift to a states' rights argument after the war?
- Why did Congress insist on the Southern states granting blacks the right to vote before the states could be readmitted to the Union?

[Stephens] After the proclamation of President Lincoln calling out the 75,000 militia [in April, 1861], under the circumstances it was issued, and blockading the southern ports, and the suspension of the writ of *habeas corpus,* the southern cause, as it was termed, received the almost unanimous support of the people of Georgia. Before that, they were very much divided on the question of the policy of secession; but afterwards they supported the cause, with very few exceptions within the range of my knowledge. There were some few exceptions, not exceeding half a dozen, I think. The impression then prevailing was that public liberty was endangered, and they supported the cause because of their zeal for constitutional rights. They still differed very much as to the ultimate object to be attained and the means to be used, but these differences yielded to the emergency of the apprehended common danger....

Question. In what particular did the people believe their constitutional liberties were assailed or endangered from the Union?

Answer. Mainly, I would say, in their internal social polity, and their apprehension from the general consolidating tendencies of the doctrines and principles of that political party which had recently succeeded in the choice of a President and Vice-President of the United States. It was the serious apprehension that if the republican organization, as then constituted, should succeed to power, it would lead ultimately to a virtual subversion of the Constitution of the United States, and all its essential guarantees of public liberty. I think that was the sincere, honest conviction in the minds of our people. Those who opposed secession did not apprehend that any such results would necessarily follow the elections which had taken place; they still thought that all their rights might be maintained in the Union and under the Constitution, especially as there were majorities in both houses who agreed with them on constitutional questions.

Question. To what feature of their internal social polity did they apprehend danger?

Answer. Principally the subordination of the African race, as it existed under their laws and institutions.

Question. In what spirit is the emancipation of the slaves received by the people?

Answer. Generally, it is acquiesced in and accepted, I think, in perfect good faith, and with a disposition to do the best that can be done in the new order of things in this particular....

Question. What is the public sentiment of Georgia with regard to the extension of the right of voting to the negroes?

Answer. The general opinion in the State is very much averse to it.... The people of Georgia, in my judgment, are perfectly willing to leave suffrage and the basis of representation where the Constitution leaves it. They look upon the question of suffrage as one belonging exclusively to the States; one over which, under the Constitution of the United States, Congress has no jurisdiction, power, or control, except in proposing amendments and not in making their acceptance and adoption by the States conditions of representation. I do not think, therefore, that the people of that State, while they are disposed, as I believe, earnestly to deal fairly, justly, and generously with the freedmen, would be willing to consent to a change in the Constitution that would give Congress jurisdiction over the question of suffrage; and especially would they be very much averse to Congress exercising any such jurisdiction without their representatives in the Senate and House being heard in the public councils upon this question that so fatally concerns their internal policy as well as the internal policy of all the States.... General, universal suffrage among the colored people, as they are now there, would by our people be regarded as about as great a political evil as could befall them....

Question. Suppose the States that are represented in Congress, and Congress itself, should be of the opinion that Georgia should not be permitted to take its place in the government of the country except upon its assent to one or the other of the two propositions suggested, is it, then, your opinion that, under such circumstances, Georgia ought to decline?...

Answer. I think she ought to decline, under the circumstances and for the reasons stated, and so ought the whole eleven. Should such an offer be made and declined, and those States, should they be kept out, a singular spectacle would be presented—a complete reversal of positions would be presented. In 1861 these States thought they could not remain safely in the Union without new guarantees, and now, when they agree to resume their former practical relations in the Union, under the Constitution, the other States turn upon them and say they cannot permit them to do so safely to their interests without new constitutional guarantees. The southern States would thus present themselves as willing for immediate union, under the Constitution, while it would be the northern States opposed to it. The former disunionists would thereby become the unionists, and the former unionists the practical disunionists....

Question. Will you state, if not indisposed to do so, the considerations or opinions which led you to identify yourself with the rebellion so far as to accept the office of Vice-President of the Confederate States of America, so-called?

Answer. I believed thoroughly in the reserved sovereignty of the several States of the Union under the compact or Constitution of 1787. I opposed secession therefore as a question of policy, and not one of right, on the part of Georgia. When the State seceded against my judgment and vote I thought my ultimate allegiance was due to her, and I preferred to cast my fortunes and destiny with hers and her people rather than take any other course, even though it might lead to my sacrifice and her ruin. In accepting a position under the new order of things my sole object was to do all the good I could in preserving and perpetuating the principles of liberty as established under the Constitution of the United States.… When the conflict arose my efforts were directed to as speedy and peaceful an adjustment of the questions as possible.…

Question. Have your opinions undergone any change since the opening of the rebellion in reference to the reserved rights of States under the Constitution of the United States?

Answer. My convictions on the original abstract question have undergone no change, but I accept the issues of the war and the result as a practical settlement of that question. The sword was appealed to to decide the question, and by the decision of the sword I am willing to abide.

SOURCE: United States Congress, Report of the Joint Committee on Reconstruction, at the First Session Thirty-Ninth Congress (Washington, 1866), pp. 159–166.

UNIT 13

America at Its Centennial

UNIT SUMMARY

In Unit 13 we observe the nation's hundredth birthday and consider how well centennial America is fulfilling the fundamental promise of equality expressed in the Declaration of Independence.

ASSIGNMENT

1. Before viewing Program 13, read this unit, and in the Appendix to *A People and a Nation* read the Declaration of Independence, the Constitution and its first fifteen amendments, and the data for the period 1790–1870 in the "Statistical Profiles."

2. View Program 13, "America at Its Centennial."

3. Visit the Web site <http://www.learner.org/biographyofamerica>. Explore the exercises for Program 13.

LEARNING OBJECTIVES

Upon completing this unit, students should be able to:

1. Discuss the significance of the Centennial Exposition in Philadelphia, and describe some of the exhibits.

2. Identify the ideals and values that the founders chose to emphasize in 1776, and assess the nation's progress toward achieving those objectives.

3. Identify fundamental problems that in 1876 remained unsolved.

4. Identify strengths and accomplishments that in 1876 held promise for the future of the United States.

PROGRAM GUIDE

As America celebrates its hundredth birthday, nearly 10 million people attend the Centennial Exposition held in Philadelphia to celebrate America's first century. The industrial transformation of the nation has led to the creation of new technologies and innovations that improve Americans' lives at work and home. Many of these are on display at the exposition. Some of the Republic's early promises, however, remain unfulfilled. Professor Miller and his team of historians examine where America is in 1876 and the question of race in America.

The nation's centennial year is the final year of Reconstruction. The Civil War era comes to a close, and many Americans think it is time to push forward the victories of laissez-faire capitalism and democracy. Not everyone is celebrating however.

Although the Sioux annihilate Custer's force at Little Big Horn about seven weeks after the exposition opens, the frontier line is moving steadily west as Indian peoples are forced to cede land and see grave threats to their traditional ways of life. The nation is turning its attention away from the struggle for racial justice and leaving blacks to their fate. Women's exasperation over their lack of voting rights is growing. The forces of free enterprise unleashed by industrialization and the resulting abuses are the focus of a national debate. But in the summer and fall of 1876, many in the nation have other concerns. It is a time for celebration as people gather in Philadelphia.

HISTORICAL OVERVIEW

America's hundredth birthday occurred at a time of profound transitions. People were searching for their place in an industrializing society that demonstrated enormous potential but created bewildering changes. While Reconstruction's end signaled the nation's failure to secure racial equality, the industrial age presaged material progress. The West continued to beckon, and immigration continued to bring strangers to America's shores. Democracy exceeded the expectations of its most ardent proponents and muted the complaints of its most vociferous critics. America in 1876 was on the move, and few desired to look back.

Centennial events occurred throughout the country, but Philadelphia was the focal point of festivities. The Centennial Exposition occupied 450 acres in Fairmount Park, within the city. Some thirty-one thousand exhibits from more than thirty-five nations filled two hundred buildings that had been constructed for the event and, with few exceptions, would be torn down after it was over. Two buildings sold nothing but popcorn—a novelty to city dwellers though not to Native Americans and country folk. The Main Hall, appropriately, was 1,876 feet long. There, and in state pavillions and buildings designated Horticultural Hall, Woman's Pavillion, Art Gallery, Machinery Hall, Carriage Building—to name just a few—crowds could see an array of artifacts, products, and informational displays: furs from Norway; chocolates and preserved fruits and jellies from London; tropical gardens; bicycles with a five-foot wheel in front and a tiny wheel in the rear; paintings and sculptures (including a butter sculpture, kept on ice, of the head and shoulders of a young girl); sugar-cured hams from Ohio; a coat, vest, and breeches worn by George Washington; inventions recently patented by women; wines from California, France, and Germany; recent innovations such as canned food and linoleum floor coverings; saddles from Egypt; Indian pottery, beadwork, tepees, and totem poles displayed by the Smithsonian Institution; a replica of the Liberty Bell made of tobacco; bone corsets; a half-mile-long exhibit of sewing machines; at the New England Log House, women wearing 1750s-style costumes serving visitors baked beans, brown bread, and a boiled dinner and demonstrating the use of fireplace cooking utensils.

The nation's industrial power, however, occupied center stage. The theme of the exposition was that machines were remaking America and would usher in a period of widespread abundance. During opening day ceremonies, President Grant and Brazil's emperor Dom Pedro II climbed the platform of the Corliss steam engine and pulled the levers that activated the huge machine, which powered all the exhibits on display in Machinery Hall. The amazed public saw machines folding paper into envelopes, printing wallpaper, sawing logs, making shoes, and in other ways demonstrating the increasing mechanization of labor. Among the new inventions to be seen were telephones, typewriters, electric lights, harvesters, high-speed printing presses, elevators, and torpedoes. Also on display in Machinery Hall was steel-wire cable to be used for the Brooklyn Bridge, begun in 1869 and completed in 1883.

America was changing rapidly in 1876, and many people were eager to leave the past behind. Eleven years had passed since the end of the Civil War and the freeing of the slaves. Reconstruction itself came to a dramatic close soon after the exposition closed. In 1876 the Supreme Court ruled in two cases, *U. S. v. Cruikshank* and *U. S. v. Reese*, to limit federal protections against discrimination. The Compromise of 1877 then reinforced the trends toward segregation, economic servitude, and disfranchisement sweeping the South. Politicians washed their hands of efforts to secure racial equality. Americans focused on other issues: organizing large, national businesses; increasing personal income; securing the right to vote for women; taking advantage of business opportunities in the West, where cheap land was still available, and in the South, still rebuilding and trying to diversify its economy.

Color and ethnicity determined the quality of justice received not only by African Americans but also by Native Americans. For them, life on the plains rapidly deteriorated after the Civil War. Pioneers moving west expected their government to remove the Indians one way or another. Treaties with the Sioux in the Dakotas and with tribes elsewhere on the plains were violated as migrants settled on sacred Indian land. The United States Army was given the task of pacifying the situation. In some parts of the country a calculated policy of genocide was implemented; elsewhere indigenous peoples were rounded up and placed on reservations. The Indians fought back. Coincidentally, on July 4, 1876, news of the massacre of Colonel George Custer and the Seventh Cavalry near Little Big Horn River by Indians led by Sioux chiefs Sitting Bull and Crazy Horse reached the halls of the Centennial Exposition in Philadelphia.

By 1876 business interests dominated society and politics, and neither business leaders nor politicians were inclined to do anything to correct the abuses that angered their critics. Ideas about regulating and restricting corporations' activities were loathsome to businessmen. Politicians tended to agree and were reluctant to regulate the economy. Working conditions and wages became a source of conflict between workers and management. Workers' efforts to organize and form unions were met by stiff resistance. Companies that experienced labor troubles resorted to terminations, private detectives to identify troublemakers, and requests for government troops to put down strikers. When depression hit the economy in 1873, conditions deteriorated. Two confrontations occurring around the time of the centennial celebration indicated the challenge for democracy: efforts—often violent— by the Molly Maguires, a secret organization of coal miners, to improve working conditions in the anthracite mines of northeastern Pennsylvania in the early 1870s, and the railroad strike of 1877 to protest wage cuts, increased workloads, and layoffs. Common to these and similar incidents was workers' struggle for workplace safety, a living wage, and dignity and self-determination.

America's industrial transformation was a development that would have surprised many of the founders—though not Alexander Hamilton. Although economic considerations played a large role in the nation's birth, the Declaration of Independence ushered in a political revolution. The Declaration proclaimed the right of the people to govern themselves. Republicanism, the idea that power emanates from the consent of the governed, the founders argued, reflected the natural condition of man in society. Jefferson's assertion that "all men are created equal, that they are endowed by their Creator with certain unalienable Rights, that among these are Life, Liberty and the pursuit of Happiness," became the nation's creed. But in 1876 it was clear that America in its first one hundred years had failed to secure equality for groups such as women and blacks and other persons of color.

PEOPLE, EVENTS, AND CONCEPTS

Identify and explain the historical significance of each item.

Centennial Exposition

Identification

Significance

Corliss steam engine

Identification

Significance

George Armstrong Custer

Identification

Significance

Civil War amendments

Identification

Significance

Susan B. Anthony and Elizabeth Cady Stanton

Identification

Significance

ESSAY QUESTIONS

1. Why did the founders not enfranchise women and abolish slavery, and why was the nation still unwilling to do either one hundred years later?

2. It has been said that the North won the Civil War but the South won Reconstruction. Do you think that is an accurate judgment? Why or why not?

3. Put yourself in the shoes of Chief Sitting Bull, Susan B. Anthony, and Frederick Douglass, and express each person's hopes for America's next 100 years.

MULTIPLE-CHOICE QUESTIONS

1. Philadelphia was a natural choice for the Centennial Exposition because
   a. it was the capital of the United States in 1876.
   b. the Declaration of Independence had been signed there in 1776.
   c. the Republican and Democratic nominating conventions were to be held there in 1876.
   d. the city itself was celebrating its hundredth birthday in 1876.

2. The Thirteenth, Fourteenth, and Fifteenth Amendments are known collectively as the
   a. Civil War amendments.
   b. Compromise of 1877.
   c. Bill of Rights.
   d. Woman's Declaration of Independence.

3. The Centennial Exposition was a celebration of
   a. the accuracy of Thomas Jefferson's vision of America.
   b. the achievement of racial equality by African Americans.
   c. the completion of the transcontinental railroad.
   d. American progress and prosperity.

4. In 1876, eleven years had passed since all of the following events *except*
   a. the assassination of President Lincoln.
   b. the impeachment of President Johnson.
   c. the end of the Civil War.
   d. the ratification of the Thirteenth Amendment.

5. United States forces commanded by Colonel Custer were massacred
   a. at Hamburg, South Carolina.
   b. soon after the Compromise of 1877 took effect.
   c. at the Battle of Little Big Horn.
   d. because conservative white southerners despised carpetbaggers.

6. All of the following factors contributed to the growth of the post–Civil War economy *except*
   a. strict government regulation of business.
   b. the availability of cheap labor.
   c. entrepreneurial skill and talent.
   d. a plentiful supply of natural resources.

7. The Fifteenth Amendment was a disappointment to feminists because it did not
   a. punish the South for causing the Civil War.
   b. halt the dispossession of Native Americans.
   c. confer citizenship on the former slaves.
   d. give women the right to vote.

8. The industry that was most central to the expansion of the post–Civil War economy was
   a. the railroad industry.
   b. the steel industry.
   c. agriculture.
   d. the petroleum industry.

Answers

1.	b	3.	d	5.	c	7.	d
2.	a	4.	b	6.	a	8.	a

PRIMARY SOURCE DOCUMENTS

The accounts of actual participants are useful for understanding the motives and thoughts of historical characters.

1.   *Leaves of Grass (1892)* **Walt Whitman**

Walt Whitman began his career as a printer and journalist, serving as editor of the Brooklyn *Eagle* until he disagreed with the publishers about the Mexican War, which he opposed. Whitman decided to write poetry that would celebrate democracy and the individual democrat. The result, published in 1855, was *Leaves of Grass*. The book, with its free-form poetry and startling allusions to sexuality, did not sell well. During the Civil War Whitman served as a volunteer nurse and later held a number of lesser government posts. He was fired from his position in the Department of the Interior in 1865 because of the increasing notoriety of his book, but then was appointed to a position in the Justice Department, which he held until 1874. Whitman devoted his energies to rewriting *Leaves of Grass* into what he saw as a single poem, the verses individual but part of the larger effort. The following selections are from Whitman's last version of *Leaves of Grass,* published the year he died.

Questions to Consider

   •   Why did so many contemporaries find Whitman obscene?

   •   Why does Whitman focus so much on himself?

One's-Self I Sing
One's-self I sing, a simple separate person,
Yet utter the word Democratic, the word En-Masse.
Of physiology from top to toe I sing,
Not physiognomy alone nor brain alone is worthy for the Muse
    —I say the Form complete is worthier far,
The Female equally with the Male I sing.
Of Life immense in passion, pulse, and power,
Cheerful, for freest action form'd under the laws divine,
The Modern Man I sing.
When Lilacs Last in the Dooryard Bloom'd
When lilacs last in the dooryard bloom'd,
And the great star early droop'd in the western sky in the night,
I mourn'd, and yet shall mourn with ever-returning spring.
Ever-returning spring, trinity sure to me you bring,
Lilac blooming perennial and drooping star in the west,
And thought of him I love.
O powerful western fallen star!
O shades of night—O moody, tearful night!
O great star disappear'd—O the black murk that hides the star!
O cruel hands that hold me powerless—O helpless soul of me!
O harsh surrounding cloud that will not free my soul....
O how shall I warble myself for the dead one there I loved?
And how shall I deck my song for the large sweet soul that has gone?
And what shall my perfume be for the grave of him I love?
Sea-winds blown from east and west,

Blown from the Eastern sea and blown from the Western sea, till there on the prairies meeting,
These and with these and the breath of my chant,
I'll perfume the grave of him I love....
Lo, body and soul—this land,
My own Manhattan with spires, and the sparkling and hurrying tides, and the ships,
The varied and ample land, the South and the North in the light, Ohio's shores and flashing Missouri,
And ever the far-spreading prairies cover'd with grass and corn....
Sing on, sing on you gray-brown bird,
Sing from the swamps, the recesses, pour your chant from the bushes,
Limitless out of the dusk, out of the cedars and pines.
Sing on dearest brother, warble your reedy song,
Loud human song, with voice of uttermost woe.
O liquid and free and tender!
O wild and loose to my soul—O wondrous singer!
You only I hear—yet the star holds me (but will soon depart),
Yet the lilac with mastering odor holds me....
Passing the visions, passing the night,
Passing, unloosing the hold of my comrades' hands,
Passing the song of the hermit bird and the tallying song of my soul,
Victorious song, death's outlet song, yet varying ever-altering song,
As low and wailing, yet clear the notes, rising and falling, flooding the night,
Sadly sinking and fainting, as warning and warning, and yet again bursting with joy,
Covering the earth and filling the spread of the heaven,
As that powerful psalm in the night I heard from recesses,
Passing, I leave thee lilac with heart-shaped leaves,
I leave thee there in the door-yard, blooming, returning with spring.
I cease from my song for thee,
From my gaze on thee in the west, fronting the west, communing with thee,
O comrade lustrous with silver face in the night.
Yet each to keep and all, retrievements out of the night,
The song, the wondrous chant of the gray-brown bird,
And the tallying chant, the echo arous'd in my soul,
With the lustrous and drooping star with the countenance full of woe,
With the holders holding my hand nearing the call of the bird,
Comrades mine and I in the midst, and their memory ever to keep, for the dead I loved so well,
For the sweetest, wisest soul of all my days and lands—and this for his dear sake,
Lilac and star and bird twined with the chant of my soul,
There in the fragrant pines and the cedars dusk and dim.
The Last Invocation
At the last, tenderly,
From the walls of the powerful fortress'd house,
From the clasp of the knitted locks, from the keep of the well-closed doors,
Let me be wafted.
Let me glide noiselessly forth;
With the key of softness unlock the locks—with a whisper,
Set ope the doors O soul.

Tenderly—be not impatient,
(Strong is your hold O mortal flesh,
Strong is your hold O love).

SOURCE: Charles W. Eliot, ed., *English Poetry in Three Volumes, Volume III: From Tennyson to Whitman* (New York, 1910), pp. 1402, 1412–1422.

2.   *Slaughter-House Cases (1873)* **U.S. Supreme Court**

Officially known as *The Butchers' Benevolent Association of New Orleans v. The Crescent City Livestock Landing and Slaughter House Company,* the Slaughter-House decision is among the most complicated and far-reaching nineteenth-century Supreme Court cases. In 1869 the Louisiana legislature granted a monopoly to the Crescent City Company to maintain slaughterhouses in the New Orleans area. The legislation prohibited "all other persons from building, keeping, or having slaughter-houses" within the New Orleans region. In return the Crescent City Company would maintain fees and sanitation standards established by the state. The Butchers' Benevolent Association sued, arguing that such economic regulation violated their new Fourteenth Amendment due process rights. The Supreme Court held that the grant of a monopoly was within the police powers of the state; in other words, the state's right to establish "regulation for the health and comfort of the people." The Court also held that the Thirteenth and Fourteenth Amendments only affected "the freedom of the African race…and their protection from the oppressions of the white men who had formerly held them in slavery." Both aspects of the Slaughter-House decision would be severely altered by Court decisions over the next twenty years.

Questions to Consider

•   Are there any limitations on the police powers of the state?

•   What, according to the Court, is the purpose of the Thirteenth and Fourteenth Amendments?

Mr. Justice Miller…delivered the opinion of the court….

That the landing of livestock in large droves, from steamboats on the bank of the river, and from railroad trains, should, for the safety and comfort of the people and the care of the animals, be limited to proper places, and those not numerous, it needs no argument to prove. Nor can it be injurious to the general community that while the duty of making ample preparation for this is imposed upon a few men, or a corporation, they should, to enable them to do it successfully, have the exclusive right of providing such landing-places, and receiving a fair compensation for the service….

The institution of African slavery, as it existed in about half the States of the Union, and the contests pervading the public mind for many years, between those who desired its curtailment and ultimate extinction and those who desired additional safeguards for its security and perpetuation, culminated in the effort, on the part of most of the States in which slavery existed, to separate from the Federal government, and to resist its authority. This constituted the war of the rebellion, and whatever auxiliary causes may have contributed to bring about this war, undoubtedly the overshadowing and efficient cause was African slavery.

In that struggle slavery, as a legalized social relation, perished. It perished as a necessity of the bitterness and force of the conflict. When the armies of freedom found themselves upon the soil of slavery they could do nothing less than free the poor victims whose enforced servitude was the foundation of the quarrel....But the war being over, those who had succeeded in re-establishing the authority of the Federal government were not content to permit this great act of emancipation to rest on the actual results of the contest or the proclamation of the Executive, both of which might have been questioned in after times, and they determined to place this main and most valuable result in the Constitution of the restored Union as one of its fundamental articles. Hence the thirteenth article of amendment of that instrument....

The process of restoring to their proper relations with the Federal government and with the other States those which had sided with the rebellion, ...developed the fact that...the condition of the slave race would, without further protection of the Federal government, be almost as bad as it was before. Among the first acts of legislation adopted by several of the States in the legislative bodies which claimed to be in their normal relations with the Federal government, were laws which imposed upon the colored race onerous disabilities and burdens, and curtailed their rights in the pursuit of life, liberty, and property to such an extent that their freedom was of little value....

These circumstances...forced upon the statesmen who had conducted the Federal government in safety through the crisis of the rebellion...the conviction that something more was necessary in the way of constitutional protection to the unfortunate race who had suffered so much. They accordingly passed through Congress...the fourteenth amendment....

...Was it the purpose of the fourteenth amendment, by the simple declaration that no State should make or enforce any law which shall abridge the privileges and immunities of *citizens of the United States,* to transfer the security and protection of all the civil rights which we have mentioned, from the States to the Federal government?...

...[S]uch a construction...would constitute this court a perpetual censor upon all legislation of the States, on the civil rights of their own citizens, with authority to nullify such as it did not approve as consistent with those rights, as they existed at the time of the adoption of this amendment. The argument we admit is not always the most conclusive which is drawn from the consequences urged against the adoption of a particular construction of an instrument. But when, as in the case before us, these consequences are so serious, so far-reaching and pervading, so great a departure from the structure and spirit of our institutions; when the effect is to fetter and degrade the State governments by subjecting them to the control of Congress, in the exercise of powers heretofore universally conceded to them of the most ordinary and fundamental character; when in fact it radically changes the whole theory of the relations of the State and Federal governments to each other and of both these governments to the people; the argument has a force that is irresistible....

We are convinced that no such results were intended by the Congress which proposed these amendments nor by the legislatures of the States which ratified them....

SOURCE: John W. Wallace, ed., *United States Reports* 16 (1873): pp. 36–130.

3. *New Orleans Race Riot (1866)* U.S. House of Representatives

Though they had lost the Civil War, Southern racists intended to win the peace. The Louisiana Constitution of 1864 limited the vote to white men only. Under these suffrage rules, former Confederates won control of the state government in 1865 and immediately passed the "black codes" eliminating any pretense of civil rights for the freedmen. Supposedly backed by the federal government, local Republicans convened a new constitutional convention at the Mechanics Institute in New Orleans on July 30, 1866. As the meeting came to order, angry whites attacked the building, leading to the deaths of thirty-eight people and the wounding of 150 others. The House of Representatives investigated this riot and other acts of violence in the South; their findings persuaded Congress to take control of the former Confederate states.

Questions to Consider

- Was Congress justified in intervening in state affairs?

- Why were the police firing on the Constitutional Convention?

New Orleans, December 24, 1866

ROBERT I. CROMWELL (colored) sworn and examined.

By the CHAIRMAN:

Q. State where you live.

A. I have lived in New Orleans since January, 1864.

Q. Were you in the convention on the 30th of June last?

A. I was. I arrived there between the hours of twelve and one on the day of the meeting of the convention, and went into the hall. I staid there from that hour until, I think, about 3 o'clock, or between three and four….

Q. State, in your own way, what facts came under your eye while you were in the hall.

A. I saw, while I was in the hall, policemen and others come in. A portion of the members had gone out. The police shot into the hall at those who remained, and I saw some parties trying to get out.

Q. Who was the shooting by; and who did you see shot?

A. I did not see any one shot. I saw policemen come in and shoot at the crowd in there; but I saw nobody shot, particularly.

Q. Did you see anybody wounded?

A. Yes sir; I saw Mr. Horton after he was wounded.

Q. Where did you go when you left the convention?

A. I jumped out of the side window down on to the pavement, between the building and the wall or brick fence, towards Canal street.

Q. Where did you go?

A. I was arrested by a policeman. When I struck the ground they came out from under the steps there, and fired at me and told me to surrender. I told them I surrendered. They then took me into a little alley way under the steps, and right under the building. I found eight or ten persons in there; one man, a Dr. Johnson, whom I knew, lay there wounded. Dr. Johnson asked me if I could not help him. I asked the policeman if I could do so, and he told me I could. I raised him up and laid him down again. I was searched and my money taken from me by the policemen. They took from me some $25 and some cents…. We were then taken out and taken to jail, where I remained till the next morning.

Q. Did you see any violence while you were on your way to the jail?

A. Yes; I saw one man who seemed to be very badly wounded; a policeman had him, kicking him and treating him very badly. They struck me with a pistol on the back of the head once after I got out.

Q. Was that by a policeman, or one of the crowd?

A. It was a policeman who did it.

Q. Was this man who was being badly treated a colored man?

A. Yes, sir.

Q. How badly treated?

A. As they had him carrying him along, one on each side, at one time his leg was let go, and they struck him and kicked him. That is what I call badly treated....

SOURCE: House of Representatives Report #16, 39th Congress, 2nd Session, 1866–67, (V1: 220), pp. 76–77.

UNIT 14

Industrial Supremacy

UNIT SUMMARY

In Unit 14 we look at the ways industry and production were organized in the early machine age and at the labor-management struggles that emerged during this era.

ASSIGNMENT

1. Before viewing Program 14, read this unit, and in *A People and a Nation* read Chapter 18, pages 487–494, and Chapter 19, pages 530–535.

2. View Program 14, "Industrial Supremacy."

3. Visit the Web site <http://www.learner.org/biographyofamerica>.
    Explore the exercises for Program 14.

LEARNING OBJECTIVES

Upon completing this unit, students should be able to:

1. Describe the changes industrialization imposed on production and manufacturing.

2. Discuss how immigration supplied the needs of business and chronicle the problems immigrants faced adapting to industrialization.

3. Describe working conditions in the new industrial age and workers' struggles against exploitation.

PROGRAM GUIDE

The industrial revolution transforms the American economic landscape. Professor Miller leads us through the stockyard and the foundry to explore the mighty engine of industrialism. Program 14 looks at the Chicago packinghouses and examines the lives of the workers and of industrialists such as Andrew Carnegie and Phillip Armour.

   The rise and domination of big business defines post-Civil War America. Americans are fascinated by the Machine Age and its inventions, its wealth, its consumerism, and its captains of industry. Cities are central to the industrial changes sweeping the nation, and by 1900, Chicago has overtaken New York as the United States' leading industrial center. The meatpacking industry transforms Chicago into a model of efficiency. While Philip Armour and Gustavus Swift vie for the title of Meat King, the masses of workers in Chicago's meatpacking plants toil in abject poverty and filth. As Andrew Carnegie, John D. Rockefeller, and J. Pierpont Morgan seize control of business and change the character of free enterprise, labor and management clash over low wages, horrendous working conditions, and long hours. Despite labor unrest, worker abuse, and corporations' monopolistic practices, industrial might propels the United States to world dominance. It is a defining moment for laissez-faire capitalism.

HISTORICAL OVERVIEW

Entrepreneurs built the corporations that came to rule the economy, and fortunes were made as economies of scale, cost-benefit analysis, and other modern accounting techniques made businesses efficient and profitable across the industrial landscape.

Railroads were the hallmark of industrial organization. They required huge pools of labor, capital, and resources, and a new class of bureaucrats organized and managed them with a keen eye on the bottom line. In an era of laissez-faire capitalism, the railroads received land subsidies, financial incentives, and loans from the federal government. In California, cheap labor in the form of immigrant Chinese was an essential ingredient in the railroads' success. During the depression in the early seventies, Irish workers in San Francisco protested the presence of Chinese in California, shouting "The Chinese must go!" In 1881 Congress passed the Chinese Exclusion Act banning further immigration.

Across America, an endless supply of immigrant labor worked for below subsistence wages. Fleeing Europe in search of a better life in the United States, they arrived with little besides their willingness to work. Industrial society was a bewildering milieu and immigrants packed themselves into the equally befuddling urban settings that were developing across the nation. Urban political machines moved into action to meet the needs of this new constituency, dispensing patronage and facilitating a steady stream of unskilled workers for industry. In exchange for votes, the boss provided jobs, housing, and other services. Workers were slow to learn the benefits of organization and solidarity, and industrialists used the waves of new immigrants to thwart organizing efforts. Thus a cycle repeated itself for decades until government regulations and labor gains forced corporations to make concessions.

Despite the difficulties facing immigrants, many recognized the opportunities of industrialization. Andrew Carnegie, a Scottish immigrant, made a fortune in steel manufacturing. A keen innovator and a shrewd manager, Carnegie employed the method of vertical integration to maximize profits and efficiency. While foundries produced steel and employed new technologies, Carnegie expanded his field of operations. He realized that the raw materials needed to make steel and the transportation links to the foundries were in the hands of middlemen. Why pay the mine and railroad operators? Carnegie bought the mines and integrated them into his overall operation. The sheer size of his enterprise enabled him to adopt new technologies that saved one cent on a pound of steel.

The modernization of industry produced many success stories, but there were costs. Corporate America ruled in industrial society and the government turned a blind eye to abuses. Efforts to regulate and restrict corporations' activities were loathsome to businessmen, and politicians were reluctant to regulate the economy. Working conditions and wages became a source of conflict between workers and management. Workers' efforts to organize and form unions were met by stiff resistance, as companies facing labor troubles resorted to terminations, private police, and even government troops. Between 1887–1906, more than 35,000 worker strikes were called in the United States. Occasionally, conflicts became bloody, as in the Railroad Strikes of 1877.

The abuses associated with industrialization are well documented. Several unions emerged to represent railway workers, miners, and steelworkers, and in the 1880s and 1890s popular resentment towards the industrialists grew. Congress eventually moved to regulate the business world and so helped to improve the poor working and living conditions associated with this industrial phase of development. Americans learned important lessons in their struggle for decency and respect in the workplace.

MAP EXERCISE

Refer to the following maps in Chapters 17 and 18 of *A People and a Nation* to answer the questions listed below.

- The Development and Natural Resources of the West (p. 469)

- Industrial Production, 1919 (p. 490)

1. How did the landscape of industrial America change with the advance of the railroads? Which sections of the nation were impacted the most and which lines served these regions?

2. Identify the nation's largest industrial centers and note the distribution of production across the country. Which were the chief industrial cities in the early-twentieth century?

PEOPLE, EVENTS, AND CONCEPTS

Identify and explain the historical significance of each item.

the Railroad Strikes of 1877

Identification

Significance

economies of scale

Identification

Significance

Andrew Carnegie

Identification

Significance

entrepreneurship

Identification

Significance

Philip Sheridan

Identification

Significance

Chicago Stockyards

Identification

Significance

vertical integration

Identification

Significance

Gustavus Swift

Identification

Significance

Chinese Exclusion Act

Identification

Significance

The Jungle

Identification

Significance

Sherman Anti-Trust Act

Identification

Significance

laissez-faire capitalism

Identification

Significance

ESSAY QUESTIONS

1. What methods were utilized by the business community to organize business with an eye on efficiency and profitability?

2. What was the role of the transcontinental railroad in the American economy and society in the age of industrialization?

3. Contrast and compare the post-Civil War phase of industrialization with that of the earlier antebellum phase of development. How did the New South fare in the second phase?

MULTIPLE-CHOICE QUESTIONS

1. The transcontinental railroad was built by
   a. Andrew Carnegie.
   b. Cornelius Vanderbilt.
   c. Gustavus Swift.
   d. none of the above.

2. The railroads facilitated industrialization by
   a. embracing laissez-faire capitalism.
   b. employing Chinese immigrants.
   c. opening the West to settlement.
   d. creating a national market system.

3. Andrew Carnegie employed all of the following methods except
   a. vertical integration.
   b. economy of scale.
   c. new technologies.
   d. the eight-hour day.

4. During the 1870s the severest threat to the new order was
   a. the Haymarket Incident.
   b. the Great Uprising.
   c. the Homestead Strike.
   d. none of the above.

5. Railroad barons were considered menaces to the public welfare because
   a. they treated the Indians brutally.
   b. they refused to pay a living wage.
   c. they bribed politicians.
   d. the railroads disrupted farming.

6. The national government tried to curtail monopolies with the
   a. Sherman Anti-Trust Act.
   b. Pure Food and Drug Act.
   c. Federal Trade Commission.
   d. Interstate Commerce Commission.

7. During the era of industrialization, workers faced
   a. declining wages and living standards.
   b. improved working conditions and shorter hours.
   c. improved standards of living but loss of work independence.
   d. declining demand for goods and loss of jobs.

8. The rise of industrial Chicago is associated with all of the following except
   a. the meat packing industry.
   b. Gustavus Swift and Phillip Armour.
   c. the first assembly line.
   d. Ellis Island.

Answers

| 1. | d | 3. | d | 5. | d | 7. | a |
| 2. | d | 4. | b | 6. | a | 8. | d |

PRIMARY SOURCE DOCUMENTS

The accounts of actual participants are useful for understanding the motives and thoughts of historical characters.

1. *The Strike of 1877 (1877)* Allan Pinkerton

Allan Pinkerton was the founder of the first large detective agency in the United States. During the Civil War he provided information of dubious quality to the U.S. government. After the war, the Pinkertons, as his agents were generically called, became the premier strikebreakers in America. Pinkertons infiltrated unions, acted as provocateurs, and served as hired thugs to beat recalcitrant workers.

Questions to Consider

- Does Pinkerton think the workers have any legitimate grievances?
- If most workers opposed the strike, as Pinkerton says, then where did these crowds come from?
- Is an alternative interpretation of these events possible?

After ascertaining that such action was of extreme necessity, in June, '77, the Pennsylvania Railroad Company announced a reduction of ten per cent. upon the wages of all officers and employees receiving more than one dollar a day the same to take effect on and after the first of July following. This order and the subsequent introduction of what is known as the "double-headers," or freight trains composed of a larger number of cars than the single train, and drawn by two engines, which economized labor, and consequently displaced a few employees, constituted the "grievances" which resulted in the reorganization of the Trainmen's Union, and eventually the strike and its terribly disastrous results.

No sooner had these measures for economy in the company's management gone into effect, than the class, and only the class—these utterly worthless employees—referred to, began their secret meetings and their seditious efforts. But it is an established fact that the great body of employees accepted the reduction with good grace…. In fact, more than three-fourths of the employees of the road, and immeasurably the most deserving, capable, and valuable class of its employees, had received the reduction in an appreciative and manly way….

At noon of Thursday, July 19th, the unexpected blow was struck; and, illustrative of the powerlessness of our State laws and imbecile inefficiency of local authorities, a handful of men, who might have been subdued by a determined corporal's guard, were permitted to precipitate what led to the most deplorable riots in history….

So swiftly did this striking fever run through the worst element of the trainmen lingering about, that scarcely an hour had elapsed before a crowd of fully five hundred employees had gathered, and all efforts at starting trains proved ineffectual....

Quick work was now made, and a sudden end put to all order and authority. Trains were run upon side-tracks and left there. Then matters on the main tracks were taken in hand, and all trains east or west were stopped. Those coming from the east were allowed to proceed into the city after the situation had been explained and their crews so thoroughly threatened and otherwise frightened that they sacredly promised to "go out," or join the strikers, as soon as Pittsburg proper had been reached, which under the circumstances they invariably did.... At night a strong guard of strikers patroled the tracks, and complete possession had been taken of the Western Division of the road....

The foolish men who had inaugurated the strike, as well as the cowardly officials who had permitted it to grow into these alarming proportions, now helplessly saw that they had unlocked the floodgates of anarchy and riot. From every quarter...men with hate in their desperate faces gathered in groups, and in low tones plotted and threatened. The slums and alleys turned out their miserable inhabitants—men with faces of brutes, women with faces of demons. Every fresh accession of communistic laborers and communistic loafers was welcomed with an intelligence only begot of murderous hate in one common purpose; ...that ignorant envy always gives to insolent outlawry....

The streets filled up with surging masses, the morning lengthened, and an ominous dread came down upon the city. Business men who had been loud in their denunciation of the Pennsylvania Railroad now shrank within their offices and stores, regretting the criminal "sympathy" they had extended to a handful of lawbreakers, out of a sickly, mawkish sentimentality, but all too late realized that the coming carnival of riot could not be checked....

At eight o'clock on the previous evening, Major-General R. M. Brinton, of Philadelphia, ...received telegraphic orders...to move his entire division, cavalry and artillery dismounted, to the scene of trouble.... Nearly one thousand men were gathered together....

A determined set of men had met a desperate set of men. For fully five minutes the soldiers slowly advanced, making but little progress in their work. The thousands of rioters behind, with yells and jeers, pushed and jammed those in front down upon the troops, who stood like a wall for a time, never uttering a word in response to the diabolical threats of their opponents, but using all their force to keep the fiends at bay.... But now a striker here and a ruffian there began to grasp the guns and lay hold of the troops roughly. This was the signal for like action all along the mob's front. At this the troops were compelled to gather back, bring their arms to a charge, and use their bayonets, when a few of the rioters were wounded. In another instant, over to the left from between the ears, a pistol-shot was heard. This was followed like a flash by the discharge of other pistol-shots and showers of stones and pieces of coal from the now infuriated mob....

Right and left the wounded soldiers began to fall, and some one poor fellow, goaded beyond forbearance, discharged his musket. In a moment more the firing became general. The mob as hotly replied with pistols, muskets taken from the Pittsburg regiments on the hill, and every manner of missile that could be lifted or hurled. But the Philadelphia troops knew how to shoot as well as to drill. The effect of their repeated volleys was terrible. The mob retreated aghast, rallied, retreated, rallied again, and through and through their numbers the deadly bullets mowed wrinkled and crumpled swaths, until upon the hill and along the tracks the wild and frenzied rioters precipitately withdrew.... But they left only to return in the blackness of the night with fury and forces increased, to bring, with them arson and flame, destruction and ruin, until the city of Pittsburg should for a time be like some doubly accursed spot to undergo the scourge of myriads of demons from the regions infernal.

...Within five days from the breaking out of the riot, Governor Hartranft...had brought together nearly six thousand troops that were admirably located at different points within the city and along the line of the Pennsylvania road, in commanding positions upon the hills, and at points where the lawless elements would be most likely to gather....

The strike really ended Sunday, July 29th, when the first freight train, after the abandonment of work by the trainmen, was moved. This train was put in motion on the Pennsylvania Central road, and successfully sent to its destination. No person would have imagined a strike had existed, save for the murmurs of a few disaffected men....

So ended the strike at Pittsburg. What had seemed a revolution resulted in a most imbecile fiasco.

Source: Allan Pinkerton, *Strikers, Communists, Tramps and Detectives* (New York, 1878), pp. 216–221, 230–231, 236–239, 282–283.

2. *Formation of the Knights of Labor (1878)* Terence V. Powderly

The Noble Order of the Knights of Labor was the first national labor union. Originally organized by the garment workers of Philadelphia in 1869, the Knights of Labor began in 1876 to expand its membership to include other skilled workers. Terence V. Powderly, a machinist from Scranton, played a key role in making the Knights of Labor into a national organization. Along with Robert Schilling, Powderly wrote the preamble of the union's constitution, which served as the guiding document of the Knights until they were supplanted by the American Federation of Labor in the 1890s. Powderly perceived that workers suffered from a social stigma which minimized the value of their labor, and hoped that the Knights would give workers a sense of their own worth.

Questions to Consider

- Why was the Knights of Labor kept secret?
- What does Powderly think are the advantages of a union?
- What reforms were necessary and why?

On January 1,1878, the representatives of the various parts of the order met in Reading, Pa. .... It was voted to call the body, which was then in session, the GENERAL ASSEMBLY OF THE KNIGHTS OF LABOR OF NORTH AMERICA....

No nominations were made except in an informal way, each representative casting his ballot for that person whom he believed to be BEST QUALIFIED TO FILL THE POSITION. The first committee on constitution of the order of the Knights of Labor, appointed by Mr. Stephens, consisted of representatives Robert Schilling, Chairman; Ralph Beaumont, Thomas King, T.V. Powderly, and George S. Boyle....

Preamble

The recent alarming development and aggression of aggregated wealth, which, unless checked, will invariably lead to the pauperization and hopeless degradation of the toiling masses, render it imperative, if we desire to enjoy the blessings of life, that a check should be placed upon its power and upon unjust accumulation, and a system adopted which will secure to the laborer the fruits of his toil; and as this much-desired object can only be accomplished by the thorough unification of labor, and the united efforts of those who obey the divine injunction that "In the sweat of thy brow shalt thou eat bread," we have formed the *****[1] with a view of securing the organization and direction, by co-operative effort, of the power of the industrial classes; and we submit to the world the objects sought to be accomplished by our organization, calling upon all who believe in securing "the greatest good to the greatest number" to aid and assist us:—

I. To bring within the folds of organization every department of productive industry, making knowledge a stand-point for action, and industrial and moral worth, not wealth, the true standard of individual and national greatness.

II. To secure to the toilers a proper share of the wealth that they create; more of the leisure that rightfully belongs to them; more societary advantages; more of the benefits, privileges, and emoluments of the world; in a word, all those rights and privileges necessary to make them capable of enjoying, appreciating, defending, and perpetuating the blessings of good government.

III. To arrive at the true condition of the producing masses in their educational, moral, and financial condition, by demanding from the various governments the establishment of bureaus of Labor Statistics.

IV. The establishment of co-operative institutions, productive and distributive.

V. The reserving of the public lands—the heritage of the people—for the actual settler;—not another acre for railroads or speculators.

VI. The abrogation of all laws that do not bear equally upon capital and labor, the removal of unjust technicalities, delays, and discriminations in the administration of justice, and the adopting of measures providing for the health and safety of those engaged in mining, manufacturing, or building pursuits.

VII. The enactment of laws to compel chartered corporations to pay their employes weekly, in full, for labor performed during the preceding week, in the lawful money of the country.

VIII. The enactment of laws giving mechanics and laborers a first lien on their work for their full wages.

IX. The abolishment of the contract system on national, State, and municipal work.

X. The substitution of arbitration for strikes, whenever and wherever employers and employes are willing to meet on equitable grounds.

XI. The prohibition of the employment of children in workshops, mines and factories before attaining their fourteenth year.

XII. To abolish the system of letting out by contract the labor of convicts in our prisons and reformatory institutions.

XIII. To secure for both sexes equal pay for equal work.

XIV. The reduction of the hours of labor to eight per day, so that the laborers may have more time for social enjoyment and intellectual improvement, and be enabled to reap the advantages conferred by the labor-saving machinery which their brains have created.

XV. To prevail upon governments to establish a purely national circulating medium, based upon the faith and resources of the nation, and issued directly to the people, without the intervention of any system of banking corporations, which money shall be a legal tender in payment of all debts, public or private.

After adopting a constitution and the preamble given above, the General Assembly elected the officers for the ensuing term, fixed upon St. Louis as the place to hold the next session, and adjourned with the following corps of officers:

Grand Master Workman—Uriah S. Stephens, of Pennsylvania.
Grand Worthy Foreman—Ralph Beaumont, of New York.
Grand Secretary—Charles H. Litchman, of Massachusetts.
Grand Assist. Secretary—John G. Laning, of Ohio....

SOURCE: T. V. Powderly, *Thirty Years of Labor: 1859 to 1889* (Columbus, OH, 1890), pp. 239, 241–246.
[1] The Knights of Labor was a secret organization until 1881, and even its name was kept confidential.—*Ed.*

3.   *What Social Classes Owe to Each Other (1883)* **William Graham Sumner**

One of the founders of sociology, William Graham Sumner believed that human conduct could be understood through scientific inquiry. Yet underneath Sumner's claim of scientific objectivity lay a powerful ideological base with obvious conservative implications. As an absolute believer in *laissez-faire* policies, Sumner dismissed nearly every effort at reform as romantic nonsense out of touch with reality. Closely aligned with Social Darwinism, Sumner believed that the early British economists Adam Smith, David Ricardo, and Thomas Malthus had discovered the great scientific facts of human behavior.

Questions to Consider

- Why should nothing be done to change social arrangements?
- What role does Sumner assign the state?
- If efforts to institute change are counterproductive, then how is social progress possible?

So far as I can find out what the classes are who are respectively endowed with the rights and duties of posing and solving social problems, they are as follows: Those who are bound to solve the problems are the rich, comfortable, prosperous, virtuous, respectable, educated, and healthy; those whose right it is to set the problems are those who have been less fortunate or less successful in the struggle for existence. The problem itself seems to be, How shall the latter be made as comfortable as the former? To solve this problem, and make us all equally well off, is assumed to be the duty of the former class; the penalty, if they fail of this, is to be bloodshed and destruction. If they cannot make everybody else as well off as themselves, they are to be brought down to the same misery as others.

During the last ten years I have read a great many books and articles, especially by German writers, in which an attempt has been made to set up "the State" as an entity having conscience, power, and will sublimated above human limitations, and as constituting a tutelary genius over us all. I have never been able to find in history or experience anything to fit this concept....

...The inadequacy of the State to regulative tasks is agreed upon, as a matter of fact, by all. Why, then, bring State regulation into the discussion simply in order to throw it out again? The whole subject ought to be discussed and settled aside from the hypothesis of State regulation....

It is commonly asserted that there are in the United States no classes, and any allusion to classes is resented. On the other hand, we constantly read and hear discussions of social topics in which the existence of social classes is assumed as a simple fact. "The poor," "the weak," "the laborers," are expressions which are used as if they had exact and well-understood definition. Discussions are made to bear upon the assumed rights, wrongs, and misfortunes of certain social classes; and all public speaking and writing consists, in a large measure, of the discussion of general plans for meeting the wishes of classes of people who have not been able to satisfy their own desires....

Now, if there are groups of people who have a claim to other people's labor and self-denial, and if there are other people whose labor and self-denial are liable to be claimed by the first groups, then there certainly are "classes," and classes of the oldest and most vicious type. For a man who can command another man's labor and self-denial for the support of his own existence is a privileged person of the highest species conceivable on earth.... We shall find that every effort to realize equality necessitates a sacrifice of liberty....

...A man who is present as a consumer, yet who does not contribute either by land, labor, or capital to the work of society, is a burden. On no sound political theory ought such a person to share in the political power of the State. He drops out of the ranks of workers and producers. Society must support him. It accepts the burden, but he must be cancelled from the ranks of the rulers likewise. So much for the pauper. About him no more need be said. ...

... [T]hose whom humanitarians and philanthropists call the weak are the ones through whom the productive and conservative forces of society are wasted. They constantly neutralize and destroy the finest efforts of the wise and industrious, and are a dead-weight on the society in all its struggles to realize any better things. Whether the people who mean no harm, but are weak in the essential powers necessary to the performance of one's duties in life, or those who are malicious and vicious, do the more mischief, is a question not easy to answer.

Under the names of the poor and the weak, the negligent, shiftless, inefficient, silly, and imprudent are fastened upon the industrious and prudent as a responsibility and a duty....

The humanitarians, philanthropists, and reformers, looking at the facts of life as they present themselves, find enough which is sad and unpromising in the condition of many members of society.... In their eagerness to recommend the less fortunate classes to pity and consideration they forget all about the rights of other classes; they gloss over all the faults of the classes in question, and they exaggerate their misfortunes and their virtues.... The man who has done nothing to raise himself above poverty finds that the social doctors flock about him, bringing the capital which they have collected from the other class, and promising him the aid of the State to give him what the other had to work for. In all these schemes and projects the organized intervention of society through the State is either planned or hoped for, and the State is thus made to become the protector and guardian of certain classes. The agents who are to direct the State action are, of course, the reformers and philanthropists.... Here it may suffice to observe that, on the theories of the social philosophers to whom I have referred, we should get a new maxim of judicious living: Poverty is the best policy. If you get wealth, you will have to support other people; if you do not get wealth, it will be the duty of other people to support you....

Every man and woman in society has one big duty. That is, to take care of his or her own self....

Society, therefore, does not need any care or supervision. If we can acquire a science of society, based on observation of phenomena and study of forces, we may hope to gain some ground slowly toward the elimination of old errors and the re-establishment of a sound and natural social order. Whatever we gain that way will be by growth, never in the world by any reconstruction of society on the plan of some enthusiastic social architect.... Society needs first of all to be freed from these meddlers—that is, to be let alone. Here we are, then, once more back at the old doctrine—*Laissez faire.* Let us translate it into blunt English, and it will read, Mind your own business. It is nothing but the doctrine of liberty....

SOURCE: William Graham Sumner, *What Social Classes Owe to Each Other* (New York, 1903), pp. 8–9, 11, 13, 15–16, 20–24, 113, 119–120.

UNIT 15

The New City

UNIT SUMMARY

In Unit 15 we look at Chicago's rise as the city that set the standard for America's new business city.

ASSIGNMENT

1. Before viewing Program 15, read this unit, and in *A People and a Nation* read Chapter 19.

2. View Program 15, "The New City."

3. Visit the Web site <http://www.learner.org/biographyofamerica>. Explore the exercises for Program 15.

LEARNING OBJECTIVES

Upon completing this unit, students should be able to:

1. Discuss the rise of Chicago as the nation's dominant commercial center.

2. Describe how machine politics secured the votes of immigrants and helped the urban business community prosper.

3. Describe the impact of both industrialization and urbanization on U.S. culture during the late nineteenth century.

4. Evaluate the conditions that led to the urban reform movement and the role of people like Jane Addams and Florence Kelly.

5. Assess the selection of Chicago for the centennial celebration and its larger meaning for the nation.

PROGRAM GUIDE

Chicago is the site of the Columbian Exposition of 1893, a world's fair held in what its architect Daniel Burnham called the "White City" built on Chicago's South Side. Chicago itself is a marvel of modern times, a commercial city with steel skyscrapers, electric lights and trolley cars, planned parks, housing developments, and department stores. Professor Miller introduces Chicago as the city to watch as it helps to redefine the people and culture of the nation entering the twentieth century, America's century.

The Great Fire of 1871 nearly destroys Chicago. By the end of the seventies, however, the city has risen from its ashes to become the nation's dominant industrial center. It is a model of efficiency in the new world of commerce. Daniel Burnham, Charles Yerkes, William LeBaron Jenney, and others figure prominently in the city's new design, as skyscrapers and the reckless pursuit of profits dub Chicago the City of Speed. Chicago is the world's first vertical city. Everything is built for efficiency, and as the city expands, people move away from the city center and out to the suburbs, aided by new mass transit. Immigrants pour into Chicago, enhancing its cosmopolitan character and providing businessmen with cheap labor. Urban squalor is characteristic of the City of Speed, and a third of Chicago's inhabitants live in crowded, unhealthy conditions. Reformers Jane Addams and Florence Kelly are key players in initiatives to effect the changes so badly needed by the masses.

HISTORICAL OVERVIEW

As the twentieth century dawned, the city emerged as the dominant expression of industrial life. Chicago typified this trend. Built for business Chicago manifested the best and worst traits in urban America. Its skyscrapers, mass transit system, and department stores defined life in the vertical city. While New York and San Francisco were uniquely transcontinental, Chicago set the rhythm and pace for the era's drive to make a dollar. Chicago was the heart of the nation in the Gilded Age.

Chicago vied with New York for the honor of hosting the Columbian Exposition in 1893. Though New Yorkers fought tenaciously for the prize, Chicago's victory attested to her position as queen of the machine age. New York had enjoyed its stature as the nation's number one industrial city throughout most of the century, but by the 1890s Chicago had surpassed all rivals in industrial might. New York had skyscrapers, but Chicago's skyscrapers were constructed with business in mind: with a keen eye on efficiency, productivity, and sales. In Chicago, the dollar was king.

After the Great Fire, Chicago was rebuilt in the age of steel. Land was surveyed on a grid system to make more money for real estate speculators. William Lebaron Jenney's steel-framed buildings were designed expressly for business. Marshall Field recognized the opportunities in the new consumerism and opened a department store, and the public came to shop. As the vertical city reached skyward, people travelled to their jobs by mass transit. Charles Yerkes built a unified system of transportation as cable car and electric trolley replaced the horse-drawn trolley. With the street car came a shift in metropolitan life: an exodus to the suburbs. As citizens left the din of the inner city for the quiet of the suburbs, they left behind them the rapidly advancing squalor of industrial and urban life. Urbanization turned Chicago inside out, from its inner core to its outer edges.

Twenty-five percent of Chicago's inhabitants lived in wretched poverty. The worse slum was Packingtown, but ghettoes dotted the landscape. Immigrants—Poles, Jews, Slovaks, blacks, and Italians—lived in their own communities. Settlement leader Jane Addams, founder of Hull House, and fellow reformer Florence Kelley fought to reduce squalor and bring compassion and dignity to urban life. They lobbied politicians to provide badly needed services to the city's diverse immigrant communities. Laws to protect women and children from sweatshop conditions helped to improve the quality of life.

Corruption was commonplace in America's industrial cities. The lurid details of New York's graft-ridden Tammany Hall outraged the public and led to some reforms, but progress was slow. Bosses controlled patronage, and the spoils system assured the loyalty of rank and file party members. Politicians winked at fraud in their administrations, distinguishing between *honest* and *dishonest* graft. The former was acceptable when it involved selling real estate to insiders for future construction projects. Dishonest graft—payoffs, bribes, and extortion—was the nature of politics in the Gilded Age. It was the cost of doing business.

Chicago's selection as the site for the Columbian Exposition recognized the city as a showplace for America's commercial prowess. The "White City" told Americans what they could expect for the future.

If Chicago exuded the confidence of the age, its cultural arrogance was another prominent feature of the time. Segregation and ethnocentrism were prominent, as Frederick Douglass noted that the accomplishments of America's toiling masses were all but ignored at the Columbian Exposition. How, he asked, could the United States advance into the next century and continue to countenance squalor, poverty, racism, and economic inequality?

MAP EXERCISE

Refer to the following maps in Chapters 19 and 20 in *A People and a Nation* to answer the questions listed below.

- Presidential Election, 1896 (p. 574)
- Urbanization 1880–1920 (p. 522)
- Sources of European-born Population, 1900 and 1920 (p. 525)

1. The nation grew rapidly in the last quarter of the century. Which cities experienced the greatest growth? Which states had emerged as the most important to presidential politics by the 1920s and why?

2. Which European nations sent the largest number of immigrants to the United States and what were the reasons for the exodus? Which cities did the immigrants populate?

PEOPLE, EVENTS, AND CONCEPTS

Identify and explain the historical significance of each item.

Daniel Burnham

Identification

Significance

Colored People's Day

Identification

Significance

William LeBaron Jenney

Identification

Significance

the White City

Identification

Significance

Columbian Exposition

Identification

Significance

Marshall Field

Identification

Significance

Charles Yerkes

Identification

Significance

Hull House

Identification

Significance

Great Fire of 1871

Identification

Significance

Florence Kelley

Identification

Significance

City of Speed

Identification

Significance

Frederick Douglass

Identification

Significance

Goliath of Graft

Identification

Significance

Theodore Dreiser

Identification

Significance

1906 earthquake

Identification

Significance

Jane Addams

Identification

Significance

Gilded Age

Identification

Significance

Graft Trials

Identification

Significance

Frederick Jackson Turner

Identification

Significance

ESSAY QUESTIONS

1. After the Great Fire of 1871, Chicago was rebuilt with business in mind. Who were the people involved in its rebirth? Describe the quintessential features of what was called *the City of Speed.*

2. Why did immigrants leave Europe and how were they greeted upon their arrival in the United States? Assess their contributions to the nation in the machine age.

3. What social problems did industrialization create for the cities? How did the political machines tailor their operations to industry's needs and why was reform necessary?

MULTIPLE-CHOICE QUESTIONS

1. Chicago's master builder and architect of the "White City" was
   a. Frederick Law Olmsted.
   b. Theodore Dreiser.
   c. Daniel Burnham.
   d. Marshall Field.
2. An early example of consumerism in urban America was
   a. factories and assembly line production.
   b. the rise of large department stores.
   c. mass transportation.
   d. centers like Hull House.
3. A large number of the immigrants coming to U.S. shores after 1880 were
   a. arriving en masse from Canada.
   b. welcomed throughout the nation.
   c. different culturally from earlier immigrants.
   d. exclusively from Central Europe.
4. Theodore Dreiser's novel *Titan* based its central character, the "Goliath of Graft," on
   a. Charles Yerkes.
   b. Marshall Field.
   c. Daniel Burnham.
   d. Louis Sullivan.
5. Jane Addams and Florence Kelley were the first in Chicago to establish centers to help
   a. labor unions.
   b. new immigrants.
   c. day-care workers.
   d. civil servants.
6. America's commercial cities expanded rapidly with innovations in technologies like the
   a. Franklin stove and pewter kettles.
   b. Corliss engine.
   c. trolleys and skyscrapers.
   d. grocery stores and malls.
7. Chicago's emergence as the dominant commercial city in the country displaced
   a. Boston.
   b. New York.
   c. New Orleans.
   d. San Francisco.
8. Historically, the wealthy lived in the center of big cities, but they left for the suburbs
   a. for the opportunities in real estate development.
   b. to escape the wretchedness of urban life.
   c. because of the frequency of fires.
   d. because they found new jobs outside the cities.

Answers

| 1. c | 3. c | 5. b | 7. b |
| 2. b | 4. a | 6. c | 8. b |

PRIMARY SOURCE DOCUMENTS

The accounts of actual participants are useful for understanding the motives and thoughts of historical characters.

1. ***The Haymarket Trials (1886)*** **Dyer D. Lum**

In the 1880s, unions concentrated their efforts on obtaining the eight-hour work day. Business leaders labeled supporters of the eight-hour work day socialists and anarchists, and, in fact, a great many of both were involved in the effort to reduce the work day. A nationwide strike in favor of the eight-hour day was called for May 1, 1886. The Chicago rally drew a large crowd, and some speakers called for violence to gain their ends. Two days later, police opened fire on a crowd of striking workers at the McCormick Harvester plant, killing one worker and wounding several others. Another mass meeting was called for at Haymarket Square to protest this official violence. Just as the meeting was breaking up, nearly two hundred police arrived and ordered everyone out of the square. At that moment, someone threw a bomb at the police, killing seven officers. The police then fired on the crowd, leading to several more deaths. The police arrested all the anarchists they could find, eight of whom were tried for murder. Though the state's only witness to claim that one of these men threw the bomb was discredited on the stand, all eight defendants were found guilty. Four of the convicted were hanged (August Spies, Adolph Fischer, George Engel, and Albert Parsons), one committed suicide in prison, and the remaining three were pardoned by Governor John Altgeld in 1893.

Questions to Consider

- Why did an eight-hour day for workers seem like such a radical idea in the 1880s?

- How could a jury find these eight men guilty based on this evidence?

On the 2d of August Hon. Carter H. Harrison, the mayor of Chicago, was placed on the witness stand as the first witness for the defense. His testimony as to the character of the meeting was clear and decisive. Following are extracts:

Q. Did you attend the Haymarket meeting on Desplaines street on the 4th of May last?

A. A part of it, not the whole. During May 4th, probably about noon, information came to me of the issuance of a circular of a very peculiar character, and a call for a meeting at the Haymarket that night. I called the chief of police and directed him that if anything should be said at that meeting as was likely to call out a recurrence of such proceedings as at McCormick's factory the meeting should be immediately dispersed. I believed that it was better for myself to be there and to disperse it myself instead of leaving it to any policemen. I thought my order would be better obeyed. I went there then for the purpose, if I felt it necessary for the best interests of the city, to disperse that meeting.

Q. How long did you remain at the meeting?

A. It was about five minutes before eight o'clock when I arrived. I should judge from the time when the bomb sounded and the time it took me to walk home, that I left the meeting between 10 and 10:05 o'clock. I heard all except probably a minute or a minute and a half of Mr. Spies' speech, and all of Mr. Parsons' up to the time I left, with the exception of a break when I left him talking and went over to the station. I was absent five or ten minutes. It was near the close of Parsons' speech. *I should judge he was looking toward a close.* I went to the station to speak to Captain Bonfield, and had determined to go home, but instead of going home I went back to hear a little more, *and then left.*

Q. Up to the time that you went to the station and had this interview with Mr. Bonfield, what was the tenor of the speeches?

A. With the exception of a portion in the earlier part of Mr. Spies' address, which, for probably a minute, was such that I feared it was leading up to a point where I should disperse the meeting, it was such that I remarked to Captain Bonfield *that it was tame.* The portion of Mr. Parsons' speech attracting most attention was the statistics as to the amount of returns given to labor from capital, and showing, if I remember rightly now, that capital got eighty-five per cent and labor fifteen per cent. It was what I should call a violent political harangue against capital.

Q. Was any action taken by you while you were at the meeting looking to the dispersal of the meeting?

A. *No!*

Q. Do you recollect any suggestion made by either of the speakers looking toward the immediate use of force or violence toward any person?

A. *There was none.* If there had been I should have dispersed them at once.

Q. How long was the interview that you had with Inspector Bonfield?

A. Probably five minutes.

Q. Will you please state what it was?

A. I went back to the station and said to Bonfield that I thought that the speeches were about over; *that nothing had occurred yet or was likely to occur to require interference, and I thought he had better issue orders to his reserves at the other stations to go home.* He replied that he thought about the same way, as he had men in the crowd who were reporting to him.

Q. Did you see any weapons in the hands of the audience?

A. No, sir; none at all….

BARTON SIMONSON, …traveling salesman…thought Mr. Parsons did say "To arms, to arms," but in what connection could not remember. "Somebody in the crowd said 'shoot' or 'hang Gould,' and he says, 'No, a great many will jump up and take his place. What Socialism aims at is not the death of individuals, but of the system.'

"Fielden spoke very loud, and as I had never attended a Socialist meeting before in my life, I thought they were a little wild…. Fielden said…two or three times, 'Now, in conclusion,' or something like that, and I became impatient. Then I heard a commotion and a good deal of noise in the audience, and somebody said, 'police.' I looked south and saw a line of police. The police moved along until the front of the column got about up to the speaker's wagon…. About the time somebody was giving that command to disperse, I distinctly heard two words coming from…the wagon. I don't know who uttered them. The words were, 'peaceable meeting.' That was a few seconds before the explosion of the bomb…. At the time the bomb exploded I was still in my position upon the stairs. There was no pistol firing by any person upon the wagon before the bomb exploded. No pistol shots anywhere before the explosion of the bomb.

"Just after the command to disperse had been given, I saw a lighted fuse, or something—I didn't know what it was at the time—come up from a point *twenty feet south* of the south line of Crane's alley, from about the center of the sidewalk on the east side of the street, from behind some boxes…. I first noticed it about six or seven feet in the air, a little above a man's head. It went in a northwest course and up about fifteen feet from the ground, and fell about the middle of the street. The explosion followed almost immediately. Something of a cloud of smoke followed the explosion. After the bomb exploded there was pistol shooting. From my position I could distinctly see the flashes of the pistols. My head was about fifteen feet above the ground. There might have been fifty to one hundred and fifty pistol shots. They proceeded from about the center of where the police were. I did not observe either the flashes of the pistol shot or hear the report of any shots from the crowd upon the police prior to the firing by the police. The police were not only shooting at the crowd, but I noticed several of them shoot just as they happened to throw their arms. I concluded that my position was possibly more dangerous than down in the crowd, and then I ran down to the foot of the stairs…. A crowd was running in the same direction…. I was in the rear of the crowd running west, the police still behind us. There were no shots from the direction to which I was running.

"I am not and never have been a member of any Socialistic party or association. Walking through the crowd before the meeting, I noticed that the meeting was composed principally of ordinary workingmen, mechanics, etc. …

"…In the course of the conversation with Capt. Bonfield at the station before the meeting that night, I asked him about the trouble in the southwestern part of the city. He says: 'The trouble there is that these'—whether he used the word Socialist or strikers, I don't know—'get their women and children mixed up with them and around them and in front of them, and we can't get at them. I would like to get 3,000 of them in a crowd without their women and children'—and to the best of my recollection he added—'and I will make short work of them.' I noticed a few women and children at the bottom of the steps where I was."

Upon cross-examination this graphic and evidently truthful narration was not weakened in the least…. The witness went to the meeting out of mere curiosity to see what Socialist meetings were, and no subsequent witness could in any manner affect his character as an exemplary citizen and Christian gentleman.

SOURCE: Dyer D. Lum, A Concise History of the Great Trial of the Chicago Anarchists in 1886 (Chicago, 1886), pp. 29–30, 112

2. *How the Other Half Lives (1890)* Jacob Riis

The rapid growth of industrialization in the United States in the 1880s created an intense need for labor. As tens of thousands of people, a great many of them immigrants, flooded into Northeastern cities, housing became a problem of major proportions. Landlords, rushing to realize quick profits, persisted in subdividing their apartments into ever smaller units, crowding the poor into the most horrid possible living conditions. In the late 1880s Jacob Riis, himself a Danish immigrant, began writing articles describing the realities of life in New York's slums. Riis was one of the first reporters to use flash photography, allowing him to take candid photos of the dark corners of poverty in New York. In 1890 he published *How the Other Half Lives,* illustrated with line drawings based on his photographs. Riis's book shocked middle-class America, which until that time had managed to avoid seeing the squalor of their own cities. A number of reform efforts followed, and Riis sparked a new brand of reporting called "muckraking."

Questions to Consider

- Why did the city government allow these conditions to persist?
- Why did the poor agree to live in such conditions?

The twenty-five cent lodging-house keeps up the pretence of a bedroom, though the head-high partition enclosing a space just large enough to hold a cot and a chair and allow the man room to pull off his clothes is the shallowest of all pretences. The fifteen-cent bed stands boldly forth without screen in a room full of bunks with sheets as yellow and blankets as foul. At the ten-cent level the locker for the sleeper's clothes disappears. There is no longer need of it. The tramp limit is reached, and there is nothing to lock up save, on general principles, the lodger. Usually the ten- and seven-cent lodgings are different grades of the same abomination. Some sort of an apology for a bed, with mattress and blanket, represents the aristocratic purchase of the tramp who, by a lucky stroke of beggary, has exchanged the chance of an empty box or ash-barrel for shelter on the quality floor of one of these "hotels." A strip of canvas, strung between rough timbers, without covering of any kind, does for the couch of the seven-cent lodger who prefers the questionable comfort of a red-hot stove close to his elbow to the revelry of the stale-beer dive. It is not the most secure perch in the world. Uneasy sleepers roll off at intervals, but they have not far to fall to the next tier of bunks, and the commotion that ensues is speedily quieted by the boss and his club. On cold winter nights, when every bunk had its tenant, I have stood in such a lodging-room more than once, and listening to the snoring of the sleepers like the regular strokes of an engine, and the slow creaking of the beams under their restless weight, imagined myself on shipboard and experienced the very real nausea of sea-sickness. The one thing that did not favor the deception was the air; its character could not be mistaken.

The proprietor of one of these seven-cent houses was known to me as a man of reputed wealth and respectability. He "ran" three such establishments and made, it was said, $8,000 a year clear profit on his investment. He lived in a handsome house quite near to the stylish precincts of Murray Hill, where the nature of his occupation was not suspected. A notice that was posted on the wall of the lodgers' room suggested at least an effort to maintain his up-town standing in the slums. It read: "No swearing or loud talking after nine o'clock." Before nine no exceptions were taken to the natural vulgarity of the place; but that was the limit.

There are no licensed lodging-houses known to me which charge less than seven cents for even such a bed as this canvas strip, though there are unlicensed ones enough where one may sleep on the floor for five cents a spot, or squat in a sheltered hallway for three. The police station lodging-house, where the soft side of a plank is the regulation couch, is next in order. The manner in which this police bed is "made up" is interesting in its simplicity. The loose planks that make the platform are simply turned over, and the job is done, with an occasional coat of whitewash thrown in to sweeten things. I know of only one easier way, but, so far as I am informed, it has never been introduced in this country. It used to be practised, if report spoke truly, in certain old-country towns. The "bed" was represented by clothes-line stretched across the room upon which the sleepers hung by the arm-pits for a penny a night. In the morning the boss woke them up by simply untying the line at one end and letting it go with its load; a labor-saving device certainly, and highly successful in attaining the desired end....

...If the tenement is here continually dragged into the eye of public condemnation and scorn, it is because in one way or another it is found directly responsible for, or intimately associated with, three-fourths of the miseries of the poor. In the Bohemian quarter it is made the vehicle for enforcing upon a proud race a slavery as real as any that ever disgraced the South. Not content with simply robbing the tenant, the owner, in the dual capacity of landlord and employer, reduces him to virtual serfdom by making his becoming *his* tenant, on such terms as he sees fit to make, the condition of employment at wages likewise of his own making. It does not help the case that this landlord employer, almost always a Jew, is frequently of the thrifty Polish race just described. ...

...Probably more than half of all the Bohemians in this city are cigarmakers, and it is the herding of these in great numbers in the so-called tenement factories, where the cheapest grade of work is done at the lowest wages, that constitutes at once their greatest hardship and the chief grudge of other workmen against them....

Men, women and children work together seven days in the week in these cheerless tenements to make a living for the family, from the break of day till far into the night. Often the wife is the original cigarmaker from the old home, the husband having adopted her trade here as a matter of necessity, because, knowing no word of English, he could get no other work. As they state the cause of the bitter hostility of the trades unions, she was the primary bone of contention in the day of the early Bohemian immigration. The unions refused to admit the women, and, as the support of the family depended upon her to a large extent, such terms as were offered had to be accepted. The manufacturer has ever since industriously fanned the antagonism between the unions and his hands, for his own advantage. The victory rests with him, since the Court of Appeals decided that the law, passed a few years ago, to prohibit cigarmaking in tenements was unconstitutional, and thus put an end to the struggle....

...I have in mind an alley—an inlet rather to a row of rear tenements—that is either two or four feet wide according as the wall of the crazy old building that gives on it bulges out or in. I tried to count the children that swarmed there, but could not. Sometimes I have doubted that anybody knows just how many there are about. Bodies of drowned children turn up in the rivers right along in summer whom no one seems to know anything about. When last spring some workmen, while moving a pile of lumber on a North River pier, found under the last plank the body of a little lad crushed to death, no one had missed a boy, though his parents afterward turned up. The truant officer assuredly does not know, though he spends his life trying to find out, somewhat illogically, perhaps, since the department that employs him admits that thousands of poor children are crowded out of the schools year by year for want of room....

SOURCE: Jacob A. Riis, *How the Other Half Lives* (New York, 1903), pp. 86–89, 136–139, 179–180.

3. *Social Ethics (1911)* Jane Addams

A social reformer of enormous energy and influence, Jane Addams began her long career by opening Hull House in 1889 to help poor immigrant families in Chicago. Over the years she launched a number of reform groups, including the Women's International League for Peace and Freedom; worked to change working conditions, housing regulations, and the juvenile courts; and was actively involved in politics, playing a leading role in Theodore Roosevelt's 1912 campaign for the presidency. Addams was often out of step with her times, a champion of both racial and gender equality and a pacifist who opposed U.S. entry into World War I. At a time of triumphant *laissez-faire* ideology, Addams insisted on the duty of the individual to help those less fortunate. In 1931 Addams was awarded the Nobel prize for peace. Addams wrote a number of books and articles encouraging people to join her progressive causes, as well as analyzing the motivations and methods of reformers. In the process she essentially created the modern job of social worker.

Questions to Consider

- Why should people devote energy to helping others?
- How can the charity worker overcome cultural differences?

Probably there is no relation in life which our democracy is changing more rapidly than the charitable relation—that relation which obtains between benefactor and beneficiary; at the same time there is no point of contact in our modern experience which reveals so clearly the lack of that equality which democracy implies. We have reached the moment when democracy has made such inroads upon this relationship, that the complacency of the old-fashioned charitable man is gone forever; while, at the same time, the very need and existence of charity, denies us the consolation and freedom which democracy will at last give....

The daintily clad charitable visitor who steps into the little house made untidy by the vigorous efforts of her hostess, the washerwoman, is no longer sure of her superiority to the latter; she recognizes that her hostess after all represents social value and industrial use, as over against her own parasitic cleanliness and a social standing attained only through status....

Added to this is a consciousness, in the mind of the visitor, of a genuine misunderstanding of her motives by the recipients of her charity, and by their neighbors. Let us take a neighborhood of poor people, and test their ethical standards by those of the charity visitor, who comes with the best desire in the world to help them out of their distress. A most striking incongruity, at once apparent, is the difference between the emotional kindness with which relief is given by one poor neighbor to another poor neighbor, and the guarded care with which relief is given by a charity visitor to a charity recipient. The neighborhood mind is at once confronted not only by the difference of method, but by an absolute clashing of two ethical standards.

A very little familiarity with the poor districts of any city is sufficient to show how primitive and genuine are the neighborly relations. There is the greatest willingness to lend or borrow anything, and all the residents of the given tenement know the most intimate family affairs of all the others. The fact that the economic condition of all alike is on a most precarious level makes the ready outflow of sympathy and material assistance the most natural thing in the world. There are numberless instances of self-sacrifice quite unknown in the circles where greater economic advantages make that kind of intimate knowledge of one's neighbors impossible. ...

...There is no doubt that this rude rule still holds among many people with whom charitable agencies are brought into contact, and that their ideas of right and wrong are quite honestly outraged by the methods of these agencies. When they see the delay and caution with which relief is given, it does not appear to them a conscientious scruple, but as the cold and calculating action of a selfish man. It is not the aid that they are accustomed to receive from their neighbors, and they do not understand why the impulse which drives people to "be good to the poor" should be so severely supervised. They feel, remotely, that the charity visitor is moved by motives that are alien and unreal. They may be superior motives, but they are different, and they are "agin nature." They cannot comprehend why a person whose intellectual perceptions are stronger than his natural impulses, should go into charity work at all. The only man they are accustomed to see whose intellectual perceptions are stronger than his tenderness of heart, is the selfish and avaricious man who is frankly; "on the make." If the charity visitor is such a person, why does she pretend to like the poor? Why does she not go into business at once? ...

Even those of us who feel most sorely the need of more order in altruistic effort and see the end to be desired, find something distasteful in the juxtaposition of the words "organized" and "charity." We say in defence that we are striving to turn this emotion into a motive, that pity is capricious, and not to be depended on; that we mean to give it the dignity of conscious duty. But at bottom we distrust a little a scheme which substitutes a theory of social conduct for the natural promptings of the heart, even although we appreciate the complexity of the situation. The poor man who has fallen into distress, when he first asks aid, instinctively expects tenderness, consideration, and forgiveness. If it is the first time, it has taken him long to make up his mind to take the step. He comes somewhat bruised and battered, and instead of being met with warmth of heart and sympathy, he is at once chilled by an investigation and an intimation that he ought to work. He does not recognize the disciplinary aspect of the situation....

We sometimes say that our charity is too scientific, but we would doubtless be much more correct in our estimate if we said that it is not scientific enough....

We have learned to condemn unthinking, ill-regulated kind-heartedness, and we take great pride in mere repression much as the stern parent tells the visitor below how admirably he is rearing the child, who is hysterically crying upstairs and laying the foundation for future nervous disorders....

We distrust the human impulse as well as the teachings of our own experience, and in their stead substitute dogmatic rules for conduct. We forget that the accumulation of knowledge and the holding of convictions must finally result in the application of that knowledge and those convictions to life itself....

SOURCE: Jane Addams, *Democracy and Social Ethics* (New York, 1911), pp. 13–14, 16, 18–20, 22–23, 25–26, 64, 67–68.

UNIT 16

The West

UNIT SUMMARY

In Unit 16 we look at the westward migrations of Americans, their settlement patterns, and their clashes with the indigenous peoples.

ASSIGNMENT

1. Before viewing Program 16, read this unit, and in *A People and a Nation* read Chapter 17 and Chapter 20, pages 563–568.

2. View Program 16, "The West."

3. Visit the Web site <http://www.learner.org/biographyofamerica>. Explore the exercises for Program 16.

LEARNING OBJECTIVES

Upon completing this unit, students should be able to:

1. Explain the impact of the railroads upon the economy and frontier settlement.

2. Discuss the role of the federal government in westward expansion and railroad building.

3. Assess the impact of westward migration and federal policies upon the life, traditions, and regional economies of the indigenous people in the decades following the Civil War.

4. Discuss the impact of industrialization on agriculture and the threats that farmers faced to their traditional ways of life.

5. Explain the rise of populism and its impact upon the political process.

PROGRAM GUIDE

Westward expansion remains a major theme in America's national development after the Civil War. Jefferson's dream of an Empire of Liberty gives way to industrialization, however, as life on the plains moves forward with the displacement of the Native Americans. Professor Scharff examines the place of railroads and ranchers, malcontents and racists on the distant frontier. The feminist movement advances the cause of women's suffrage, while farmers form the Populist Party to organize against monopolies.

The west opens for business with passage of the Pacific Railway and Homestead acts. It takes two months to reach Oregon by the Oregon Trail; it takes only six days by rail. The path leading west is fraught with danger, however, Native Americans stand in the path of the settlers and subsequent "pacification" campaigns destroy the indigenous culture through warfare, ethnocide, and forced relocations to reservations. The shame of these events is chronicled by Helen Hunt Jackson in *A Century of Dishonor*. Although the federal government implements a more humane policy, the Dawes Act, in 1887, which grants land to Indian families, tribal life barely survives. Farmers settling the lands of the natives find life difficult on the frontier. Commercial agriculture presents unique demands that are characteristic of the new industrial age: debt, problems with machinery, and environmental exploitation. Jefferson's Empire of Liberty is in serious trouble. The democratic spirit of resistance, however, leads to a full-scale rebellion by farmers against businessmen and politicians. Populism sweeps the country at the end of the nineteenth century and Americans stand ready, as populist leader Mary Lease says, "to raise less corn and more hell."

HISTORICAL OVERVIEW

The railroad building era that followed the Civil War opened the frontier to further settlement, and Manifest Destiny, slowed by the war, captured the nation's imagination again. Farmers, miners, cattle ranchers, and other enterprising settlers went west in search of new opportunities. The Homestead Act, which allotted 160 acres to citizens who could live on and improve the land, was a powerful incentive to pioneers, and railroads contributed to the building of the national economy as they moved the nation west. Settlers' dreams did not always materialize, given the harsh environments and the rapid changes wrought by industrialization. Centuries of conflict with Native Americans climaxed with the closing of the frontier. Americans ushered in a new century unsure about the meaning of modernity and their place in industrial society, but they remained optimistic about the future.

Pioneers headed west in the 1870s, encouraged by Congressional Geological Survey reports advertising the vastness of the national domain and by news of gold and silver strikes in California and Nevada. Mining booms transformed the region. In the second half of the century, discoveries of mineral wealth in Colorado, Wyoming, and Arizona brought a new wave of settlements into lands once isolated and unknown. Places like Denver, Virginia City, and Tombstone captured the nation's attention as new cities dotted the remote desert and mountain landscapes. Railroads carried passengers and cargoes to lands that Americans had once deemed unfit for human habitation.

Railroad building proceeded at full speed in the seventies and eighties. This phase of economic development required capital, risk taking, and lots of labor. Once the job was completed, workers often bought land and settled into farming or other enterprises. The west offered tremendous opportunities to men fresh from mining and railroad experiences. New lands provided work in fishing, lumber, real estate, railroads, farming, cattle ranching, and more, and settlers quickly transformed isolated regions.

White settlers' rapacious appetite for land brought them into conflict with Native Americans. While Washington pursued a policy of forcing Indians onto reservations, the settlers were eager to displace and destroy indigenous peoples everywhere. The military was sent in to keep the peace, but more frequently engaged in pacification and eradication campaigns. General Philip Sheridan, national commander of Indian pacification, made it clear that "the only good Indian was a dead one." Where the Indians resisted, ethnocide stamped out opposition. The 1890 massacre of old men, women, and children at Wounded Knee signaled the end of this tragic era.

The frontier was a land of endless opportunities and settlers pursued their dreams with reckless abandonment. The pursuit of riches quickly took its toll on the environment. Water policy determined the development of all western states. The Colorado River continues to experience the detrimental effect of Americans' ceaseless need for water. Dams, diversions, and irrigation projects brought water to the desert and semi-arid lands of Colorado, Arizona, and California. Settlers' demands were met, but without proper environmental planning. Gold mining in the Sierra-Nevada Mountains caused tremendous erosion and destruction of the pristine mountain rivers, and the pattern was repeated throughout the west. Settlements around the San Francisco Bay Area rapidly destroyed the redwood forests and filled the bay and wetlands with pollutants. Strip mining in Arizona, New Mexico, and Colorado poisoned the environment. Voices of protest began to question the pace of progress and development.

Natural resources seemed available in abundance, but the reality was different. George Catlin, Ralph Waldo Emerson, Henry David Thoreau and others had earlier questioned the wisdom of unbridled progress. In the 1870s and 1880s the public began to listen to the voices of restraint and to realize that the wilderness needed protection and stewardship. It was Catlin who made the public aware of the uniqueness of Yellowstone. Thanks to the energies of people like Catlin and the naturalist John Muir and assisted by President Theodore Roosevelt, the national government began to remove lands from private exploitation and set them aside for protection and conservation projects. Roosevelt appointed the first chief forester, Gifford Pinchot, to administer the nation's resources, and millions of acres subsequently came under the control of the National Forest System.

Jefferson's vision of independent farmers living in a land of liberty failed to materialize in the age of machines. Farming became a commercial enterprise, and commodities like grain, cotton, and cattle were at the mercy of market forces. Railroads, banks, and insurance companies became the nemesis of farmers across rural America, and farming communities organized into Granges, which pressed for so-called Granger laws to regulate transportation and storage rates. What began as a regional response to industrialization became a national movement as the Populist Party called for further reforms and gave birth to progressivism.

The 1920 census confirmed what many had recognized at the beginning of the new century: the United States was now an urban nation. Frederick Jackson Turner proclaimed that the frontier had vanished and a new era of American history was at hand.

MAP EXERCISE

Refer to the following maps in Chapter 17 of *A People and a Nation* to answer the questions listed below.

- The United States, 1876–1912 (p. 473)

- The Development and Natural Resources of the West (p. 469)

- Agricultural Regions of the United States, 1890 (p. 478)

    1. What states were admitted after the Civil War? What attracted settlers to those states and what economies dominated in those states?

    2. Which cities were linked by the emerging western railroad network and which were left out? Why?

    3. How did the agricultural revolution affect regional developments in the west? Did one product dominate in a given region?

PEOPLE, EVENTS, AND CONCEPTS

Identify and explain the historical significance of each item.

Sierra Nevada

Identification

Significance

Empire of Liberty

Identification

Significance

John Muir

Identification

Significance

California Solution

Identification

Significance

Ghost Dance

Identification

Significance

Colonel John Chivington

Identification

Significance

Yellowstone Park

Identification

Significance

Helen Hunt Jackson

Identification

Significance

Mullan Tunnel

Identification

Significance

Anaconda Copper Company

Identification

Significance

Arapaho and Cheyenne

Identification

Significance

Continental Divide

Identification

Significance

Homestead Act

> *Identification*

> *Significance*

Mary Lease

> *Identification*

> *Significance*

Wounded Knee

> *Identification*

> *Significance*

Knights of Labor

> *Identification*

> *Significance*

William Jennings Bryan

> *Identification*

> *Significance*

Rural Free Delivery

> *Identification*

> *Significance*

Dawes Act

Identification

Significance

Sitting Bull

Identification

Significance

Grangers

Identification

Significance

barbed wire

Identification

Significance

Omaha, Nebraska

Identification

Significance

Populist Party

Identification

Significance

Sand Creek

Identification

Significance

Central Pacific

Identification

Significance

ESSAY QUESTIONS

1. Discuss the problems faced by Western settlers that led to the populist movement. What effect did populism have on farmers' lives?

2. How did industrialization transform life on the plains? Which technological innovations had the greatest impact and why?

3. Frontier settlements varied from region to region. How were mining, cattle ranching, and farming communities affected by the era's industrial methods?

4. Plains Indians were the last tribes to submit to federal authority. What policy was used against them and what was its impact upon their culture? Did the Dawes Act represent a significant shift in policy? Explain.

5. The western environment suffered dramatically with settlement. Who were some of the leaders of preservationist efforts and how did their energies lead to governmental involvement?

MULTIPLE-CHOICE QUESTIONS

1. The settlers who moved to the far west were mostly
   a. cattle ranchers.
   b. new immigrants.
   c. slave owners looking for new lands.
   d. farmers from the midwest.
2. People most commonly moved west to
   a. live in a healthy environment.
   b. seek greater business opportunities.
   c. look for land.
   d. trap for furs.

3. What was the national government's policy toward the Plains Indian tribes?
   a. The government intended to restock the plains with buffalo.
   b. The government wanted to eliminate the tribes.
   c. The government gave the states total authority to deal with the tribes.
   d. The government offered tribes a program of "protective custody."
4. In the end, the Plains tribes were defeated by
   a. improved weapons from the Civil War.
   b. their own religious and moral convictions.
   c. the mass destruction of the buffalo herds.
   d. their own political system.
5. The farmers who peopled the west after the Civil War were primarily
   a. the families of soldiers who came west to fight the natives.
   b. migrants from the eastern United States and Eastern Europe.
   c. searching for gold and silver.
   d. carrying the message of Christianity to the natives.
6. Farming communities on the plains and out west expanded with
   a. a decline in the fortunes of the mining communities.
   b. natural increases in the birthrate.
   c. the arrival of settlers from the east and Europe.
   d. the collapse of the cattle industry.
7. The conscience of the American public was aroused to the treatment of Indians by
   a. A Century of Dishonor.
   b. Poverty and Progress.
   c. Uncle Tom's Cabin.
   d. The Red Record.
8. The founder of the Sierra Club, the father of preservationism, and advocate for Yosemite National Park was
   a. Theodore Roosevelt.
   b. Gifford Pinchot.
   c. John Muir.
   d. Philip Sheridan.

Answers

1. d	3. d	5. b	7. a
2. c	4. c	6. a	8. c

PRIMARY SOURCE DOCUMENTS

The accounts of actual participants are useful for understanding the motives and thoughts of historical characters.

1. *Granger Resolutions (1873)* **The Illinois State Farmers' Association**

The Civil War accelerated the industrialization of the United States. In the years following the war Congress removed all controls over industry, to the benefit of the largest corporations. In contrast, farmers in the old Midwest saw profits vanish as prices for farm products began a thirty-year decline at the same time that costs increased, as a result of the mechanization of agriculture. Many farmers felt themselves the victims of economic change, objecting most particularly to what they saw as the avaricious practices of the railroads. In the 1870s, meetings of farmers' associations in several states began what is known as the Granger Movement, demanding state regulation of the railroads. The

Illinois resolutions were among the first such public calls for a reversal of the prevailing *laissez-faire* attitude.

Questions to Consider

- Why do the Grangers feel that unrestrained capitalism poses a danger to their way of life?
- What exactly do the Grangers expect of the government?

_____

The Resolutions

A resolution was offered and passed, condemning the back-pay steal, and censuring the President for signing the bill. The committee appointed to draft resolutions submitted the following:

Resolved, By the Farmers of Illinois in Mass Meeting Assembled, That all chartered monopolies, not regulated and controlled by law, have proved in that respect detrimental to the public prosperity, corrupting in their management, and dangerous to republican institutions.

Resolved, That the railways of the world, except in those countries where they have been held under the strict regulation and supervision of the government, have proved themselves arbitrary, extortionate, and as opposed to free institutions and free commerce between States as were the feudal barons of the middle ages.

Resolved, That we hold, declare, and resolve that this despotism, which defies our laws, plunders our shippers, impoverishes our people, and corrupts our government, shall be subdued and made to subserve the public interest at whatever cost.

Resolved, That we believe the State did not and could not confer any of its sovereign power upon any corporation, and that now is the most favorable time to settle the question, so that it may never be hereafter misunderstood that a State can not create a corporation it can not thereafter control.

Resolved, That in view of the present extortions, we look with alarm upon the future of an interest which can combine in the hands of a few men a capital of nearly $250,000,000, and we believe it essential to the prosperity of all classes that this contest continue until these corporations acknowledge the supremacy of law.

Resolved, That we regard it as the undoubted power, and the imperative duty of the legislature, to pass laws fixing reasonable maximum rates for freight and passengers, without classification of roads, and that we urge upon our General Assembly the passage of such laws.

Resolved, That the existing statute, providing for a classification of railroads with a view to adjusting a tariff of charges according to the gross amount of earnings, is a delusion and a snare, and is so framed that the railroads are able to classify themselves, and that it ought to be carefully modified or repealed.

Resolved, That inasmuch as the Supreme Court has clearly pointed out the way to reach unjust discriminations made by the railroads of this State, we can see no reason for delay on the part of the Legislature in enacting the necessary laws on the subject, and we urge immediate action thereon.

Resolved, That we urge the passage of a bill enforcing the principle that railroads are public highways, and requiring railroads to make connections with all roads whose tracks meet or cross their own, and to receive and transmit cars and trains offered over their roads at reasonable maximum rates, whether offered at such crossings, or at stations along their roads, and empowering the making of connections by municipal corporations for that purpose, and for the public use.

Resolved, That we heartily indorse the action of the General Assembly looking to the enforcement of the performance of their duties by monopolies as common carriers; and that, in addition thereto, we believe that railroads should be required to carry all freight and passengers offered from the country through which they pass, and not permitted to limit the amount of their business and destroy its natural increase.

Resolved, That the constitution and laws of Illinois are as binding upon railroad corporations as upon the citizens, and that the State must require obedience to the laws from all alike, whether the same be deemed constitutional or not by the parties affected, until repealed or declared unconstitutional.

Resolved, That we indorse most fully the action of those who tender legal rates of fare upon the railroads, and refuse to pay more; and that it is the duty of the Legislature to provide by law for the defense by the State of Illinois of suits commenced, or that hereafter may be commenced, by railroad companies against individuals who have in good faith insisted, or hereafter may insist, upon the right to ride on railroads at legal rates.

Resolved, That the presentation of railroad passes to our legislators, whatever may be the spirit and intent with which they are accepted, are demoralizing in their influence; and we look to our Legislature, now in session, to rise above personal considerations of pecuniary interest or convenience, and to pass a law making it a misdemeanor for any Senator, or other State or county officers, to accept any railroad pass, knowing, as we do, that the people look upon the acceptance of these passes with decided and almost universal disapprobation.

WHEREAS, The Constitution of 1848 [of Illinois], Article X, prohibits the Legislature from granting special railroad charters in the following words: "And corporations not possessing banking powers or privileges, may be formed under general law, but shall not be created by special acts, except for municipal purposes; and in cases where, in the judgment of the General Assembly, the objects of the corporation can not be attained under general laws," therefore,

Resolved, That it is extremely doubtful whether any railroad charter granted since April 1, 1848, by the Legislature of Illinois is of any validity, and that the vested rights of railroad monopolies in this State exist only by assumption of the monopolies and the sufferance of the people.

WHEREAS, The Constitution of 1870 [of Illinois], Article XI, Section 13, prohibits any railroad company from issuing watered stock, in these words: "No railroad corporation shall issue any stock or bonds except for money, labor, or property actually received and applied to the purposes for which such corporation was created; and all stock, dividends, and other fictitious increase of the capital, stock, or indebtedness of any such corporation shall be void…;" and,

WHEREAS, This article of the Constitution has probably been violated by nearly all the railroad companies in the State; therefore,

Resolved, That it is the duty of the Railroad Commissioners to look carefully into this matter, and to commence proceedings…against all railroad companies which have disregarded this important provision of the organic law of the State.

Resolved, That we regard the improvement of the Illinois River as not sectional, but of great importance; and we request the members of the House of Representatives to vote for the bill now pending for the improvement of that river, as it will give our State absolutely into the hands of the people.

Resolved, That we demand of Congress a repeal of all laws preventing the competition of small vessels, which may choose to engage in the carrying trade on our inland lakes between ports in the United States, without regard to nationality.

Resolved, That we are in favor of the immediate repeal of the protective duties on iron, steel, lumber, and all materials which enter into the construction of railroad cars, steamships, sailing vessels, agricultural implements, etc., and that we urge upon Congress immediate action for this purpose, that cheap railroads and cheap ships are necessary to cheap freights; and that we invite the railroad companies to co-operate with us to that end.

SOURCE: Jonathan Periam, A History of the Origins, Aims, and Progress of the Farmer's Movement (Cincinnati, 1874), pp. 286–289.

2. *A White Heron (1886)* Sarah Orne Jewett

In an age of moralizing authors, Sarah Orne Jewett stood out for her simple and honest characterizations. Her stories, which so accurately recreated the life of small town New England, influenced writers as diverse as Henry James and Willa Cather. This story, "A White Heron," was first published in 1886.

Questions to Consider

- What connection exists between Sylvia and the heron?
- What brings Sylvia to the countryside, and how does that motivation compare to the hunter's?

I

The woods were already filled with shadows one June evening, just before eight o'clock, though a bright sunset still glimmered faintly among the trunks of the trees. A little girl was driving home her cow, a plodding, dilatory, provoking creature in her behavior, but a valued companion for all that. They were going away from the western light, and striking deep into the dark woods, but their feet were familiar with the path, and it was no matter whether their eyes could see it or not.

There was hardly a night the summer through when the old cow could be found waiting at the pasture bars; on the contrary, it was her greatest pleasure to hide herself away among the high huckleberry bushes, and though she wore a loud bell she had made the discovery that if one stood perfectly still it would not ring. So Sylvia had to hunt for her until she found her, and call Co'! Co'! with never an answering Moo, until her childish patience was quite spent. If the creature had not given good milk and plenty of it, the case would have seemed very different to her owners. Besides, Sylvia had all the time there was, and very little use to make of it. Sometimes in pleasant weather it was a consolation to look upon the cow's pranks as an intelligent attempt to play hide and seek, and as the child had no playmates she lent herself to this amusement with a good deal of zest. Though this chase had been so long that the wary animal herself had given an unusual signal of her whereabouts, Sylvia had only laughed when she came upon Mistress Moolly at the swamp-side, and urged her affectionately homeward with a twig of birch leaves. The old cow was not inclined to wander farther, she even turned in the right direction for once as they left the pasture, and stepped along the road at a good pace. She was quite ready to be milked now, and seldom stopped to browse. Sylvia wondered what her grandmother would say because they were so late. It was a great while since she had left home at half past five o'clock, but everybody knew the difficulty of making this errand a short one. Mrs. Tilley had chased the hornéd torment too many summer evenings herself to blame any one else for lingering, and was only thankful as she waited that she had Sylvia, nowadays, to give such valuable assistance. The good woman suspected that Sylvia loitered occasionally on her own account; there never was such a child for straying about out-of-doors since the world was made! Everybody said that it was a good change for a little maid who had tried to grow for eight years in a crowded manufacturing town, but, as for Sylvia herself, it seemed as if she never had been alive at all before she came to live at the farm. She thought often with wistful compassion of a wretched dry geranium that belonged to a town neighbor.

"'Afraid of folks,'" old Mrs. Tilley said to herself, with a smile, after she had made the unlikely choice of Sylvia from her daughter's houseful of children, and was returning to the farm. "'Afraid of folks,' they said! I guess she won't be troubled no great with 'em up to the old place!" When they reached the door of the lonely house and stopped to unlock it, and the cat came to purr loudly, and rub against them, a deserted pussy, indeed, but fat with young robins, Sylvia whispered that this was a beautiful place to live in, and she never should wish to go home.

The companions followed the shady wood-road, the cow taking slow steps, and the child very fast ones. The cow stopped long at the brook to drink, as if the pasture were not half a swamp, and Sylvia stood still and waited, letting her bare feet cool themselves in the shoal water, while the great twilight moths struck softly against her. She waded on through the brook as the cow moved away, and listened to the thrushes with a heart that beat fast with pleasure. There was a stirring in the great boughs overhead. They were full of little birds and beasts that seemed to be wide-awake, and going about their world, or else saying good-night to each other in sleepy twitters. Sylvia herself felt sleepy as she walked along. However, it was not much farther to the house, and the air was soft and sweet. She was not often in the woods so late as this, and it made her feel as if she were a part of the gray shadows and the moving leaves. She was just thinking how long it seemed since she first came to the farm a year ago, and wondering if everything went on in the noisy town just the same as when she was there; the thought of the great red-faced boy who used to chase and frighten her made her hurry along the path to escape from the shadow of the trees.

Suddenly this little woods-girl is horror-stricken to hear a clear whistle not very far away. Not a bird's whistle, which would have a sort of friendliness, but a boy's whistle, determined, and somewhat aggressive. Sylvia left the cow to whatever sad fate might await her, and stepped discreetly aside into the bushes, but she was just too late. The enemy had discovered her, and called out in a very cheerful and persuasive tone, "Halloa, little girl, how far is it to the road?" and trembling Sylvia answered almost inaudibly, "A good ways."

She did not dare to look boldly at the tall young man, who carried a gun over his shoulder, but she came out of her bush and again followed the cow, while he walked alongside.

"I have been hunting for some birds," the stranger said kindly, "and I have lost my way, and need a friend very much. Don't be afraid," he added gallantly. "Speak up and tell me what your name is, and whether you think I can spend the night at your house, and go out gunning early in the morning."

Sylvia was more alarmed than before. Would not her grandmother consider her much to blame? But who could have foreseen such an accident as this? It did not appear to be her fault, and she hung her head as if the stem of it were broken, but managed to answer "Sylvy," with much effort when her companion again asked her name.

Mrs. Tilley was standing in the doorway when the trio came into view. The cow gave a loud moo by way of explanation.

"Yes, you'd better speak up for yourself, you old trial! Where'd she tucked herself away this time, Sylvy?" Sylvia kept an awed silence; she knew by instinct that her grandmother did not comprehend the gravity of the situation. She must be mistaking the stranger for one of the farmer-lads of the region.

The young man stood his gun beside the door, and dropped a heavy game-bag beside it; then he bade Mrs. Tilley good-evening, and repeated his wayfarer's story, and asked if he could have a night's lodging.

"Put me anywhere you like," he said. "I must be off early in the morning, before day; but I am very hungry, indeed. You can give me some milk at any rate, that's plain."

"Dear sakes, yes," responded the hostess, whose long slumbering hospitality seemed to be easily awakened. "You might fare better if you went out on the main road a mile or so, but you're welcome to what we've got. I'll milk right off, and you make yourself at home. You can sleep on husks or feathers," she proffered graciously. "I raised them all myself. There's good pasturing for geese just below here towards the ma'sh. Now step round and set a plate for the gentleman, Sylvy!" And Sylvia promptly stepped. She was glad to have something to do, and she was hungry herself.

It was a surprise to find so clean and comfortable a little dwelling in this New England wilderness. The young man had known the horrors of its most primitive housekeeping, and the dreary squalor of that level of society which does not rebel at the companionship of hens. This was the best thrift of an old-fashioned farmstead, though on such a small scale that it seemed like a hermitage. He listened eagerly to the old woman's quaint talk, he watched Sylvia's pale face and shining gray eyes with ever growing enthusiasm, and insisted that this was the best supper he had eaten for a month; then, afterward, the new-made friends sat down in the doorway together while the moon came up.

Soon it would be berry-time, and Sylvia was a great help at picking. The cow was a good milker, though a plaguy thing to keep track of, the hostess gossiped frankly, adding presently that she had buried four children, so that Sylvia's mother, and a son (who might be dead) in California were all the children she had left. "Dan, my boy, was a great hand to go gunning," she explained sadly. "I never wanted for pa'tridges or gray squer'ls while he was to home. He's been a great wand'rer, I expect, and he's no hand to write letters. There, I don't blame him, I'd ha' seen the world myself if it had been so I could.

"Sylvia takes after him," the grandmother continued affectionately, after a minute's pause. "There ain't a foot o' ground she don't know her way over, and the wild creatur's counts her one o' themselves. Squer'ls she'll tame to come an' feed right out o' her hands, and all sorts o' birds. Last winter she got the jay-birds to bangeing here, and I believe she'd 'a' scanted herself of her own meals to have plenty to throw out amongst 'em, if I hadn't kep' watch. Anything but crows, I tell her, I'm willin' to help support,—though Dan he went an' tamed one o' them that did seem to have reason same as folks. It was round here a good spell after he went away. Dan an' his father they didn't hitch,—but he never held up his head ag'in after Dan had dared him an' gone off."

The guest did not notice this hint of family sorrows in his eager interest in something else.

"So Sylvy knows all about birds, does she?" he exclaimed, as he looked round at the little girl who sat, very demure but increasingly sleepy, in the moonlight. "I am making a collection of birds myself. I have been at it ever since I was a boy." (Mrs. Tilley smiled.) "There are two or three very rare ones I have been hunting for these five years. I mean to get them on my own ground if they can be found."

"Do you cage 'em up?" asked Mrs. Tilley doubtfully, in response to this enthusiastic announcement.

"Oh, no, they're stuffed and preserved, dozens and dozens of them," said the ornithologist, "and I have shot or snared every one myself. I caught a glimpse of a white heron three miles from here on Saturday, and I have followed it in this direction. They have never been found in this district at all. The little white heron, it is," and he turned again to look at Sylvia with the hope of discovering that the rare bird was one of her acquaintances.

But Sylvia was watching a hop-toad in the narrow footpath.

"You would know the heron if you saw it," the stranger continued eagerly. "A queer tall white bird with soft feathers and long thin legs. And it would have a nest perhaps in the top of a high tree, made of sticks, something like a hawk's nest."

Sylvia's heart gave a wild beat; she knew that strange white bird, and had once stolen softly near where it stood in some bright green swamp grass, away over at the other side of the woods. There was an open place where the sunshine always seemed strangely yellow and hot, where tall, nodding rushes grew, and her grandmother had warned her that she might sink in the soft black mud underneath and never be heard of more. Not far beyond were the salt marshes and beyond those was the sea, the sea which Sylvia wondered and dreamed about, but never had looked upon, though its great voice could often be heard above the noise of the woods on stormy nights.

"I can't think of anything I should like so much as to find that heron's nest," the handsome stranger was saying. "I would give ten dollars to anybody who could show it to me," he added desperately, "and I mean to spend my whole vacation hunting for it if need be. Perhaps it was only migrating, or had been chased out of its own region by some bird of prey."

Mrs. Tilley gave amazed attention to all this, but Sylvia still watched the toad, not divining, as she might have done at some calmer time, that the creature wished to get to its hole under the doorstep, and was much hindered by the unusual spectators at that hour of the evening. No amount of thought, that night, could decide how many wished-for treasures the ten dollars, so lightly spoken of, would buy.

The next day the young sportsman hovered about the woods, and Sylvia kept him company, having lost her first fear of the friendly lad, who proved to be most kind and sympathetic. He told her many things about the birds and what they knew and where they lived and what they did with themselves. And he gave her a jack-knife, which she thought as great a treasure as if she were a desert-islander. All day long he did not once make her troubled or afraid except when he brought down some unsuspecting singing creature from its bough. Sylvia would have liked him vastly better without his gun; she could not understand why he killed the very birds he seemed to like so much. But as the day waned, Sylvia still watched the young man with loving admiration. She had never seen anybody so charming and delightful; the woman's heart, asleep in the child, was vaguely thrilled by a dream of love. Some premonition of that great power stirred and swayed these young foresters who traversed the solemn woodlands with soft-footed silent care. They stopped to listen to a bird's song; they pressed forward again eagerly, parting the branches,—speaking to each other rarely and in whispers; the young man going first and Sylvia following, fascinated, a few steps behind, with her gray eyes dark with excitement.

She grieved because the longed-for white heron was elusive, but she did not lead the guest, she only followed, and there was no such thing as speaking first. The sound of her own unquestioned voice would have terrified her,—it was hard enough to answer yes or no when there was need of that. At last evening began to fall, and they drove the cow home together, and Sylvia smiled with pleasure when they came to the place where she heard the whistle and was afraid only the night before.

II

Half a mile from home, at the farther edge of the woods, where the land was highest, a great pine-tree stood, the last of its generation. Whether it was left for a boundary mark, or for what reason, no one could say; the woodchoppers who had felled its mates were dead and gone long ago, and a whole forest of sturdy trees, pines and oaks and maples, had grown again. But the stately head of this old pine towered above them all and made a landmark for sea and shore miles and miles away. Sylvia knew it well. She had always believed that whoever climbed to the top of it could see the ocean; and the little girl had often laid her hand on the great rough trunk and looked up wistfully at those dark boughs that the wind always stirred, no matter how hot and still the air might be below. Now she thought of the tree with a new excitement, for why, if one climbed it at break of day, could not one see all the world, and easily discover whence the white heron flew, and mark the place, and find the hidden nest?

What a spirit of adventure, what wild ambition! What fancied triumph and delight and glory for the later morning when she could make known the secret! It was almost too real and too great for the childish heart to bear.

All night the door of the little house stood open, and the whippoorwills came and sang upon the very step. The young sportsman and his old hostess were sound asleep, but Sylvia's great design kept her broad awake and watching. She forgot to think of sleep. The short summer night seemed as long as the winter darkness, and at last when the whippoorwills ceased, and she was afraid the morning would after all come too soon, she stole out of the house and followed the pasture path through the woods, hastening toward the open ground beyond, listening with a sense of comfort and companionship to the drowsy twitter of a half-awakened bird, whose perch she had jarred in passing. Alas, if the great wave of human interest which flooded for the first time this dull little life should sweep away the satisfactions of an existence heart to heart with nature and the dumb life of the forest!

There was the huge tree asleep yet in the paling moonlight, and small and hopeful Sylvia began with utmost bravery to mount to the top of it, with tingling, eager blood coursing the channels of her whole frame, with her bare feet and fingers, that pinched and held like bird's claws to the monstrous ladder reaching up, up, almost to the sky itself. First she must mount the white oak tree that grew alongside, where she was almost lost among the dark branches and the green leaves heavy and wet with dew; a bird fluttered off its nest, and a red squirrel ran to and fro and scolded pettishly at the harmless housebreaker. Sylvia felt her way easily. She had often climbed there, and knew that higher still one of the oak's upper branches chafed against the pine trunk, just where its lower boughs were set close together. There, when she made the dangerous pass from one tree to the other, the great enterprise would really begin.

She crept out along the swaying oak limb at last, and took the daring step across into the old pine-tree. The way was harder than she thought; she must reach far and hold fast, the sharp dry twigs caught and held her and scratched her like angry talons, the pitch made her thin little fingers clumsy and stiff as she went round and round the tree's great stem, higher and higher upward. The sparrows and robins in the woods below were beginning to wake and twitter to the dawn, yet it seemed much lighter there aloft in the pine-tree, and the child knew that she must hurry if her project were to be of any use.

The tree seemed to lengthen itself out as she went up, and to reach farther and farther upward. It was like a great main-mast to the voyaging earth; it must truly have been amazed that morning through all its ponderous frame as it felt this determined spark of human spirit creeping and climbing from higher branch to branch. Who knows how steadily the least twigs held themselves to advantage this light, weak creature on her way! The old pine must have loved his new dependent. More than all the hawks, and bats, and moths, and even the sweet-voiced thrushes, was the brave, beating heart of the solitary gray-eyed child. And the tree stood still and held away the winds that June morning while the dawn grew bright in the east.

Sylvia's face was like a pale star, if one had seen it from the ground, when the last thorny bough was past, and she stood trembling and tired but wholly triumphant, high in the tree-top. Yes, there was the sea with the dawning sun making a golden dazzle over it, and toward that glorious east flew two hawks with slow-moving pinions. How low they looked in the air from that height when before one had only seen them far up, and dark against the blue sky. Their gray feathers were as soft as moths; they seemed only a little way from the tree, and Sylvia felt as if she too could go flying away among the clouds. Westward, the woodlands and farms reached miles and miles into the distance; here and there were church steeples, and white villages; truly it was a vast and awesome world.

The birds sang louder and louder. At last the sun came up bewilderingly bright. Sylvia could see the white sails of ships out at sea, and the clouds that were purple and rose-colored and yellow at first began to fade away. Where was the white heron's nest in the sea of green branches, and was this wonderful sight and pageant of the world the only reward for having climbed to such a giddy height? Now look down again, Sylvia, where the green marsh is set among the shining birches and dark hemlocks; there where you saw the white heron once you will see him again; look, look! a white spot of him like a single floating feather comes up from the dead hemlock and grows larger, and rises, and comes close at last, and goes by the landmark pine with steady sweep of wing and outstretched slender neck and crested head. And wait! wait! do not move a foot or a finger, little girl, do not send an arrow of light and consciousness from your two eager eyes, for the heron has perched on a pine bough not far beyond yours, and cries back to his mate on the nest, and plumes his feathers for the new day!

The child gives a long sigh a minute later when a company of shouting cat-birds comes also to the tree, and vexed by their fluttering and lawlessness the solemn heron goes away. She knows his secret now, the wild, light, slender bird that floats and wavers, and goes back like an arrow presently to his home in the green world beneath. Then Sylvia, well satisfied, makes her perilous way down again, not daring to look far below the branch she stands on, ready to cry sometimes because her fingers ache and her lamed feet slip. Wondering over and over again what the stranger would say to her, and what he would think when she told him how to find his way straight to the heron's nest.

"Sylvy, Sylvy!" called the busy old grandmother again and again, but nobody answered, and the small husk bed was empty, and Sylvia had disappeared.

The guest waked from a dream, and remembering his day's pleasure hurried to dress himself that it might sooner begin. He was sure from the way the shy little girl looked once or twice yesterday that she had at least seen the white heron, and now she must really be persuaded to tell. Here she comes now, paler than ever, and her worn old frock is torn and tattered, and smeared with pine pitch. The grandmother and the sportsman stand in the door together and question her, and the splendid moment has come to speak of the dead hemlock-tree by the green marsh.

But Sylvia does not speak after all, though the old grandmother fretfully rebukes her, and the young man's kind appealing eyes are looking straight in her own. He can make them rich with money; he has promised it, and they are poor now. He is so well worth making happy, and he waits to hear the story she can tell.

No, she must keep silence! What is it that suddenly forbids her and makes her dumb? Has she been nine years growing, and now, when the great world for the first time puts out a hand to her, must she thrust it aside for a bird's sake? The murmur of the pine's green branches is in her ears, she remembers how the white heron came flying through the golden air and how they watched the sea and the morning together, and Sylvia cannot speak; she cannot tell the heron's secret and give its life away.

Dear loyalty, that suffered a sharp pang as the guest went away disappointed later in the day, that could have served and followed him and loved him as a dog loves! Many a night Sylvia heard the echo of his whistle haunting the pasture path as she came home with the loitering cow. She forgot even her sorrow at the sharp report of his gun and the piteous sight of thrushes and sparrows dropping silent to the ground, their songs hushed and their pretty feathers stained and wet with blood. Were the birds better friends than their hunter might have been,—who can tell? Whatever treasures were lost to her, woodlands and summer-time, remember! Bring your gifts and graces and tell your secrets to this lonely country child!

SOURCE: Sarah Orne Jewett, *Tales of New England* (Boston, 1894), pp. 138–158.

3. *Wounded Knee (1890)* James Mooney

Originally it was called the Battle of Wounded Knee. The U.S. Army claimed that the soldiers had acted in self-defense and awarded commendations to its men, including the Congressional Medal of Honor to one soldier who continued to shoot fleeing Indians even after burning his hand on his overheated Hotchkiss gun. James Mooney of the Bureau of Ethnology was on hand to interview the survivors. The Bureau had sent Mooney west to observe the Ghost Dance, a religious revival among the Plains Indians that many in Washington saw as a threat. The nativist spiritualism of the Ghost Dance convinced many people, especially among the Sioux, to flee their reservations and seek salvation in the old ways. The efforts of the Army to return the Sioux to their reservation led to the tragedy now known as the Massacre of Wounded Knee.

Questions to Consider

- Did the Army have any alternative to opening fire on the Indians?
- What accounts for the willingness of these soldiers to kill fleeing civilians?
- What recourse did the Indians have after Wounded Knee?

On the morning of December 29, 1890, preparations were made to disarm the Indians preparatory to taking them to the agency and thence to the railroad. In obedience to instructions the Indians had pitched their tipis on the open plain a short distance west of the creek and surrounded on all sides by the soldiers. In the center of the camp the Indians had hoisted a white flag as a sign of peace and a guarantee of safety. Behind them was a dry ravine running into the creek, and on a slight rise in the front was posted the battery of four Hotchkiss machine guns, trained directly on the Indian camp. In front, behind, and on both flanks of the camp were posted the various troops of cavalry, a portion of two troops, together with the Indian scouts, being dismounted and drawn up in front of the Indians at the distance of only a few yards from them….

Shortly after 8 o'clock in the morning the warriors were ordered to come out from the tipis and deliver their arms. They came forward and seated themselves on the ground in front of the troops. They were then ordered to go by themselves into their tipis and bring out and surrender their guns. The first twenty went and returned in a short time with only two guns. It seemed evident that they were unwilling to give them up, and after consultation of the officers part of the soldiers were ordered up to within ten yards of the group of warriors, while another detachment of troops was ordered to search the tipis. After a thorough hunt these last returned with about forty rifles, most of which, however, were old and of little value. The search had consumed considerable time and created a good deal of excitement among the women and children, as the soldiers found it necessary in the process to overturn the beds and other furniture of the tipis and in some instances drove out the inmates. All this had its effect on their husbands and brothers, already wrought up to a high nervous tension and not knowing what might come next. While the soldiers had been looking for the guns Yellow Bird, a medicine-man, had been walking about among the warriors, blowing on an eagle-bone whistle, and urging them to resistance, telling them that the soldiers would become weak and powerless, and that the bullets would be unavailing against the sacred "ghost shirts," which nearly every one of the Indians wore…. Suddenly…a young Indian…drew a rifle from under his blanket and fired at the soldiers, who instantly replied with a volley directly into the crowd of warriors and so near that their guns were almost touching. From the number of sticks set up by the Indians to mark where the dead fell, as seen by the author a year later, this one volley must have killed nearly half the warriors…. The survivors sprang to their feet, throwing their blankets from their shoulders as they rose, and for a few minutes there was a terrible hand to hand struggle, where every man's thought was to kill. Although many of the warriors had no guns, nearly all had revolvers and knives in their belts under their blankets, together with some of the murderous warclubs still carried by the Sioux….

At the first volley the Hotchkiss guns trained on the camp opened fire and sent a storm of shells and bullets among the women and children, who had gathered in front of the tipis to watch the unusual spectacle of military display. The guns poured in 2-pound explosive shells at the rate of nearly fifty per minute, mowing down everything alive…. In a few minutes 200 Indian men, women, and children, with 60 soldiers, were lying dead and wounded on the ground, the tipis had been torn down by the shells and some of them were burning above the helpless wounded, and the surviving handful of Indians were flying in wild panic to the shelter of the ravine, pursued by hundreds of maddened soldiers and followed up by a raking fire from the Hotchkiss guns, which had been moved into position to sweep the ravine.

There can be no question that the pursuit was simply a massacre, where fleeing women, with infants in their arms, were shot down after resistance had ceased and when almost every warrior was stretched dead or dying on the ground…. Commissioner Morgan in his official report says that "Most of the men, including Big Foot, were killed around his tent, where he lay sick. The bodies of the women and children were scattered along a distance of two miles from the scene of the encounter."

SOURCE: James Mooney, *The Ghost-Dance Religion and Wounded Knee* (Washington, D.C., 1896), pp. 868–870.

UNIT 17
Capital and Labor

_____

UNIT SUMMARY

In Program 17 we look at the growing conflict between labor and capital.

ASSIGNMENT

1. Before viewing Program 17, read this unit, and in *A People and a Nation* read Chapter 18, pages 495–515, Chapter 20, pages 551–563 and 568–576, and Chapter 21, pages 581–582.

2. View Program 17, "Capital and Labor."

3. Visit the Web site <http://www.learner.org/biographyofamerica>. Explore the exercises for Program 17.

LEARNING OBJECTIVES

Upon completing this unit, students should be able to:

1. Discuss the role of financier J. P. Morgan and the influence he wielded over the American economy.

2. Discuss the prevailing practices of capital and their adverse impact upon the working class.

3. Assess the efforts of labor to organize and the problems that it faced within and without its ranks.

4. Describe the impact of Edward Bellamy's *Looking Backward* on public sentiment at the end of the nineteenth century.

5. Evaluate the validity of President Lincoln's negative assessment concerning the rise of capital.

PROGRAM GUIDE

Laissez-faire capitalism creates serious problems of social inequality in the last decades of the nineteenth century. The making of money pits workers against capitalists. Industrialization widens the chasm between rich and poor, as the affluent live the life of conspicuous consumption and the masses live in squalor and poverty. Professor Miller examines the miners' struggle for dignity and the fight to unionize, as workers make their stand against the reigning capitalists of the age. Investigative journalists expose the abuses that accompany the age of free enterprise, and photojournalist Jacob Riis documents the pathetic tenement life of workers and immigrants in *How the Other Half Lives*.

But industrialists and financiers rule America, and the pre-eminent capitalist of the age is J. P. Morgan. His life typifies the greedy acquisitiveness of corporate titans. Empire building is the order of the day, and Morgan collects businesses like a collector amasses art. Morgan controls billions of dollars—his power alone ends the economic Panic of 1906—and his mines, railroads, and foundries together answer the nation's insatiable demand for steel. In the coal mines, miners suffer the indignities of exploitation and frequently lose their lives for their efforts. John Mitchell, president of the United Mine Workers, organizes his followers to do battle against this system, although a constant stream of immigration makes organizing difficult, and the power of the state and capital make the job virtually impossible. Nevertheless, the plutocrats are slowly reigned in, and a new breed of political reformers leads the nation into an era of progressive reforms.

HISTORICAL OVERVIEW

Corporations ruled with impunity in the age of laissez-faire capitalism, and America's leaders enabled businesses' monopolistic practices. Abraham Lincoln worried about the dominance of big business and the corporate greed he saw destroying the republic. After the Civil War, the nation faced new challenges to national unity. "An era of corruption in high places *had* followed and corporations *were* exploiting the popular prejudices of the people allowing for the concentration of wealth into the hands of the few," as Lincoln had warned. Could democracy survive in the world of Wall Street and the plutocrats? How could the Carnegies, the Rockefellers, and the Morgans be made to consider the needs of the general public?

Although the captains of industry wielded tremendous power, some moved to curtail its worse abuses. Insurgents organized against the malefactors of wealth, as reformers called them, aided by muckrakers, investigative reporters who exposed the prevailing practices of monopolies and their corrupt partners, the politicians. Edward Bellamy, author of *Looking Backward,* the most widely read novel of the late nineteenth century, imagined a utopian solution to the conflict between labor and capital.

Corporations had assumed a dominant position in the American economy by 1870 and their methods of raising capital were fraught with corruption. Railroads, incorporated by the federal government, were the first modern businesses. The Pacific Railway Act in 1862 created the Central Pacific and Union Pacific railroad companies, and during the Civil War years agents for the two corporations issued bonds, borrowed money, and made grandiose promises to the federal government and stockholders in order to raise capital to begin operations. Colis P. Huntington, Leland Stanford, Mark Hopkins, and Charles Crocker owned and operated the western railroads. The "Big Four" resorted to all types of chicanery to get their companies up and running. Stanford, governor of California and president of Central Pacific, secured political and financial support. Crocker used federal monies specifically and exclusively intended for Central Pacific's construction on his own pet schemes. Huntington traveled to New York and Washington to sell bonds at a fraction of their value and bribe congressmen to gain favorable legislation. Thomas Durant, president of Union Pacific, speculated on and manipulated competing railroads' bonds while seeking government aid for his own company. Durant, who had smuggled Confederate cotton during the war, created the Credit Mobilier construction company to build Union Pacific railroad. Stockholders gave the construction company huge contracts. They siphoned off money from the Union Pacific, a company in which they owned little stock, to Credit Mobilier, where they owned a majority of the stock. The Union Pacific received government subsidies and funds; the investors stole government money. The stockholders then tried to avoid investigation by bribing members of Congress with gifts of stock, but the Credit Mobiler scandal broke in 1872. But corruption and bribery had become a part of doing business.

Immigrants played a vital role in the building of industrial society, and industrialists exercised enormous control over their workers' lives. Charles Crocker contracted Chinese laborers for the dangerous work of getting the railroad across the Sierra Nevada. Although he recognized them for their diligence and dedication, Crocker paid the Chinese lower wages than he paid white men and exploited their willingness to work. Crocker's exploitation was not the exception. Coal was essential to the nineteenth century economy, in everything from moving goods by rail to heating homes. Coal mining was dangerous work, and miners working for twenty-five cents a day in the coal fields of West Virginia had no job security nor protection from unsafe working conditions. The mines were located in isolated regions where company towns controlled all aspects of life: workers were paid in script that could only be redeemed in company stores; schools and churches taught only company-approved doctrine; cribbing, in which the coal-weighing scales shorted the true weight of workers' toil, robbed miners of a decent day's wage; and children worked—and for substandard wages.

Laborers were at a grave disadvantage across industrial America throughout the nineteenth century. Corporations exploited workers as the one variable cost of doing business. Businessmen enjoyed the advantages of massive immigration to the United States in the closing decades of the century. These immigrants, primarily from eastern Europe, came with little education or skill. Industrialists hired them for backbreaking, monotonous, and debilitating work. "Hyphenated Americans," as they were called, having come with nothing, were willing to work for substandard wages.

Labor fought long and hard to win the right to organize and bargain collectively. The history of the union movement began in the early days of industrialization. In the 1940s, women in the textile mills of Lowell, Massachusetts organized the first labor movement in the state, going on strike to protest what they called wage slavery. On the eve of the Civil War more than 20,000 shoemakers left their jobs in a protest over wages. After the Civil War, the Knights of Labor emerged as the nation's largest union. Knights sought to organize from a broad spectrum of the working class: skilled and unskilled, women and racial minorities. Terence Powderly, the union's president, envisioned a future where workers' cooperatives would own and operate industries. Powderly and other union leaders were opposed to strikes, though they resorted to them upon occasion, saying that strikes legitimized the existence of the wage system. Workers created the lion-share of industrial wealth they said, but it was expropriated by businessmen. The Knights' goal, Ponderly said, was "to secure to the workers the full enjoyment of the wealth they create." Craftsworkers also formed unions to protect their trades and eventually formed the American Federation of Labor to strengthen their bargaining position (the AFL was and still is a loose confederation of skilled workers from different trades). Workers themselves were often at cross purposes, and building solidarity within the ranks proved illusive among the diverse immigrant communities.

Free enterprise practices produced periods of grave uncertainty. During the final quarter of the nineteenth century, the depressions of 1873 and 1893 brought economic ruin to banks, railroads, states, industries, and especially to the masses. Laissez-faire capitalists accepted the idea that collapses were normal features of the business cycle; they claimed that no remedial measures were necessary. The Great Uprising of 1877, the Homestead Strike of 1892, and the Pullman Strike of 1893 all attest to the growing conflicts between labor and management. Although the public came to view the unrest associated with these disputes as labor radicalism, it was clear that the prevailing economic system required reforms and regulations. The real crisis of the Gilded Age, as Lincoln had noted, was that *the monied power would stop at nothing until all wealth aggregated in the hands of the few and the republic would be destroyed.* Middle-class Americans worried about the possibility of revolution.

Reformers criticized the prevailing practices of capitalism. Henry George called for a single tax upon the landed monopolies in *Poverty and Progress.* The economist Thorstein Veblen attacked the growing inequality in wealth as dangerous to the safety and security of society and argued for government regulation of the economy. Class conflict threatened the future of American capitalism. One author captured the imagination of the public in a novel about a world without social strife. Edward Bellamy's *Looking Backward* begins in the year 1887. Labor unrest was ubiquitous, and the central character, Julian West, goes to sleep one day during this time of heightened tensions and fears, and when he awakes from his sleep, the year is 2000. The national government has taken control of the economy and a utopian world is unveiled. People in the twenty-first century enjoy employment in jobs based upon their specific talents and interest and everyone works: poverty does not exist, and class conflict has vanished. The book was hugely popular. Nationalist clubs (Bellamy called his new order *nationalism*) sprang up around the country, and a new movement was born. Americans wanted solutions to the problems associated with unbridled free enterprise. The workers' struggles against predatory capitalism continued over the ensuing decades.

MAP EXERCISE

Refer to the following figures and table in Chapter 18 of *A People and a Nation* to answer the question below.

- Distribution of Occupational Categories Among Employed Men and Women, 1880–1920 (p. 496)

- Children in the Labor Force, 1880–1930 (p. 497)

- American Living Standards, 1890–1910 (p. 505)

1. What do the graphs reveal about the trends in living standards and the distribution of employment between men and women? How do children fit into the picture?

PEOPLE, EVENTS, AND CONCEPTS

Identify and explain the historical significance of each item.

Theodore Dreiser

Identification

Significance

Mulberry Bend

Identification

Significance

Morganization

Identification

Significance

Jacob Riis

Identification

Significance

Credit Mobilier

Identification

Significance

Hercules' Club

Identification

Significance

J. P. Morgan

Identification

Significance

black lung

Identification

Significance

Stephen Crane

Identification

Significance

anthracite

Identification

Significance

William Jennings Bryan

Identification

Significance

Wall Street

Identification

Significance

William McKinley

Identification

Significance

Tammany Hall

Identification

Significance

Eight-hour League
Identification

Significance

Mark Hanna
Identification

Significance

Haymarket
Identification

Significance

Molly McGuires
Identification

Significance

John Mitchell
Identification

Significance

Knights of Labor
Identification

Significance

Lincoln Steffens

Identification

Significance

cooperatives

Identification

Significance

Terence Powderly

Identification

Significance

Full Dinner Pail

Identification

Significance

ESSAY QUESTIONS

1. Who were the muckrakers? How did their efforts help to mobilize the public in the reform movement?

2. J. P. Morgan was described as a constructive capitalist. What did his admirers mean by this, and what was constructive about his activities?

3. Discuss the problems facing coal miners in the later part of the nineteenth century. How did they respond to the conditions in the mines? How successful was their struggle against exploitation?

4. Why did labor unions find it difficult to organize industrial workers in the latter part of the nineteenth century?

MULTIPLE-CHOICE QUESTIONS

1. During the heyday of railroad building the major cost was paid by
    a. state governments.
    b. federal taxes.
    c. land, loans, and bounties from the national government.
    d. private investments.
2. The national government began to regulate industry when it established the
    a. Federal Deposit Insurance Corporation.
    b. Interstate Commerce Commission.
    c. Clayton Anti-Trust Act.
    d. Pendleton Act.
3. Company towns controlled the lives of their workers by all of the following means except
    a. their method of paying employees.
    b. their hiring practices.
    c. the doctrines workers were taught in company schools and churches.
    d. compensating miners who had black lung disease.
4. The railroad strike of 1877 started when
    a. the president sent in troops to nationalize operations.
    b. the four largest railroads cut salaries by ten percent.
    c. the companies cut working hours.
    d. the companies brought in strike breakers.
5. Who purchased and created the first billion-dollar corporation?
    a. John D. Rockefeller
    b. Andrew Carnegie
    c. J. P. Morgan
    d. Jay Gould
6. According to the Knights of Labor, labors woes would disappear when
    a. government nationalized industry.
    b. labor owned and operated businesses.
    c. all unions joined together in confederation.
    d. the Republicans were forced from office.
7. By the turn of the century, the national economy had shifted to reveal
    a. sharper class distinctions.
    b. greater earning power for workers.
    c. effective government planning.
    d. government support for collective bargaining.
8. In *Poverty and Progress*, Henry George argued that unearned profits should be
    a. used by industrialists exclusively for capital investments.
    b. returned to the workers.
    c. confiscated in the form of taxes.
    d. invested in social programs.

Answers

1. c	3. d	5. c	7. a
2. b	4. b	6. b	8. c

PRIMARY SOURCE DOCUMENTS

The accounts of actual participants are useful for understanding the motives and thoughts of historical characters.

1. *The Cross of Gold (1896)* William Jennings Bryan

The election of 1896 hinged largely on the question of currency. The Republicans insisted on the gold standard, while the Democrats were leaning toward bimetallism (gold and silver) when they met in Chicago in July. The last speaker on the silver question was a thirty-six-year-old former representative from Nebraska, William Jennings Bryan. His speech electrified the convention, which burst into sustained cheering and shouting for an hour. The following day Bryan was selected as the Democratic nominee for president. He lost the election to Republican William McKinley.

Questions to Consider

- What difference did it make whether the United States had a gold or a silver standard?

- Why was Bryan's speech so remarkably effective?

The humblest citizen in all the land when clad in the armor of a righteous cause is stronger than all the whole hosts of error that they can bring. I come to speak to you in defense of a cause as holy as the cause of liberty, the cause of humanity....

Never before in the history of this country has there been witnessed such a contest as that through which we have passed. Never before in the history of American politics has a great issue been fought out as this issue has been by the voters themselves....

In this contest brother has been arrayed against brother and father against father. The warmest ties of love and acquaintance and association have been disregarded. Old leaders have been cast aside when they refused to give expression to the sentiments of those whom they would lead, and new leaders have sprung up to give direction to this cause of truth....

We say to you that you have made too limited in its application the definition of the business man. The man who is employed for wages is as much a business man as his employer.... The farmer who goes forth in the morning and toils all day, begins in the spring and toils all summer, and by the application of brain and muscle to the natural resources of this country creates wealth, is as much a business man as the man who goes upon the board of trade and bets upon the price of grain. The miners who go a thousand feet into the earth or climb two thousand feet upon the cliffs and bring forth from their hiding-places the precious metals to be poured in the channels of trade are as much business men as the few financial magnates who in a back room corner the money of the world.

We come to speak for this broader class of business men. Ah, my friends, we say not one word against those who live upon the Atlantic coast; but those hardy pioneers who braved all the dangers of the wilderness, who have made the desert to blossom as the rose—those pioneers away out there, rearing their children near to nature's heart, where they can mingle their voices with the voices of the birds; out there where they have erected schoolhouses for the education of their young, and churches where they praise their Creator, and cemeteries where sleep the ashes of their dead, are as deserving of the consideration of this party as any people in this country. ...

It is for these that we speak. We do not come as aggressors. Our war is not a war of conquest. We are fighting in the defense of our homes, our families, and posterity. ...We have petitioned, and our petitions have been scorned. We have entreated, and our entreaties have been disregarded. We have begged and they have mocked, and our calamity came. We beg no longer. We entreat no more. We petition no more. We defy them....

We say in our platform that we believe that the right to coin money and issue money is a function of government. We believe it. We believe it is a part of sovereignty, and can no more, with safety, be delegated to private individuals than we could afford to delegate to private individuals the power to make penal statutes or to levy laws for taxation....

The sympathies of the Democratic party, as described by the platform, are on the side of the struggling masses, who have ever been the foundation of the Democratic party. ...There are two ideas of government. There are those who believe that if you just legislate to make the well-to-do prosperous, their prosperity will leak through on those below. The Democratic idea has been that if you legislate to make the masses prosperous their prosperity will find its way up and through every class and rest upon it. ...

You come to us and tell us that the great cities are in favor of the gold standard. I tell you that the great cities rest upon these broad and fertile prairies. Burn down your cities and leave our farms, and your cities will spring up again as if by magic. But destroy our farms and the grass will grow in the streets of every city in this country. ...

...Having behind us the commercial interests, and the laboring interests, and all the toiling masses, we shall answer their demands for a gold standard by saying to them, you shall not press down upon the brow of labor this crown of thorns. You shall not crucify mankind upon a cross of gold.

SOURCE: C. M. Stevans, ed., *Bryan and Sewall and the Great Issue of 1896* (New York, 1896), pp. 68–72, 76–78.

2. *Wealth and Its Uses (1907)* Andrew Carnegie

The living symbol of America's rag-to-riches mythology, Andrew Carnegie emigrated from Scotland with his family in 1848, and by 1900 was one of the richest men in the world. In 1901 Carnegie's companies formed the core of the new United States Steel Corporation. After the formation of this giant industry, Carnegie retired from business, devoting himself to philanthropy and spreading his personal philosophy, "The Gospel of Wealth," arguing that the rich should hold their wealth in trust for the public good. Carnegie lived up to his ideal of giving, donating $350,000,000 to build libraries, promote higher education, and establish the Carnegie Endowment for International Peace.

Questions to Consider

- Why does Carnegie think the rich should give away much of their wealth?
- What are the advantages of poverty?
- How does inherited wealth fit into Carnegie's philosophy?

It is the fashion nowadays to bewail poverty as an evil, to pity the young man who is not born with a silver spoon in his mouth; but I heartily subscribe to President Garfield's doctrine, that "The richest heritage a young man can be born to is poverty." ... It is not from the sons of the millionnaire or the noble that the world receives its teachers, its martyrs, its inventors, its statesmen, its poets, or even its men of affairs. It is from the cottage of the poor that all these spring.... There is nothing so enervating, nothing so deadly in its effects upon the qualities which lead to the highest achievement, moral or intellectual, as hereditary wealth. And if there be among you a young man who feels that he is not compelled to exert himself in order to earn and live from his own efforts, I tender him my profound sympathy....

The principal complaint against our industrial conditions of to-day is that they cause great wealth to flow into the hands of the few. ... It was formerly so.... To-day it is not true. Wealth is being more and more distributed among the many. The amount of the combined profits of labour and capital which goes to labour was never so great as to-day, the amount going to capital never so small....

You may be sure, gentlemen, that the question of the distribution of wealth is settling itself rapidly under present conditions, and settling itself in the right direction. The few rich are getting poorer, and the toiling masses are getting richer. Nevertheless, a few exceptional men may yet make fortunes, but these will be more moderate than in the past. This may not be quite as fortunate for the masses of the people as is now believed, because great accumulations of wealth in the hands of one enterprising man who still toils on are sometimes most productive of all the forms of wealth....

The bees of a hive do not destroy the honey-making bees, but the drones. It will be a great mistake for the community to shoot the millionnaires, for they are the bees that make the most honey, and contribute most to the hive even after they have gorged themselves full. It is a remarkable fact that any country is prosperous and comfortable in proportion to the number of its millionnaires....

But assuming that surplus wealth flows into the hands of a few men, what is their duty? How is the struggle for dollars to be lifted from the sordid atmosphere surrounding business and made a noble career? Now, wealth has hitherto been distributed in three ways: The first and chief one is by willing it at death to the family. Now, beyond bequeathing to those dependent upon one the revenue needful for modest and independent living, is such a use of wealth either right or wise? I ask you to think over the result, as a rule, of millions given over to young men and women, the sons and daughters of the millionnaire.... Nothing is truer than this, that as a rule the "almighty dollar" bequeathed to sons or daughters by millions proves an almighty curse. It is not the good of the child which the millionnaire parent considers when he makes these bequests, it is his own vanity....

There is a second use of wealth, less common than the first, which is not so injurious to the community, but which should bring no credit to the testator. Money is left by millionnaires to public institutions when they must relax their grasp upon it. There is no grace, and can be no blessing, in giving what cannot be withheld. It is no gift, because it is not cheerfully given, but only granted at the stern summons of death. The miscarriage of these bequests, the litigation connected with them, and the manner in which they are frittered away seem to prove that the Fates do not regard them with a kindly eye. We are never without a lesson that the only mode of producing lasting good by giving large sums of money is for the millionnaire to give as close attention to its distribution during his life as he did to its acquisition....

The third use, and the only noble use of surplus wealth, is this: That it be regarded as a sacred trust, to be administered by its possessor, into whose hands it flows, for the highest good of the people. Man does not live by bread alone, and five or ten cents a day more revenue scattered over thousands would produce little or no good. Accumulated into a great fund and expended as Mr. Cooper expended it for the Cooper Institute, it establishes something that will last for generations. It will educate the brain, the spiritual part of man. It furnishes a ladder upon which the aspiring poor may climb; and there is no use whatever, gentlemen, trying to help people who do not help themselves. You cannot push any one up a ladder unless he be willing to climb a little himself. When you stop boosting, he falls, to his injury. Therefore, I have often said, and I now repeat, that the day is coming, and already we see its dawn, in which the man who dies possessed of millions of available wealth which was free and in his hands ready to be distributed will die disgraced....

SOURCE: Andrew Carnegie, *Empire of Business* (Buffalo, 1907), pp. 125–126, 135–136, 138–139, 141–144.

3. The Money Trust Investigation *(1913)* The Pujo Committee

Throughout 1912, a special subcommittee of the House Committee on Banking and Currency, chaired by Arsene Pujo of Louisiana, investigated accusations that a "money trust" dominated the American economy. The Pujo

Committee's findings validated the suspicions of many Progressives. Their detailed accounting of big business's "interlocking directorates"—the first such study—appeared to support the view that the nation's finances were controlled by a small number of people. The Pujo Committee's report, issued on February 28, 1913, argued that the concentration of economic power was increasing. The new president, Woodrow Wilson, used the report to buttress his calls for such reform as the Federal Reserve System. [Exhibit citations have been removed.]

Questions to Consider

• What is wrong with a few people controlling the flow of money?

• What can be done legally to limit this concentration of wealth?

Concentration of *control* of money, and consequently of credit, more particularly in the city of New York, is the subject of this inquiry....

The resources of the banks and trust companies of the city of New York in 1911 were $5,121,245,175, which is 21.73 per cent of the total banking resources of the country as reported to the Comptroller of the Currency. This takes no account of the unknown resources of the great private banking houses whose affiliations to the New York financial institutions we are about to discuss....

This increased concentration of control of money and credit has been effected principally as follows:

First, through consolidations of competitive or potentially competitive banks and trust companies, which consolidations in turn have recently been brought under sympathetic management.

Second, through the same powerful interests becoming large stockholders in potentially competitive banks and trust companies. This is the simplest way of acquiring control, but since it requires the largest investment of capital, it is the least used, although the recent investments in that direction for that apparent purpose amount to tens of millions of dollars in present market values.

Third, through the confederation of potentially competitive banks and trust companies by means of the system of interlocking directorates.

Fourth, through the influence which the more powerful banking houses, banks, and trust companies have secured in the management of insurance companies, railroads, producing and trading corporations, and public utility corporations, by means of stockholdings, voting trusts, fiscal agency contracts, or representation upon their boards of directors, or through supplying the money requirements of railway, industrial, and public utilities corporations and thereby being enabled to participate in the determination of their financial and business policies.

Fifth, through partnership or joint account arrangements between a few of the leading banking houses, banks, and trust companies in the purchase of security issues of the great interstate corporations, accompanied by understandings of recent growth—sometimes called "banking ethics"—which have had the effect of effectually destroying competition between such banking houses, banks, and trust companies in the struggle for business or in the purchase and sale of large issues of such securities....

[The committee examines the structure of Morgan & Co. and its related firms and offers the following summary.]

...It appears there that firm members or directors of these institutions together hold:

One hundred and eighteen directorships in 34 banks and trust companies having total resources of $2,679,000,000 and total deposits of $1,983,000,000.

Thirty directorships in 10 insurance companies having total assets of $2,293,000,000.

One hundred and five directorships in 32 transportation systems having a total capitalization of $11,784,000,000 and a total mileage (excluding express companies and steamship lines) of 150,200.

Sixty-three directorships in 24 producing and trading corporations having a total capitalization of $3,339,000,000.

Twenty-five directorships in 12 public utility corporations having a total capitalization of $2,150,000,000.

In all, 341 directorships in 112 corporations having aggregate resources or capitalization of $22,245,000,000....

Your committee is satisfied from the proofs submitted, even in the absence of data from the banks, that there is an established and well-defined identity and community of interest between a few leaders of finance, created and held together through stock ownership, interlocking directorates, partnership and joint account transactions, and other forms of domination over banks, trust companies, railroads, and public-service and industrial corporations, which has resulted in great and rapidly growing concentration of the control of money and credit in the hands of these few men....

To us the peril is manifest. But the remedy is not so easily found or applied, having due regard, as we should, to the encouragement of enterprise.

As the first and foremost step in applying a remedy and also for reasons that seem to us conclusive, independently of that consideration, we recommend that interlocking directorates in potentially competing financial institutions be abolished and prohibited, so far as lies in the power of Congress to bring about that result....

It is manifestly improper and repugnant to the theory and practice of competition that the same person or members of the same firm shall undertake to act in such inconsistent capacities.... When we find...the same man a director in a half dozen or more banks and trust companies all located in the same section of the same city, doing the same class of business and with a like set of associates similarly situated all belonging to the same group and representing the same class of interests, all further pretense of competition is useless....

SOURCE: U.S. Congress, Report of the Committee Appointed Pursuant to House Resolutions 429 and 504 to Investigate the Concentration of Money and Credit, House Report No. 1593, 3 vols. (Washington, D.C., 1913), III: pp. 55–56, 89, 129, 140.

Unit 18

Theodore Roosevelt and Woodrow Wilson

UNIT SUMMARY

In Unit 18 we look at the personalities of Theodore Roosevelt and Woodrow Wilson and contrast their philosophies and presidencies.

ASSIGNMENT

1. Before viewing Program 18, read this unit, and in *A People and a Nation* read Chapter 21, pages 596–605, Chapter 22, and Chapter 23.

2. View Program 18, "Theodore Roosevelt and Woodrow Wilson."

3. Visit the Web site <http://www.learner.org/biographyofamerica>. Explore the exercises for Program 18.

LEARNING OBJECTIVES

Upon completing this unit, students should be able to:

1. Discuss the stature of the presidency following the Civil War and the styles of presidential leadership through 1900.

2. Describe Theodore Roosevelt's rise to power and the political philosophy that he embraced and contrast it with Woodrow Wilson's.

3. Discuss the two presidents' approaches to foreign policy and the ways in which their initiatives reinforced and differed from one another's.

4. Compare their presidencies in terms of legislative achievements and leadership in the progressive era.

PROGRAM GUIDE

The presidencies of Theodore Roosevelt and Woodrow Wilson restore the chief executive as the nation's true leader. After Lincoln's assassination, a series of weak and middling presidents, lacking vision and leadership, assumed office. Another assassination, this time President William McKinley's, elevates to the presidency a man described as "a steam engine in trousers": Theodore Roosevelt. Roosevelt brings to the Oval Office boundless energy and an American sense of superiority. TR and, eleven years later, Woodrow Wilson usher in the modern imperial presidency. Professor Brinkley examines their distinctive styles of leadership. Both men assume office during the upheavals of progressivism at home and imperialism abroad. Whereas TR wields a big stick in diplomatic affairs, using his office as a bully pulpit to shape the nation's course, Wilson wages a moral crusade for a new democratic world order. Both exercise bold leadership in world affairs with an unabashed faith in their own correctness. The Roosevelt and Wilson presidencies mark America's rise as a world power, redefining the notions of democracy, its possibilities and its limitations.

HISTORICAL OVERVIEW

The United States entered the twentieth century as a world power. While at home the nation wrestled with the problems associated with industrialization, abroad the nation's leaders defined a new role for America. The presidencies of Theodore Roosevelt and Woodrow Wilson were intimately associated with both trends. Both men helped to redefine the nature of the presidency, though their approaches were dramatically different. Roosevelt used his power to reign in what he called "the bad trust" and sought a square deal for the workingman. Wilson promised to dismantle the monopolies but later made compromises that led to the demise of progressivism. Roosevelt resorted to brute force in Panama to get what he felt was in the nation's best interest, while Wilson sought to define U.S. foreign interests in moral terms of black vs. white, good vs. evil, and democracy vs. tyranny. Both men advanced the nation's power globally.

The presidency fell into the hands of lackluster and mediocre leaders following the Civil War, and political power coalesced around the Congress, the Supreme Court, and the political parties. Presidents mostly dispensed with patronage and acted as figureheads in domestic affairs. The laissez-faire attitude of the national government in the age of big business contributed to this lack of presidential leadership. Ironically, presidents showed initiative in the one area where they were least prepared to lead: foreign policy. During the Spanish-American War, it was reported, President McKinley asked for a map so he could locate the Philippines.

Theodore Roosevelt's ascendancy to the presidency ended the reign of mediocrity. His credentials as a long-standing reformer in the Republican party worried the party hierarchy, and party bosses moved Roosevelt into the vice presidency in 1900, thinking he would fade into obscurity. Their calculations misfired when President McKinley was assassinated in 1901. Although he was, at age 43, the youngest man ever to assume the presidency, Roosevelt had been in politics his entire adult life. He craved power and had very firm ideas about how to use it. During the first year of his presidency, a strike in the coal mining industry gave TR an opportunity to demonstrate his leadership. When the coal operators refused to negotiate further with the miners, Roosevelt's threat to nationalize the industry encouraged them into arbitration and an agreement. Declaring that his policies would control the corporations, protect the consumers, and conserve the nation's resources, Roosevelt articulated what he called a "Square Deal" for everybody:

> "When I say I believe in a square deal I do not mean to give every man the best hand. If the cards do not come to any man, or if they do come, and he does not got the power to play them that is his affair. All I mean is that there shall be no crookedness in the dealing."

Victory in the Spanish-American War in 1898 had transformed the United States into an imperial republic. Americans had mixed feelings about reigning over an empire, but Roosevelt embraced the opportunities imperialism offered. Early in his first term he moved quickly to secure rights to ownership of a transoceanic canal in Panama. His notorious "big stick" foreign policy approach alienated much of the Latin American world, but the Roosevelt Corollary to the Monroe Doctrine warned the region and assured the world of America's mandate:

> "Chronic wrongdoing ... may in America, as elsewhere, ultimately require intervention by some civilized nation, and in the Western Hemisphere the adherence of the United States to the Monroe Doctrine may force the United States, however reluctantly, in flagrant cases of such wrongdoing or impotence, to the exercise of an international police power."

At the height of his popularity, TR fulfilled an earlier promise not to seek reelection in 1908. Roosevelt had left a clear agenda for his hand-picked successor, William Howard Taft. But while the ex-president watched impatiently from the sidelines, Taft caved in to special interests. In 1912, the Bull Moose Party nominated Theodore Roosevelt for president. He campaigned aggressively on a reform platform in a three-way contest against Taft and Woodrow Wilson. When Republicans divided their votes between Taft and Roosevelt, Woodrow Wilson won the election. The new president called on Congress to enact a host of progressive measures, and child labor, anti-trust, and fiscal reforms quickly followed in the spring of 1913. Although President Wilson revealed his skill in domestic matters, he soon found his administration overwhelmed by foreign affairs.

Wilson followed Roosevelt's lead in defending American interests in the Western Hemisphere during the Mexican Revolution, sending troops into Mexico "to teach these republics to elect good men!" The Pershing Expedition and invasions in the Caribbean and Central America followed. Wilson parted company with TR's world view in World War I, however, announcing that a nation could be "too proud to fight." While Democrats thundered during the 1916 re-election campaign that "he kept us out of war," in 1917 the U.S. went to war against Germany. Wilson turned America's involvement in the Great War into a crusade, announcing in 1917 that the nation had no territorial ambitions but instead stood for making the world safe for democracy. After the war, Wilson announced his Fourteen Points, a framework for a new world order (see primary source document 2). Despite Wilson's best intentions, European leaders were in no mood to support his call for a new world order. They were determined to punish Germany for the sins of WWI, thus setting the background to WWII.

American politics changed rapidly during the Roosevelt and Wilson presidencies. A new overseas empire required aggressive action, while the ills of industrial society demanded assertive leadership. Roosevelt and Wilson revitalized the office of the presidency and provided badly needed leadership in domestic and foreign affairs. Both presidents boldly shaped national policy, and their legacies remain strong today.

MAP EXERCISE

Refer to the following maps in Chapters 21, 22, and 23 of *A People and a Nation* to answer the questions listed below.

- Presidential Election, 1912 (p. 601)

- Imperialism in Asia. Turn of the Century (p. 625)

- U.S. Hegemony in the Caribbean and Latin America (p. 628)

- Europe Transformed by War and Peace (p. 658)

1. The 1912 election catapulted Wilson to power. Does the vote tally suggest a different outcome in a two-man race?

2. How far did the United States' empire extend into the Pacific at the turn of the century? Who were the nation's chief competitors in the imperial race?

3. Where did the Roosevelt Corollary come into play and what were the motivations behind it?

4. How was the map of Europe redrawn following WWI? Which nations appear to have suffered and which to have benefited from this transformation?

PEOPLE, EVENTS, AND CONCEPTS

Identify and explain the historical significance of each item.

John Burroughs

Identification

Significance

square deal

Identification

Significance

Veracruz

Identification

Significance

John Milton Cooper

Identification

Significance

bully pulpit

Identification

Significance

Jeannette Rankin

Identification

Significance

Monroe Doctrine

Identification

Significance

Edith Bolling Wilson

Identification

Significance

Roosevelt Corollary

Identification

Significance

Panama Canal

Identification

Significance

Fourteen Points

Identification

Significance

the Philippines

Identification

Significance

Mark Hanna

Identification

Significance

League of Nations

Identification

Significance

John Burroughs

Identification

Significance

Mexican Revolution

Identification

Significance

John L. Lewis

Identification

Significance

Versailles Treaty

Identification

Significance

ESSAY QUESTIONS

1. Describe the political and economic reforms sought by progressives? What were they supposed to accomplish? Assess their successes and shortcomings.

2. Why did President Roosevelt promote conservation? How did the nation benefit from this program? Can it be defined as progressive? Explain.

3. What methods were used by TR to promote U.S. imperial interests? Select a specific nation and evaluate the president's methods.

4. Overseas expansion created dissension at home. Opponents claimed that imperialism undermined democratic values. What do you think and why?

5. Woodrow Wilson entered the presidency at the height of progressivism. When his presidency came to a close, progressivism had stalled. What was Wilson's role?

6. How did Wilson's Fourteen Points—calling for national self determination, demilitarization, neutral rights, among other things—reflect the diplomatic needs of the era? Was Wilson ahead of his time? Discuss why his crusade for a new world order failed.

MULTIPLE-CHOICE QUESTIONS

1. Theodore Roosevelt advocated all of the following as part of his reform program except the idea that
   a. corporations should be controlled.
   b. labor needed restraints.
   c. consumers needed protection.
   d. our natural resources should be conserved.

2. Theodore Roosevelt felt that the national government should adopt which policy toward trusts?
   a. They should be destroyed to ensure competition.
   b. They should be given total freedom.
   c. They should be regulated.
   d. They should be accepted, because they were too powerful to control.

3. Theodore Roosevelt's assault on trusts was an attempt to
   a. stop activities that harmed the public interest.
   b. stop the break-up of large industries.
   c. make clear who ran the United States.
   d. make the trusts more efficient.

4. President Wilson pursued a progressive policy that
   a. favored the expansion of monopolies.
   b. realized the federal government could not enforce regulation.
   c. stopped the movement toward greater economic consolidation.
   d. proved ineffective and was highly discriminatory toward consumers.
5. The immediate cause behind the U.S. declaration of war against Germany was
   a. Germany's failure to resolve its debts.
   b. the Villista raids on U.S. border towns.
   c. Germany's encouragement of terror attacks in the United States.
   d. the resumption of unrestricted submarine warfare.
6. The most important element in Wilson's Fourteen Points was the call for
   a. reduction of armaments.
   b. a League of Nations.
   c. respect for neutral rights.
   d. the right of self determination.
7. According to the Roosevelt Corollary to the Monroe Doctrine
   a. the United States promised to protect Caribbean nations from invasions.
   b. Latin American nations had to pay all their debts upon demand.
   c. the United States would help to raise living standards in the hemisphere.
   d. regional order was essential to America's prosperity and security.
8. The major difference between Roosevelt and Wilson on foreign affairs was
   a. that TR was a pragmatist and Wilson was an idealist.
   b. that Roosevelt refused to get embroiled in European affairs.
   c. that Wilson refused to resort to force to achieve his goals.
   d. none of the above

Answers

1.	b	3.	a	5.	d	7.	d
2.	c	4.	c	6.	b	8.	a

PRIMARY SOURCE DOCUMENTS

The accounts of actual participants are useful for understanding the motives and thoughts of historical characters.

1. *Fifth Annual Message (1905)* Theodore Roosevelt

Twice during Theodore Roosevelt's presidency, European nations made military efforts to force Latin American nations to pay their debts—in Venezuela in 1902 and the Dominican Republic in 1904. In each instance Roosevelt intervened with naval forces and insisted on U.S. mediation. In his annual message to Congress, delivered in December 1905, Roosevelt sought to legitimatize such actions with what would become known as Roosevelt's Corollary to the Monroe Doctrine. In Roosevelt's view, the Monroe Doctrine justified the United States in behaving as a sort of policeman for the entire Western Hemisphere.

Questions to Consider

- What gives the United States the right to police the Western Hemisphere?

- What limitations does Roosevelt place on American power?

- Is Roosevelt suggesting some fundamental change in American foreign policy?

Our aim is righteousness. Peace is normally the hand-maiden of righteousness; but when peace and righteousness conflict then a great and upright people can never for a moment hesitate to follow the path which leads toward righteousness, even though that path also leads to war....

One of the most effective instruments for peace is the Monroe Doctrine as it has been and is being gradually developed by this Nation and accepted by other nations.... It is useful at home, and is meeting with recognition abroad because we have adapted our application of it to meet the growing and changing needs of the hemisphere. When we announce a policy such as the Monroe Doctrine we thereby commit ourselves to the consequences of the policy, and those consequences from time to time alter. It is out of the question to claim a right and yet shirk the responsibility for its exercise. Not only we, but all American republics who are benefited by the existence of the doctrine, must recognize the obligations each nation is under as regards foreign peoples no less than its duty to insist upon its own rights.

That our rights and interests are deeply concerned in the maintenance of the doctrine is so clear as hardly to need argument....

There are certain essential points which must never be forgotten as regards the Monroe Doctrine. In the first place we must as a Nation make it evident that we do not intend to treat it in any shape or way as an excuse for aggrandizement on our part at the expense of the republics to the south.... All that this country desires is that the other republics on this continent shall be happy and prosperous; and they cannot be happy and prosperous unless they maintain order within their boundaries and behave with a just regard for their obligations toward outsiders. It must be understood that under no circumstances will the United States use the Monroe Doctrine as a cloak for territorial aggression.... There are, of course, limits to the wrongs which any self-respecting nation can endure. It is always possible that wrong actions toward this Nation, or toward citizens of this Nation, in some State unable to keep order among its own people, ...may result in our having to take action to protect our rights; but such action...will be taken...only with extreme reluctance and when it has become evident that every other resource has been exhausted.

Moreover, we must make it evident that we do not intend to permit the Monroe Doctrine to be used by any nation on this Continent as a shield to protect it from the consequences of its own misdeeds against foreign nations. If a republic to the south of us commits a tort [wrongful act] against a foreign nation, ...then the Monroe Doctrine does not force us to interfere to prevent punishment of the tort, save to see that the punishment does not assume the form of territorial occupation in any shape. The case is more difficult when it refers to a contractual obligation. Our own Government has always refused to enforce such contractual obligations on behalf of its citizens by an appeal to arms. It is much to be wished that all foreign governments would take the same view. But they do not; and in consequence we are liable at any time to be brought face to face with disagreeable alternatives. On the one hand, this country would certainly decline to go to war to prevent a foreign government from collecting a just debt; on the other hand, it is very inadvisable to permit any foreign power to take possession, even temporarily, of the custom houses of an American Republic in order to enforce the payment of its obligations; for such temporary occupation might turn into a permanent occupation. The only escape from these alternatives may at any time be that we must ourselves undertake to bring about some arrangement by which so much as possible of a just obligation shall be paid....

Moreover, for the United States to take such a position offers the only possible way of insuring us against a clash with some foreign power. The position is, therefore, in the interest of peace as well as in the interest of justice. It is of benefit to our people; it is of benefit to foreign peoples; and most of all it is really of benefit to the people of the country concerned.

This brings me to what should be one of the fundamental objects of the Monroe Doctrine. We must ourselves in good faith try to help upward toward peace and order those of our sister republics which need such help. Just as there has been a gradual growth of the ethical element in the relations of one individual to another, so we are, even though slowly, more and more coming to recognize the duty of bearing one another's burdens, not only as among individuals, but also as among nations....

SOURCE: James D. Richardson, ed., *A Compilation of the Messages and Papers of the Presidents* 16 (New York, 1920): pp. 7372, 7374–7377.

2. *The Fourteen Points (1918)* Woodrow Wilson

As American troops finally entered combat in Europe, Woodrow Wilson attempted to give shape to the nation's war aims, while suggesting the terms under which peace could be attained short of total victory. Delivered before Congress on January 8, 1918, this "program of the world's peace," which became known as the "Fourteen Points," transformed Wilson into an international leader of great moral authority. Clearly a great many common people in America and Europe shared Wilson's vision for the postwar world. When Germany finally sued for peace, its government did so with the expectation that the Fourteen Points would serve as the basis for all future negotiations.

Questions to Consider

- Why would America's enemies come to find hope in the Fourteen Points?
- How did Wilson think that his program would produce world peace?

We entered this war because violations of right had occurred which touched us to the quick and made the life of our own people impossible unless they were corrected and the world secured once for all against their recurrence. What we demand in this war, therefore, is nothing peculiar to ourselves. It is that the world be made fit and safe to live in; and particularly that it be made safe for every peace-loving nation which, like our own, wishes to live its own life, determine its own institutions, be assured of justice and fair dealings by the other peoples of the world, as against force and selfish aggression. All the peoples of the world are in effect partners in this interest, and for our own part we see very clearly that unless justice be done to others it will not be done to us....

I.—Open covenants of peace, openly arrived at, after which there shall be no private international understandings of any kind, but diplomacy shall proceed always frankly and in the public view.

II.—Absolute freedom of navigation upon the seas, outside territorial waters, alike in peace and in war, except as the seas may be closed in whole or in part by international action for the enforcement of international covenants.

III.—The removal, so far as possible, of all economic barriers and the establishment of an equality of trade conditions among all the nations consenting to the peace and associating themselves for its maintenance.

IV.—Adequate guarantees given and taken that national armaments will be reduced to the lowest point consistent with domestic safety.

V.—Free, open-minded, and absolutely impartial adjustment of all colonial claims, based upon a strict observance of the principle that in determining all such questions of sovereignty the interests of the population concerned must have equal weight with the equitable claims of the Government whose title is to be determined.

VI.—The evacuation of all Russian territory and such a settlement of all questions affecting Russia as will secure the best and freest cooperation of the other nations of the world in obtaining for her an unhampered and unembarrassed opportunity for the independent determination of her own political development and national policy, and assure her of a sincere welcome into the society of free nations under institutions of her own choosing; and, more than a welcome, assistance also of every kind that she may need and may herself desire....

VII.—Belgium, the whole world will agree, must be evacuated and restored, without any attempt to limit the sovereignty which she enjoys in common with all other free nations....

VIII.—All French territory should be freed and the invaded portions restored, and the wrong done to France by Prussia in 1871 in the matter of Alsace-Lorraine, which has unsettled the peace of the world for nearly fifty years, should be righted, in order that peace may once more be made secure in the interest of all.

IX.—A readjustment of the frontiers of Italy should be effected along clearly recognizable lines of nationality.

X.—The peoples of Austria-Hungary, whose place among the nations we wish to see safeguarded and assured, should be accorded the freest opportunity of autonomous development.

XI.—Rumania, Serbia, and Montenegro should be evacuated; occupied territories restored; Serbia accorded free and secure access to the sea; and the relations of the several Balkan States to one another determined by friendly counsel along historically established lines of allegiance and nationality; and international guarantees of the political and economic independence and territorial integrity of the several Balkan States should be entered into.

XII.—The Turkish portions of the present Ottoman Empire should be assured a secure sovereignty, but the other nationalities which are now under Turkish rule should be assured an undoubted security of life and an absolutely unmolested opportunity of autonomous development, and the Dardanelles should be permanently opened as a free passage to the ships and commerce of all nations under international guarantees.

XIII.—An independent Polish State should be erected which should include the territories inhabited by indisputably Polish populations, which should be assured a free and secure access to the sea, and whose political and economic independence and territorial integrity should be guaranteed by international covenant.

XIV.—A general association of nations must be formed under specific covenants for the purpose of affording mutual guarantees of political independence and territorial integrity to great and small states alike....

SOURCE: Supplement to the Messages and Papers of the Presidents, Covering the Second Term of Woodrow Wilson, March 4, 1917, to March 4, 1921 (Washington, D.C., 1921), pp. 8423–8425.

3. *Monopoly or Opportunity? (1912)* Woodrow Wilson

The right to create monopolies was the essential issue of the 1912 election. Theodore Roosevelt, the Progressive candidate, held that monopolies were an unavoidable part of the modern economy, but that they could be regulated for the benefit of society. The Democratic candidate, Woodrow Wilson, hoped to prevent the creation of monopolies through a federal regulation that would foster competition. Wilson maintained faith in the ability of small businesses to fuel economic growth. In his campaign speeches, such as the following, Wilson promised a "New Freedom" based on a renewal of competition.

Questions to Consider

- Is there a nostalgic component to Wilson's views?

- Can big business be restrained from dominating government?

I admit the popularity of the theory that the trusts have come about through the natural development of business conditions in the United States, and that it is a mistake to try to oppose the processes by which they have been built up, because those processes belong to the very nature of business in our time, and that therefore the only thing we can do, and the only thing we ought to attempt to do, is to accept them as inevitable arrangements and make the best out of it that we can by regulation.

I answer, nevertheless, that this attitude rests upon a confusion of thought. Big business is no doubt to a large extent necessary and natural. The development of business upon a great scale, upon a great scale of cooperation, is inevitable, and, let me add, is probably desirable. But that is a very different matter from the development of trusts, because the trusts have not grown. They have been artificially created; they have been put together, not by natural processes, but by the will, the deliberate planning will, of men who were more powerful than their neighbors in the business world, and who wished to make their power secure against competition....

Did you ever look into the way a trust was made? It is very natural, in one sense, in the same sense in which human greed is natural. If I haven't efficiency enough to beat my rivals, then the thing I am inclined to do is to get together with my rivals and say: "Don't let's cut each other's throats; let's combine and determine prices for ourselves; determine the output, and thereby determine the prices: and dominate and control the market." That is very natural. That has been done ever since freebooting was established. That has been done ever since power was used to establish control. The reason that the masters of combination have sought to shut out competition is that the basis of control under competition is brains and efficiency. I admit that any large corporation built up by the legitimate processes of business, by economy, by efficiency, is natural; and I am not afraid of it, no matter how big it grows. It can stay big only by doing its work more thoroughly than anybody else. And there is a point of bigness,—as every business man in this country knows, though some of them will not admit it,—where you pass the limit of efficiency and get into the region of clumsiness and unwieldiness. You can make your combine so extensive that you can't digest it into a single system; you can get so many parts that you can't assemble them as you would an effective piece of machinery. The point of efficiency is overstepped in the natural process of development oftentimes, and it has been overstepped many times in the artificial and deliberate formation of trusts....

Talk of that as sound business? Talk of that as inevitable? It is based upon nothing except power. It is not based upon efficiency. It is no wonder that the big trusts are not prospering in proportion to such competitors as they still have in such parts of their business as competitors have access to; they are prospering freely only in those fields to which competition has no access....

For my part, I want the pigmy to have a chance to come out. And I foresee a time when the pigmies will be so much more athletic, so much more astute, so much more active, than the giants, that it will be a case of Jack the giant-killer. Just let some of the youngsters I know have a chance and they'll give these gentlemen points. Lend them a little money. They can't get any now. See to it that when they have got a local market they can't be squeezed out of it. Give them a chance to capture that market and then see them capture another one and another one, until these men who are carrying an intolerable load of artificial securities find that they have got to get down to hard pan to keep their foothold at all....

SOURCE: Woodrow Wilson, *The New Freedom* (New York, 1913), pp. 164–170.

UNIT 19

A Vital Progressivism

UNIT SUMMARY

In Unit 19 we look at the meaning of progressivism and the struggle for equality waged by African Americans, Mexican Americans, Asian Americans, and Native Americans.

ASSIGNMENT

1. Before viewing Program 19, read this unit, and in *A People and a Nation* read Chapter 17, pages 459–469, Chapter 20, pages 560–563, and Chapter 21, pages 577–596.

2. View Program 19, "A Vital Progressivism."

3. Visit the Web site <http://www.learner.org/biographyofamerica>. Explore the exercises for Program 19.

LEARNING OBJECTIVES

Upon completing this unit, students should be able to:

1. Discuss the Progressive movement and the struggles of minorities to find a place in the new industrial society.

2. Describe abuses associated with big business and industrialization.

3. Describe Euro-Americans' approach to "saving" the Native Americans.

4. Assess the role of women in the reform movements.

PROGRAM GUIDE

The Progressive movement is a national crusade to alleviate the social, economic, and political ills of the industrial age. It is predominantly a middle-class movement in an age when reformist politics enjoy increasing popular support. Professor Martin argues that the reformist spirit can be seen most vividly in the struggles of non-Euro-Americans to achieve their dreams in the new industrial society.

The monopolistic practices of big business after the Civil War lead to many abuses: laboring children, tenement housing, long hours, and poor wages. Urbanization reinforces exploitation, squalor, and suffering. Immigrants to the United States find the new world befuddling, and their bewilderment is made worse by the overcrowded conditions in which they live. Reformers seek to raise public awareness of these and other woes associated with the industrial age. One arena of reform that receives scant public attention, however, is the struggle for civil rights. The Progressive movement in America often neglects racial minorities. At the end of the program, Professors Scharff and Miller join Professor Martin in a discussion affirming the roles of Native Americans, Latinos, Asian Americans, and Blacks in the fight for equality against enormous odds.

HISTORICAL OVERVIEW

W. E. B. DuBois, the noted scholar, sociologist, and historian, wrote in *The Soul of Black Folks* that: "The problem of the twentieth century is the problem of the color line…and the struggle of racial minorities was to overcome their feelings of twoness." DuBois described how having African ancestry (or Chinese, Mexican, or Native American) carried a perceived stigma of inferiority. Blacks were Americans, but they lived in a land of bigotry and prejudice. How could this dilemma be resolved in the era of Jim Crow segregation? Although passage of the Fourteenth and Fifteenth Amendments had theoretically secured the rights of *freedmen*, or former slaves, as American citizens, the South in alliance with the Supreme Court continued to affirm color as a mark of inferiority. The high court ruled in Plessy v. Ferguson (1896) that states had the right to regulate race relations, and segregation affected the lives of all racial minorities. A system of *apartheid*, or separation of the races, mandated separate facilities: churches and schools, water fountains and bathrooms, hospitals and graveyards, department stores and hotels and, ultimately, justice. In her exposé "The Red Record," journalist Ida Wells Barnett documented the illegal and barbaric lynchings perpetrated upon blacks throughout the South. The federal government ignored Barnett's domestic and international campaign to stop the lynchings and took no action until the 1940s.

Color and ethnicity determined the quality of justice for Americans. The emphasis on acculturation forced Indians into farming, while no thought of protecting their cultural uniqueness entered into anyone's mind. Thousands of Native American children were taken from their parents and sent to boarding schools to be properly instructed in Euro-American ways. The philosophy of the Carlisle Indian School in Pennsylvania reflected the popular attitude that it was necessary to "kill the Indian to save the man." Suzette and Susan la Flesche, Omaha Indians whose brother suffered the humiliation of the Carlisle experience, fought for citizenship protections and lobbied Congress to extend constitutional guarantees to Indians, and the distinguished service of Native Americans in WWI led Congress to enact legislation extending full citizenship rights in 1924.

Chinese sailed across the Pacific because of the discovery of gold in California. Their presence in San Francisco and in the Mother Lode led to hostilities, as California was, as Anglo-Americans said, a white man's land. After the gold rush, a new wave of Chinese arrived in the west as contracted workers to build the railroads. Once their work was finished, they searched for new jobs in agriculture, fishing, and service-oriented occupations. During the Terrible Seventies, when depression struck California, Euro-Americans rallied against the Chinese. As efforts to harass, intimidate, and legislate against Asian immigrants escalated, Congress took action. The Chinese Exclusion Act of 1881 banned further immigration. Congress did not repeal the law until the beginning of World War II.

Mexicans, who were extended citizenship rights by the 1848 Treaty of Guadalupe-Hidalgo, sought economic opportunities in a land of bigotry and discrimination and endured the injustices, hardships, and humiliations of a people viewed as aliens in their own land. In communities across the Southwest—Tucson, El Paso, San Antonio, Los Angeles—Jim Crow laws relegated them to second-class citizenship. Later, Mexicans fled their country during the Mexican Revolution and World War I searching for work and safety. Racist resentment against them led to a dual wage system, as Mexicans were routinely paid less than their Anglo counterparts. When Mexican workers organized to protest these conditions, as they did in Bisbee, Arizona, the authorities responded by sending them back to Mexico as undesirable aliens. Even American citizens were rounded up and forced back across the Mexican border. The League of United Latin American Citizens was founded to challenge these and other injustices.

Efforts to redress the inequities associated with discrimination met with little success in the Progressive era. The disenfranchised organized to improve their situations, however, and slowly advanced their cause. The formation of the National Association for the Advancement of Colored

People, or NAACP, and litigation efforts in the courts had some effect, but it took two world wars and decades of organizational efforts to improve conditions for minorities in the United States. As the public forged new alliances with government, racial minorities began to challenge American society's discriminatory practices. We shall see in future programs that the struggle for equality continues into the twenty-first century.

MAP EXERCISE

Refer to the following map in Chapter 21 of *A People and a Nation* to answer the question listed below.

- Woman Suffrage Before 1920 (p. 595)

1. Where did women have the right to vote before the nineteenth amendment was ratified? How did the Progressive era help clarify women's issues?

PEOPLE, EVENTS, AND CONCEPTS

Identify and explain the historical significance of each item.

W. E. B. DuBois

Identification

Significance

Carlisle Indian School

Identification

Significance

progressivism

Identification

Significance

Zeferino Ramirez

Identification

Significance

Gold Rush California

Identification

Significance

Jim Crow laws

Identification

Significance

ethnocentrism

Identification

Significance

Ida B. Welles

Identification

Significance

Wounded Knee

Identification

Significance

nativist

Identification

Significance

Booker T. Washington

Identification

Significance

sharecropper

Identification

Significance

Frederick Douglass

Identification

Significance

Red Progressives

Identification

Significance

the LaFlesche Sisters

Identification

Significance

Bisbee, Arizona

Identification

Significance

Great Migration

Identification

Significance

Wovoka

Identification

Significance

ESSAY QUESTIONS

1. You are a social progressive. Choose one cause—education, housing, women workers—explain the problems, and propose a solution.

2. W. E. B. DuBois wrote that "the problem of the twentieth century is the color line." Evaluate the quality of life for African-Americans at the beginning of the twentieth century and explain the barriers to full citizenship. What methods did DuBois advocate to combat discrimination?

3. Contrast the approaches to civil rights promoted by Booker T. Washington and W. E. B. DuBois. Who is the accommodation advocate? Who opposes accommodation and why?

4. What drew the Chinese to the west coast? How did the public respond to their presence and why?

5. Evaluate the effect of reservation policy on native culture and how the Dawes Severalty Act changed the policy.

MULTIPLE-CHOICE QUESTIONS

1. All of the following were used by southern whites to deny African Americans the right to vote except
   a. a grandfather clause.
   b. a poll tax.
   c. limits on black education.
   d. country of birth.

2. The Indian Wars were caused by all of the following except
   a. the Indians were defending their land.
   b. the Indians wanted to avenge massacres committed by whites.
   c. the Indians wanted to protest broken treaties.
   d. the Indians wanted their women returned from exile.

3. The attitude of most humanitarians towards Indians expressed
   a. very little respect for traditional Indian culture.
   b. a desire for traditions like the Ghost Dance to continue.
   c. no need for new laws like the Dawes Act.
   d. disdain for all U.S. efforts towards acculturation.

4. Which of the following changes in Indian life was *not* a result of the Dawes Act?
   a. Many Indian tribes lost their status as a legal entity.
   b. White attempted to make Indians into rugged individualists.
   c. Whites tried to remove tribal ownership of land.
   d. The sacred Sun Dance was outlawed.

5. In California, Chinese faced an angry public and efforts to restrict them by
   a. making them ineligible for citizenship.
   b. placing them into relocation camps.
   c. passing of the Chinese Exclusion Act.
   d. passing laws to repatriate them back to China.

6. According to the Treaty of Guadalupe-Hidalgo, Mexicans were to
   a. be returned to Mexico as aliens and undesirables.
   b. be granted all their rights as citizens of the United States.
   c. work only the fields of California as farm workers.
   d. remain in the territories but be denied due process rights.

7. The National Association for the Advancement of Colored People
   a. spoke exclusively for the southern sharecropper.
   b. refused to accept people of other nationalities.
   c. fought for the reversal of discrimination in the courts.
   d. emphasized separation and segregation of the races.
8. Mexican-American miners in the southwest faced discrimination in the form of
   a. the dual wage system.
   b. losing all their rights of American citizenship.
   c. being forced into janitorial positions.
   d. being arrested for their socialist activities.

Answers

1. d	3. a	5. c	7. c
2. d	4. d	6. b	8. a

PRIMARY SOURCE DOCUMENTS

The accounts of actual participants are useful for understanding the motives and thoughts of historical characters.

1. ***The Niagara Movement (1905) W. E. B. Du Bois***

In his "Atlanta Compromise" of 1895, Booker T. Washington proposed that black Americans would not question their political and social subjugation as long as they were allowed to develop economically. Many other African Americans objected to Washington's willingness to accept racism as a fact of life. Meeting secretly in 1905 on the Canadian side of the border at Niagara Falls (not Buffalo, as Du Bois writes), a group of prominent black intellectuals, led by W. E. B. Du Bois, formed the Niagara Movement to fight for full human rights. The organization enjoyed some small successes and garnered a great deal of attention, but suffered from a serious lack of funds. In 1910, at Du Bois's urging, the Niagara Movement disbanded and reformed in an alliance with white liberals as the National Association for the Advancement of Colored People (NAACP).

Questions to Consider

- What were the attractions of the Niagara Movement for black Americans?
- Why was it dominated by intellectuals?

What is the Niagara Movement? The Niagara Movement is an organization composed at present of fifty-four men resident in eighteen states of the United States. These men having common aspirations have banded themselves together into an organization. This organization was perfected at a meeting held at Buffalo, N. Y., July 11, 12 and 13, 1905, and was called "The Niagara Movement." The present membership, which of course we hope to enlarge as we find others of like thought and ideal, consists of ministers, lawyers, editors, business men and teachers. The honor of founding the organization belongs to F. L. McGhee, who first suggested it; C. C. Bentley, who planned the method of organization and W. M. Trotter, who put the backbone into the platform.

The organization is extremely simple and is designed for effective work. Its officers are a general secretary and treasurer, a series of state secretaries and a number of secretaries of specific committees. Its membership in each State constitutes the State organization under the State secretary.

Why this organization is needed. The first exclamation of any one hearing of this new movement will naturally be: "Another!" Why, we may legitimately be asked, should men attempt another organization after the failures of the past? We answer soberly but earnestly, "For that very reason."

Failure to organize Negro-Americans for specific objects in the past makes it all the more imperative that we should keep trying until we succeed. Today we have no organization devoted to the general interests of the African race in America. The Afro-American Council, while still in existence, has done practically nothing for three years, and is today, so far as effective membership and work is concerned, little more than a name. For specific objects we have two organizations, the New England Suffrage League and the Negro Business League. There is, therefore, without the slightest doubt room for a larger national organization. What now is needed for the success of such an organization? If the lessons of the past are read aright there is demanded:

1. Simplicity of organization.

2. Definiteness of aim.

The country is too large, the race too scattered and the rank and file too unused to organized effort to attempt to impose a vast machine-like organization upon a wavering, uncertain constituency. This has been the mistakes of several efforts at united work among us. Effective organization must be simple—a banding together of men on lines essentially as simple as those of a village debating club. What is the essential thing in such organization. Manifestly it is like-mindedness. Agreement in the object to be worked for, or in other words, *definiteness of aim.*

Among ten million people enduring the stress under which we are striving there must of necessity be great and far-reaching differences of opinions. It is idle, even nonsensical, to suppose that a people just beginning self-mastery and self-guidance should be able from the start to be in perfect accord as to the wisdom or expediency of certain policies. And some universal agreement is impossible. The best step is for those who agree to unite for the realization of those things on which they have reached agreement. This is what the Niagara movement has done. It has simply organized and its members agree as to certain great ideals and lines of policy. Such people as are in agreement with them it invites to co-operation and membership. Other persons it seeks to convert to its way of thinking; it respects their opinion, but believes thoroughly in its own. This the world teaches us is the way of progress.

What the Niagara Movement proposes to do. What now are the principles upon which the membership of the Niagara Movement are agreed? As set forth briefly in the constitution, they are as follows:

(a)   Freedom of speech and criticism.

(b)   An unfettered and unsubsidized press.

(c)   Manhood suffrage.

(d)   The abolition of all caste distinctions based simply on race and color.

(e)   The recognition of the principle of human brotherhood as a practical present creed.

(f)   The recognition of the highest and best training as the monopoly of no class or race.

(g)   A belief in the dignity of labor.

(h)   United effort to realize these ideals under wise and courageous leadership.

All these things we believe are of great and instant importance; there has been a determined effort in this country to stop the free expression of opinion among black men; money has been and is being distributed in considerable sums to influence the attitude of certain Negro papers; the principles of democratic government *are* losing ground, and caste distinctions are growing in all directions. Human brotherhood is spoken of today with a smile and a sneer; effort is being made to curtail the educational opportunities of the colored children; and while much is said about money-making, not enough is said about efficient, self-sacrificing toil of head and hand. Are not all these things worth striving for? *The Niagara Movement* proposes to gain these ends. All this is very well, answers the objector, but the ideals are impossible of realization. We can never gain our freedom in this land. To which we reply: We certainly cannot unless we try. If we expect to gain our rights by nerveless acquiescence in wrong, then we expect to do what no other nation ever did. What must we do then? We must complain. Yes, plain, blunt complaint, ceaseless agitation, unfailing exposure of dishonesty and wrong—this is the ancient, unerring way to liberty, and we must follow it. I know the ears of the American people have become very sensitive to Negro complaints of late and profess to dislike whining. Let that worry none. No nation on earth ever complained and whined so much as this nation has, and we propose to follow the example. Next we propose to work. These are the things that we as black men must try to do:

To press the matter of stopping the curtailment of our political rights.
To urge Negroes to vote intelligently and effectively.
To push the matter of civil rights.
To organize business co-operation.
To build school houses and increase the interest in education.
To open up new avenues of employment and strengthen our hold on the old.
To distribute tracts and information in regard to the laws of health.
To bring Negroes and labor unions into mutual understanding.
To study Negro history.
To increase the circulation of honest, unsubsidized newspapers and periodicals.
To attack crime among us by all civilized agencies. In fact to do all in our power by word or deed to increase the efficiency of our race, the enjoyment of its manhood, rights and the performance of its just duties.

This is a large program. It cannot be realized in a short time. But something can be done and we are going to do something. It is interesting to see how the platform and program has been received by the country. In not a single instance has the justice of our demands been denied. The *Law Register* of Chicago acknowledges openly that "the student of legal and political history is aware that every right secured by men either individually or as a nation has been won only after asserting the right and sometimes fighting for it. And when a people begin to voice their demand for a right and keep it up, they ultimately obtain the right as a rule." The *Mail and Express* says that this idea is "that upon which the American white man has founded his success."—all this *but*—and then have come the excuses: The *Outlook* thinks that "A child should use other language." It is all right for the white men says the *Mail and Express,* but black men—well they had better "work." Complaint has a horrible and almost a treasonable sound to the *Tribune* while the *Chicago Record-Herald* of course makes the inevitable discovery of "Social Equality." Is not this significant? Is justice in the world to be finally and definitely labelled white and that with your apathetic consent? Are we not men enough to protest, or shall the sneer of the *Outlook* and its kind be proven true that out of ten millions there are only a baker's dozen who will follow these fifty Negro-Americans and dare to stand up and be counted as demanding every single right that belongs to free American citizens? This is the critical time, Black men of America; the staggering days of Emancipation, of childhood are gone.

"God give us men! A time like this demands
Strong minds, great hearts, true faith, and ready hands;
Men whom lust of office does not kill;
Men whom the spoils of office cannot buy;
Men who possess opinions and a will;
Men who have honor, men who will not lie;
Men who can stand before a demagogue,

And damn his treacherous flatterers without winking.
Tall men, sun-crowned, who live above the fog
In public duty and private thinking.
For when the rabble, with their thumb worn creeds,
Their large professions and their little deeds,
Mingle in selfish strife—lo, Freedom weeps,
Wrong rules the land, and waiting Justice sleeps."

SOURCE: W. E. B. Du Bois, "The Niagara Movement," *The Voice of the Negro* vol. 2, no. 9 (September 1905), pp. 619-622.

2.   *The Chinese Boycott (1906)* John W. Foster

In 1879, responding to pressure from Western representatives, Congress excluded Chinese immigrants from the United States. President Rutherford B. Hayes vetoed the bill as a violation of the 1868 Burlingame Treaty between the United States and China. After the revision of that treaty in 1880, Congress passed the Chinese Exclusion Act prohibiting the immigration of Chinese workers—the first time that a specific ethnic group had been denied the right to emigrate to the United States. The Exclusion Act was revised for another ten years in 1892 and made permanent in 1902. The people of China responded with a boycott of all American goods. In the following article, John Foster describes the consequences of American policy.

Questions to Consider

   •   What justification did Congress have for excluding Chinese laborers from the United States?

   •   Does Foster offer evidence that the legislation was the result of bigotry rather than economic policy?

The Chinese boycott of American goods is a striking evidence of an awakening spirit of resentment in the great Empire against the injustice and aggression of foreign countries. It seems singular that its first manifestation of resentment should be directed against the nation whose government has been most conspicuous in defending its integrity and independence. The explanation of this is that the boycott movement owes its initiative, not to the Chinese government, but to individual and popular influence, and is almost entirely the outgrowth of the ill-feeling of the people who have been the victims of the harsh exclusion laws and the sufferers by the race hatred existing in certain localities and classes in the United States....

I do not know how I can better illustrate the kind of protection, or want of protection, extended to the Chinese, as guaranteed by the Constitution, the treaties, and the solemn promises of the government of the United States, than by recalling a notorious case which occurred, not on the sand lots of California, not under the auspices of labor agitators, but in the enlightened city of Boston and under the conduct of Federal officials.

...At about half past seven o'clock on the evening of Sunday, October 11, 1902, a number of United States officials of Boston, New York, and other cities charged with the administration of the Chinese exclusion laws, assisted by a force of the local police, made a sudden and unexpected descent upon the Chinese quarter of Boston. The raid was timed with a refinement of cruelty which did greater credit to the shrewdness of the officials than to their humanity. It was on the day and at the hour when the Chinese of Boston and its vicinity were accustomed to congregate in the quarter named for the purpose of meeting friends and enjoying themselves after a week of steady and honest toil. The police and immigration officials fell upon their victims without giving a word of warning. The clubs, restaurants, other public places where Chinese congregated, and private houses, were surrounded. Every avenue of escape was blocked. To those seized no warrant for arrest or other paper was read or shown.

Every Chinese who did not at once produce his certificate of residence was taken in charge, and the unfortunate ones were rushed off to the Federal Building without further ceremony. There was no respect of persons with the officials; they treated merchants and laborers alike. In many cases no demand was made for certificates, the captives were dragged off to imprisonment, and in some instances the demand was not made till late at night or the next morning, when the certificates were in the possession of the victims at the time of their seizure.

In the raid no mercy was shown by the government officials. The frightened Chinese who had sought to escape were dragged from their hiding-places, and stowed like cattle upon wagons or other vehicles, to be conveyed to the designated place of detention. On one of those wagons or trucks from seventy to eighty persons were thrown, and soon after it moved it was overturned. A scene of indescribable confusion followed, in which the shrieks of those attempting to escape mingled with the groans of those who were injured....

About two hundred and fifty Chinese were thus arrested and carried off to the Federal Building. Here they were crowded into two small rooms where only standing space could be had, from eight o'clock in the evening, all through the night, and many of them till late in the afternoon of the next day. There was no sleep for any of them that night, though some of them were so exhausted that they sank to the floor where they stood. Their captors seemed to think that they had to do with animals, not human beings....

...The official report of the chief officer soon after the event showed that two hundred and thirty-four Chinese were imprisoned, that one hundred and twenty-one were released without trial or requirement of bail, and that only five had so far been deported....

Even as to the guilty Chinese the arrest and confinement was without warrant of law. But what justification can be offered for the arrest of the two hundred peaceable and law-abiding Chinese,— the indignities, hardships, and insults to which they were subjected? Although earnest complaint was made by the Chinese Minister to the government at Washington, not a single officer was punished or even censured for his illegal and brutal conduct, and no reparation was obtained by the Chinese....

Tom Kim Yung, the military attaché of the Chinese Legation in Washington, was in 1903 sent to San Francisco on a temporary duty. One night, after spending the evening dining with the president of the Chinese Merchants' Association, when returning to his lodgings at the Consulate General, and near that place, he was accosted by a policeman in most indecent language and struck with gross indignity. This resulted in an encounter participated in by another policeman. The attaché was beaten and severely bruised, and finally handcuffed and tied by his queue to a fence until the arrival of a patrol wagon, into which he was forced and taken to the police station. Here he was kept for some time, until released on bail given by a Chinese merchant, about half past one o'clock at night.

He was held for trial on a charge of assaulting a police officer, and when his diplomatic character was brought to the attention of the chief of police by the consul general, that officer refused to dismiss the charge. The excuse of the policeman for his conduct was that he mistook the attaché for another Chinaman for whom he was on the look-out. The attaché, not being able to secure the dismissal of the charges or any punishment of the policeman, was greatly chagrined; he felt that he had "lost face" with his countrymen; and brooding over what he regarded as his disgrace, he committed suicide....

SOURCE: John W. Foster, "The Chinese Boycott," *Atlantic Monthly* 97 (1906): pp. 118–127.

3. *Lynch Law (1907)* Benjamin Tillman

In Brownsville, Texas, on August 13, 1906, a company of black soldiers got in a gunfight with the local police after a series of racist provocations. That incident became a national issue, leading many Southern members of Congress to argue that no blacks should be allowed to serve in the military. One of those endorsing that position was South Carolina's Senator Benjamin "Pitchfork Ben" Tillman. In the following speech, delivered on the floor of the United States Senate on January 21, 1907, Tillman constructed an imagined history of the South since the Civil War as a justification for the denial of rights to, and the lynching of, black Americans.

Questions to Consider

- How does Tillman justify stealing elections through such methods as "stuffed ballot boxes"?
- Why does Tillman refer to African Americans as "creatures"?
- Is lynching a form of law?

I will repeat the statement of fact and circumstances. It was in 1876, …and the people of South Carolina had been living under negro rule for eight years. There was a condition bordering upon anarchy. Misrule, robbery, and murder were holding high carnival. The people's substance was being stolen, and there was no incentive to labor. Our legislature was composed of a majority of negroes, most of whom could neither read nor write. They were the easy dupes and tools of as dirty a band of vampires and robbers as ever preyed upon a prostrate people. There was riotous living in the statehouse and sessions of the legislature lasting from year to year.

…We felt the very foundations of our civilization crumbling beneath our feet, that we were sure to be engulfed by the black flood of barbarians who were surrounding us and had been put over us by the Army under the reconstruction acts…. Life ceased to be worth having on the terms under which we were living, and in desperation we determined to take the government away from the negroes.

We reorganized the Democratic party with one plank, and only one plank, namely, that "this is a white man's country and white men must govern it." Under that banner we went to battle….

Clashes came. The negro militia grew unbearable and more and more insolent…. The Hamburg riot was one clash, in which seven negroes and one white man were killed. A month later we had the Ellenton riot, in which no one ever knew how many negroes were killed, but there were forty or fifty or a hundred. It was a fight between barbarism and civilization, between the African and the Caucasian, for mastery.

It was then that "we shot them;" it was then that "we killed them;" it was then that "we stuffed ballot boxes." … [W]e had decided to take the government away from men so debased as were the negroes—I will not say baboons; I never have called them baboons; I believe they are men, but some of them are so near akin to the monkey that scientists are yet looking for the missing link. We saw the evil of giving the ballot to creatures of this kind, and saying that one vote shall count regardless of the man behind the vote and whether that vote would kill mine. …

…Then it was that we stuffed ballot boxes, because desperate diseases require desperate remedies, and having resolved to take the State away, we hesitated at nothing.

…I want to say now that we have not shot any negroes in South Carolina on account of politics since 1876. We have not found it necessary. [Laughter.] …

…It took the State fifteen years to recover and begin to move forward again along the paths of development and progress; and in consequence of the white men interpreting the word "liberty" to mean the liberty of white people and not the license of black ones, the State is to-day in the very vanguard of southern progress, and can point to the result as the absolute justification for every act which we performed in '76, however lawless our acts may be in the eyes of the Senator from Wisconsin....

Have I ever advocated lynch law at any time or at any place? I answer on my honor, "Never!" I have justified it for one crime, and one only, and I have consistently and persistently maintained that attitude for the last fourteen years. As governor of South Carolina I proclaimed that, although I had taken the oath of office to support the law and enforce it, I would lead a mob to lynch any man, black or white, who had ravished a woman, black or white. This is my attitude calmly and deliberately taken, and justified by my conscience in the sight of God....

Now let me suppose a case. Let us take any Senator on this floor.... Let us carry this Senator to the backwoods in South Carolina, put him on a farm miles from a town or railroad, and environed by negroes. We will suppose he has a fair young daughter just budding into womanhood: and recollect this, the white women of the South are in a state of siege; the greatest care is exercised that they shall at all times where it is possible not be left alone or unprotected, but that can not always and in every instance be the case. That Senator's daughter...is left home alone for a brief while. Some lurking demon who has watched for the opportunity seizes her: she is choked or beaten into insensibility and ravished, her body prostituted, her purity destroyed, her chastity taken from her, and a memory branded on her brain as with a red-hot iron to haunt her night and day as long as she lives....

In other words, a death in life. This young girl thus blighted and brutalized drags herself to her father and tells him what has happened. Is there a man here with red blood in his veins who doubts what impulses the father would feel? Is it any wonder that the whole countryside rises as one man and with set, stern faces seek the brute who has wrought this infamy? Brute, did I say? Why, Mr. President, this crime is a slander on the brutes. No beast of the field forces his female. He waits invitation. It has been left for something in the shape of a man to do this terrible thing. And shall such a creature, because he has the semblance of a man, appeal to the law? ...So far as I am concerned he has put himself outside the pale of the law, human and divine.... He has invaded the holy of holies. He has struck civilization a blow, the most deadly and cruel that the imagination can conceive. It is idle to reason about it; it is idle to preach about it. Our brains reel under the staggering blow and hot blood surges to the heart. Civilization peels off us, any and all of us who are men, and we revert to the original savage type whose impulses under any and all such circumstances has always been to "kill! kill! kill!"...

SOURCE: *The Congressional Record – Senate*, 59th Congress, 2d Session, vol. 41, pt. 2 (January, 1907), pp. 1440–1441.

UNIT 20

The Twenties

UNIT SUMMARY

In Unit 20 we look at the Roaring Twenties, when Henry Ford's "Tin Lizzie" was the symbol of speed, status, and freedom, and people pursued their dreams in prosperous cities like Los Angeles.

ASSIGNMENT

1. Before viewing Program 20, read this unit, and in *A People and a Nation* read Chapter 24.

2. View Program 20, "The Twenties."

3. Visit the Web site <http://www.learner.org/biographyofamerica>.
   Explore the exercises for Program 20.

LEARNING OBJECTIVES

Upon completing this unit, students should be able to:

1. Discuss the importance of Henry Ford and how his innovations in the auto industry revolutionized production.

2. Assess the relationship between government and business and their joint efforts to build an environment for economic prosperity.

3. Describe the economic and social changes of the era and their impact upon American values and popular culture.

4. Discuss the growth and development of Los Angeles.

5. Explain the causes of the Great Depression.

PROGRAM GUIDE

Americans enter the twenties dreaming of prosperity, material comfort, and progress, Professor Miller tells us. The ultimate symbol of liberation, the automobile, is now affordable, thanks to the pioneering efforts of the assembly line and the mass production innovations of Henry Ford. No city exhibits the character of this new freedom better than Los Angeles. It is the city of dreams, and Hollywood, the center of the movie-making industry, tells the nation that the sky's the limit.

Henry Ford claims to have invented the modern age. As we see in this program, Ford, like his fellow countrymen, loves to dream big. He offers the people a new future by making the "Tin Lizzie," as the Model T was affectionately called, affordable for the masses. The car is the status symbol of the age, and speed, sex, mobility, and movies become national pastimes and obsessions. The car also redefines city life, and no city captures the dreams of a people on the go like Los

Angeles. Once a sleepy pueblo of the Mexican and American republics, LA rumbles into the national limelight during the twenties. The city radiates out in all directions as highway construction expands and bedroom communities like Hollywood attract filmmakers and a new industry. Despite the sense of unlimited possibilities, however, the hype promised by the California dreamers crashes into the economic realities of the Great Depression.

HISTORICAL OVERVIEW

"The business of America is business," proclaimed President Calvin Coolidge. "The man who builds a factory builds a temple." The United States economy was poised for prosperity as the nation moved into the twenties. Henry Ford promised to steer Americans into the modern age with his Model T. While the automobile reshaped traditional American values, other trends helped redefine the country. Movies, music, and sports competed for dominance as the nation's favorite pastime. Americans rushed to acquire the latest comforts as businesses scrambled to manufacture both the desire and the goods to meet demand. But consumerism tells only part of the story in this time of rapid change. The frenzy of materialistic pursuits blinded leaders and the public to economic realities. Prosperity was built upon an uneven foundation of speculation and trickle down economics. The twenties opened with great hopes and promises, but it came crashing to a close with the Great Depression.

Republicans sought to rally the nation with their call for "A Return to Normalcy" in 1920. The public had grown tired of reformers seeking to correct the ills of industrial society. Nostalgia appealed to a public anxious for fewer commitments. Warren G. Harding, the new president, promised prosperity. His Treasury Secretary, Andrew Mellon, devised an economic plan calling for tax cuts that would trickle down to the masses. Mellon's prescription for prosperity claimed that the economy would thrive once it was released from the burdens of regulation. The American economy appeared to fulfill its promise through the decade as the stock market boomed. Workers' real wages declined throughout the twenties, however, and jeopardized prosperity as supply outstripped consumer demand. But producers continued to embrace the faith of endless possibilities, and the goods kept rolling off the assembly lines.

Cars redefined American lifestyles, and the Model T altered the national economy in many ways. Car ownership was a status symbol, and Henry Ford wanted everyone to participate in the joys of mobility. Ford focused on making the assembly line more efficient in order to drive down prices, and costs plummeted. By 1927 the Model T cost $295, down from $825 in 1913. While the national government assisted the auto industry's growth by building highways, the car industry had a ripple effect across the economic landscape. People took to the highways with their new-found freedom, giving rise to new enterprises: gas stations, motels, grocery stores, and more.

The car and the mobility it offered changed American city life, and no city experienced a greater transformation than Los Angeles. Spain had settled Los Angeles back in the eighteenth century. Although the gold rush had changed California overnight, the southern part of the state was isolated from the rush's earliest developments. The railroads broke down that isolation in the last quarter of the nineteenth century. During the boom of the eighties, which was centered in Southern California, railroad rate wars led to two-dollar fares from the midwest to LA. Advertisements describing the region's idyllic climate and agricultural potential lured people west. Population growth transformed Los Angeles' bedroom communities overnight and attracted the entertainment industry that today is synonymous with LA.

The movie industry moved west in the first decades of the new century. The climate, the geography, the sun, and the money all favored Hollywood as the filmmaking capitol of the world. Hollywood became "the Greatest Show on Earth," and the nickelodeon made movies accessible to the masses. After seeing *The Birth of a Nation,* Woodrow Wilson exclaimed that, "it is like writing history with lightning." The public went to the movies for entertainment and to escape the mundane aspects of their daily lives. The era of matinee idols commenced, as cowboys, vaudevillians, and hearthrobs blazed across the silver screen: Charlie Chaplin, Mary Pickford, Tom Mix, Clara Bow, Rudolph Valentino, Greta Garbo. Audiences were further awed in 1927 by the first talkie, *The Jazz Singer*. Movie moguls like Cecil B. De Mille produced films for visual pleasure and spectacle and built beautiful theaters in which to show them. Some civic groups charged that movies adversely shaped cultural norms and glorified violence, corruption, and sex; reformers fought for more wholesome films.

Businessmen recognized the tremendous potential for profit taking in the twenties. The extension of credit made purchasing goods easier, though it also increased debt. Advertisement agencies shaped consumers' wants and together with manufacturers reaped huge profits from the sale of everything from mouthwash to washing machines. Automobiles led the way in defining purchasing trends. Style surpassed utility, and upstarts like Alfred Sloan built General Motors on the notion that people wanted choices. His Chevrolet competed with the Model T, which was re-issued every year in the same style, but the Buick, Oldsmobile, Pontiac, and Cadillac all offered alternatives. The idea of planned obsolescence found its way into consumerism as new models rolled off the assembly line with brighter colors, luxurious interiors, and fancier designs. Each new car's appeal faded with next year's model. Buyers could even trade in their old car and buy a new one on an installment plan. The national government contributed to the boom in auto manufacturing by making highway building the second largest expenditure in the national budget.

Despite the anticipation of profit making in the twenties, there was an undercurrent of disillusionment. Farmers were losing their lands at record rates as prices for goods plummeted after the war. There was no governmental assistance, and foreclosures seized farms that had been in families for generations. Workers' real wages declined, making it difficult to purchase the radios, refrigerators, and other appliances vital to economic prosperity. The Nineteenth Amendment gave women the right to vote, but they still lacked the rights of full citizenship. Prohibition ushered in a new national pastime: sneaking into speakeasies and smuggling rum, whiskey, and scotch from overseas. African Americans redefined their role in society in an explosion of artistic defiance and resistance, the Harlem Renaissance. Intellectuals, meanwhile, lamented America's drift in a sea of materialism at the cost of selling its soul for a dollar.

The architects of prosperity neglected to heed some early deficiencies characteristic of the boom. Several key indicators revealed that prosperity was built upon a shaky foundation. Tax cuts benefited the wealthy, and a misdistribution of wealth made it difficult for consumers to buy producers' inventories. Surplus production was just one threat to economic stability. A number of industries—mining, textiles, farming, and railroading—drifted into a tailspin. Deregulation and the revival of monopolies also threatened the economy. However, the key ingredients of prosperity that brought the economy down were, ironically, the elements of economic success: confidence and optimism. When the stock market crashed in October of 1929, the American people had lost faith in their leaders, money, and, ultimately, themselves.

MAP EXERCISE

Refer to the following figures in Chapter 24 of *A People and a Nation* to answer the questions listed below.

- Changing Dimensions of Paid Female Labor, 1910–1930 (p. 679)

- Sources of Immigration, 1907 and 1927 (p. 683)

1. Although immigration restrictions in the 1920s curtailed the flow of Europeans, other nationals came in larger numbers. Who were they and how do you explain their increasing numbers?

2. World War I altered employment patterns. How did women's roles change between 1910 and 1930? Where did they experience greater opportunities? Did women of color benefit? Explain.

PEOPLE, EVENTS, AND CONCEPTS

Identify and explain the historical significance of each item.

Henry Ford

Identification

Significance

the Jazz Age

Identification

Significance

Calvin Coolidge

Identification

Significance

Birth of a Nation

Identification

Significance

the City of Freedom

Identification

Significance

Will Rogers

Identification

Significance

Tin Lizzie

Identification

Significance

Harlem Renaissance

Identification

Significance

Alfred Sloan

Identification

Significance

Black Tuesday

Identification

Significance

Tinseltown

Identification

Significance

Samuel Goldwyn

Identification

Significance

Teapot Dome

Identification

Significance

Louis B. Mayer

Identification

Significance

River Rouge plant

Identification

Significance

Henry E. Huntington

Identification

Significance

Return to Normalcy

Identification

Significance

Wall Street

Identification

Significance

ESSAY QUESTIONS

1. Choose one of the major technological developments of the 1920's (auto, radio, electrification) and explain its effect on the life of the average citizen.

2. Although the twenties held out the prospect of prosperity, there was an underlying sense of anxiety. How do you explain the era in terms of these two contradictory ideas? Which best describes the decade? Cite examples and explain your viewpoint.

3. What hidden indicators led to the economic collapse of 1929? How did each contribute to the crash?

4. The emergence of Los Angeles as the city of dreams revealed significant changes in the national economy and in the nation's growth. What were these changes and what did they reveal about modernity?

MULTIPLE-CHOICE QUESTIONS

1. Henry Ford's main contribution to the automobile industry was
    a. his introduction of mass produced and affordable autos.
    b. the large variety of colors and models in his cars.
    c. the increased speed of his cars.
    d. his consistent models year after year.
2. Automobiles, radios, and motion pictures
    a. proved not to be very popular.
    b. helped standardize U.S. life.
    c. had little impact on the nation.
    d. were too expensive for the average person.
3. Which amendment to the Constitution gave women the right to vote?
    a. The Seventeenth
    b. The Eighteenth
    c. The Nineteenth
    d. The Twentieth
4. The Volstead Act became the basis for the law concerning
    a. prostitution.
    b. prohibition.
    c. immigration quotas.
    d. illicit drugs crossing state lines.
5. President Wilson cited the historical accuracy of *The Clansman* in the movie
    a. The Jazz Singer.
    b. Sons of the South.
    c. All Quiet on the Western Front.
    d. Birth of a Nation.
6. The growth of Los Angeles can be attributed to all of the following except
    a. the location of the film industry in southern California.
    b. popular accounts of LA's climate and agricultural potential.
    c. its tolerance for Spanish-speaking peoples.
    d. the railroad rate wars in the 1880s.

7. Prohibition, or the "noble experiment," was
   a. well enforced and respected by the public.
   b. applied specifically to the Irish and Germans.
   c. responsible for the rise in gangsterism and profiteering.
   d. an effort to raise revenue with government controls.
8. One cause of the Depression was the uneven distribution of wealth resulting from
   a. increased production but declining demand.
   b. the failure of business to expand output.
   c. Americans' lack of savings to invest in the stock market.
   d. consumers purchasing more goods from overseas than at home.

Answers

1. a	3. c	5. d	7. c
2. b	4. b	6. c	8. a

PRIMARY SOURCE DOCUMENTS

The accounts of actual participants are useful for understanding the motives and thoughts of historical characters.

1. *Return to Normalcy (1921)* Warren G. Harding

President Woodrow Wilson had promised that U.S. involvement in the First World War would make "the world safe for democracy." Within a year of the war's end, it was obvious that this hope would remain unfulfilled. The Republican Party, sensing that the public was exhausted and disillusioned, promised in the 1920 elections that they would deliver "a return to normalcy." Their presidential candidate, Senator Warren G. Harding, was an appropriately obscure and innocuous man to reverse recent trends established by such activists as Wilson and Theodore Roosevelt. On April 12, 1921, just five weeks after his inauguration, President Harding appeared before a special session of Congress to present his minimalist agenda.

Questions to Consider

- According to Harding, what are the key issues facing the United States in the 1920s?
- What are the attractions of normalcy?
- Is there any contradiction between Harding's call for both minimal government and increased participation in such new industries as radio, highway construction, and aviation?

I know of no more pressing problem at home than to restrict our national expenditures within the limits of our national income…and at the same time measurably lift the burdens of war taxation from the shoulders of the American people.

…The unrestrained tendency to heedless expenditure and the attending growth of public indebtedness, extending from Federal authority to that of State and municipality and including the smallest political subdivision, constitute the most dangerous phase of government to-day. The Nation can not restrain except in its own activities, but it can be exemplar in a wholesome reversal.

The staggering load of war debt must be cared for in orderly funding and gradual liquidation…. In the fever of war our expenditures were so little questioned, the emergency was so impelling, appropriation was so unimpeded that we little noted millions and counted the Treasury inexhaustible. It will strengthen our resolution if we ever keep in mind that a continuation of such a course means inevitable disaster.

Our current expenditures are running at the rate of approximately five billions a year, and the burden is unbearable. There are two agencies to be employed in correction: One is rigid resistance in appropriation and the other is the utmost economy in administration. Let us have both....

The urgency for an instant tariff enactment, emergency in character and understood by our people that it is for the emergency only, can not be too much emphasized. I believe in the protection of American industry, and it is our purpose to prosper America first. ... The privileges of the American market to the foreign producer are offered too cheaply to-day, and the effect on much of our own productivity is the destruction of our self-reliance....

The maturer revision of our tariff laws should be based on the policy of protection, resisting that selfishness which turns to greed, but ever concerned with that productivity at home which is the source of all abiding good fortune. It is agreed that we can not sell unless we buy, but ability to sell is based on home development and the fostering of home markets. There is little sentiment in the trade of the world. Trade can and ought to be honorable, but it knows no sympathy....

A very important matter is the establishment of the Government's business on a business basis. There was toleration of the easy-going, unsystematic method of handling our fiscal affairs, when indirect taxation held the public unmindful of the Federal burden. But there is knowledge of the high cost of government to-day, and high cost of living is inseparably linked with high cost of government. There can be no complete correction of the high living cost until government's cost is notably reduced....

Somewhat related to the foregoing human problems is the race question. Congress ought to wipe the stain of barbaric lynching from the banners of a free and orderly, representative democracy.... I am convinced that in mutual tolerance, understanding, charity, recognition of the interdependence of the races, and the maintenance of the rights of citizenship lies the road to righteous adjustment....

Neither branch of the Government can be unmindful of the call for reduced expenditure for these departments of our national defense. The Government is in accord with the wish to eliminate the burdens of heavy armament....

...In the existing League of Nations, world-governing with its superpowers, this Republic will have no part. ...There can be no misinterpretation, and there will be no betrayal of the deliberate expression of the American people in the recent election, ...it is only fair to say to the world in general, and to our associates in war in particular, that the League covenant can have no sanction by us....

SOURCE: *Congressional Record*, 67th Congress, 1st session (1921), pp. 169–170, 172.

2. *The National Economic Condition (1929)* Herbert Hoover

Herbert Hoover was certainly one of the more qualified men to hold the office of president. A very successful engineer and famous humanitarian who had led the relief effort in postwar Europe, Hoover served as secretary of commerce from 1921 to 1929. In 1928 he easily beat the Democratic candidate, Alfred E. Smith, a New York Catholic. Hoover hoped to bring the United States into alignment with modern technology and science, but all his plans were ruined by the stock market crash in October 1929. The crash terrified many Americans, who feared its long-range economic consequences. In a news conference held on November 5, 1929, Hoover exuded confidence, promising a quick rebound in the economy. It was not a good prediction.

Questions to Consider

- What economic indicators assured Hoover of continued prosperity?
- How was it possible for Hoover to so misread the situation?

I haven't anything of any news here to announce. I thought perhaps you might like that I discuss the business situation with you just a little, but not from the point of view of publication at all—simply for your own information. I see no particular reasons for making any public statements about it, either directly or indirectly.

The question is one somewhat of analysis. We have had a period of overspeculation that has been extremely widespread, one of those waves of speculation that are more or less uncontrollable, as evidenced by the efforts of the Federal Reserve Board, and that ultimately results in a crash due to its own weight. That crash was perhaps a little expedited by the foreign situation, in that one result of this whole phenomenon has been the congestion of capital in the loan market in New York in the driving up of money rates all over the world....There has been a very great movement out of New York into the interior of the United States, as well as some movement out of New York into foreign countries. The incidental result of that is to create a difficult situation in New York, but also to increase the available capital in the interior. In the interior there has been, in consequence, a tendency for interest rates to fall at once because of the unemployed capital brought back into interior points.

Perhaps the situation might be clearer on account of its parallel with the last very great crisis, 1907–1908. In that crash the same drain of money immediately took place into the interior. In that case there was no Federal Reserve System. There was no way to acquaint of capital movement over the country, and the interest rates ran up to 300 percent. The result was to bring about a monetary panic in the entire country.

Here with the Federal Reserve System and the activity of the Board, and the ability with which the situation has been handled, there has been a complete isolation of the stock market phenomenon from the rest of the business phenomena in the country. The Board, in cooperation with the banks in New York, has made ample capital available for the call market in substitution of the withdrawals. This has resulted in a general fall of interest rates, not only in the interior, but also in New York, as witness the reduction of the discount rate. So that instead of having a panic rise in interest rates with monetary rise following it, we have exactly the reverse phenomenon—we have a fallen interest rate. That is the normal thing to happen when capital is withdrawn from the call market through diminution in values.

The ultimate result of it is a complete isolation of the stock market phenomenon from the general business phenomenon. In other words, the financial world is functioning entirely normal and rather more easily today than it was 2 weeks ago, because interest rates are less and there is more capital available.

The effect on production is purely psychological. So far there might be said to be from such a shock some tendency on the part of people through alarm to decrease their activities, but there has been no cancellation of any orders whatsoever. There has been some lessening of buying in some of the luxury contracts, but that is not a phenomenon itself.

The ultimate result of the normal course of things would be that with a large release of capital from the speculative market there will be more capital available for the bond and mortgage market....The sum of it is, therefore, that we have gone through a crisis in the stock market, but for the first time in history the crisis has been isolated to the stock market itself. It has not extended into either the production activities of the country or the financial fabric of the country, and for that I think we may give the major credit to the constitution of the Federal Reserve System.

And that is about a summary of the whole situation as it stands at this moment.

SOURCE: Public Papers of the Presidents of the United States: Herbert Hoover, 1929 (Washington, D.C., 1974), pp. 366–369.

3. *Financing Relief Efforts (1931)* Herbert Hoover

President Herbert Hoover, though a man of great compassion, was seriously constrained by his laissez-faire attitudes in responding to the emergency of the Great Depression. Hoover flatly rejected the notion of government spending, even in the face of malnutrition and record unemployment. Hoover found precedent for this view in his nineteenth-century Democratic predecessor, President Grover Cleveland, who had vetoed a bill to feed starving farmers. Hoover's refusal to support federal efforts at public relief handed the Democratic nominee in 1932, Franklin Delano Roosevelt, the perfect political issue. The following speech was delivered on February 3, 1931.

Questions to Consider

- What would happen if charities did not respond to the crisis?
- Why does Hoover feel that the expenditure of public moneys would have a negative impact on Americans?

Certain Senators have issued a public statement to the effect that unless the President and the House of Representatives agree to appropriations from the Federal Treasury for charitable purposes they will force an extra session of Congress. I do not wish to add acrimony to a discussion, but would rather state this case as I see its fundamentals.

This is not an issue as to whether people shall go hungry or cold in the United States. It is solely a question of the best method by which hunger and cold shall be prevented. It is a question as to whether the American people on one hand will maintain the spirit of charity and mutual self-help through voluntary giving and the responsibility of local government as distinguished on the other hand from appropriations out of the Federal Treasury for such purposes. My own conviction is strongly that if we break down this sense of responsibility of individual generosity to individual and mutual self-help in the country in times of national difficulty and if we start appropriations of this character we have not only impaired something infinitely valuable in the life of the American people but have struck at the roots of self-government. Once this has happened it is not the cost of a few score millions, but we are faced with the abyss of reliance in future upon Government charity in some form or other. The money involved is indeed the least of the costs to American ideals and American institutions.

President Cleveland, in 1887, confronted with a similar issue stated in part:

A prevalent tendency to disregard the limited mission of this power and duty should, I think, be steadfastly resisted, to the end that the lesson should be constantly enforced that though the people support the Government, the Government should not support the people.

The friendliness and charity of our countrymen can always be relied upon to relieve their fellow citizens in misfortune. This has been repeatedly and quite lately demonstrated.

Federal aid in such cases encourages the expectation of paternal care on the part of the

Government and weakens the sturdiness of our national character, while it prevents the indulgence among our people of that kindly sentiment and conduct which strengthens the bonds of a common brotherhood.

And there is a practical problem in all this. The help being daily extended by neighbors, by local and national agencies, by municipalities, by industry and a great multitude of organizations throughout the country today is many times any appropriation yet proposed. The opening of the doors of the Federal Treasury is likely to stifle this giving and thus destroy far more resources than the proposed charity from the Federal Government.

The basis of successful relief in national distress is to mobilize and organize the infinite number of agencies of self-help in the community. That has been the American way of relieving distress among our own people and the country is successfully meeting its problem in the American way today.

We have two entirely separate and distinct situations in the country—the first is the drought area; the second is the unemployment in our large industrial centers—for both of which these appropriations attempt to make charitable contributions.

Immediately upon the appearance of the drought last August, I convoked a meeting of the Governors, the Red Cross and the railways, the bankers and other agencies in the country and laid the foundations of organization and the resources to stimulate every degree of self-help to meet the situation which it was then obvious would develop. The result of this action was to attack the drought problem in a number of directions. The Red Cross established committees in every drought county, comprising the leading citizens of those counties, with instructions to them that they were to prevent starvation among their neighbors and, if the problem went beyond local resources, the Red Cross would support them.

The organization has stretched throughout the area of suffering, the people are being cared for today through the hands and with sympathetic understanding and upon the responsibility of their neighbors who are being supported, in turn, by the fine spirit of mutual assistance of the American people. The Red Cross officials, whose long, devoted service and experience is unchallenged, inform me this morning that, except for the minor incidents of any emergency organization, no one is going hungry and no one need go hungry or cold.

To reinforce this work at the opening of Congress I recommended large appropriations for loans to rehabilitate agriculture from the drought and provision of further large sums for public works and construction in the drought territory which would give employment in further relief to the whole situation. These Federal activities provide for an expenditure of upward of $100 million in this area and it is in progress today.

The Red Cross has always met the situations which it has undertaken. After careful survey and after actual experience of several months with their part of the problem they have announced firmly that they can command the resources with which to meet any call for human relief in prevention of hunger and suffering in drought areas and that they accept this responsibility. They have refused to accept Federal appropriations as not being consonant either with the need or the character of their organization. The Government departments have given and are giving them every assistance. We possibly need to strengthen the Public Health Service in matters of sanitation and to strengthen the credit facilities of that area through the method approved by the Government departments to divert some existing appropriations to strengthen agricultural credit corporations.

In the matter of unemployment outside of the drought areas important economic measures of mutual self-help have been developed such as those to maintain wages, to distribute employment equitably, to increase construction work by industry, to increase Federal construction work from a rate of about $275 million a year prior to the depression to a rate now of over $750 million a year, to expand State and municipal construction—all upon a scale never before provided or even attempted in any depression. But beyond this to assure that there shall be no suffering, in every town and county voluntary agencies in relief of distress have been strengthened and created and generous funds have been placed at their disposal. They are carrying on their work efficiently and sympathetically.

But after and coincidentally with voluntary relief, our American system requires that municipal, county, and State governments shall use their own resources and credit before seeking such assistance from the Federal Treasury.

I have indeed spent much of my life in fighting hardship and starvation both abroad and in the Southern States. I do not feel that I should be charged with lack of human sympathy for those who suffer, but I recall that in all the organizations with which I have been connected over these many years, the foundation has been to summon the maximum of self-help. I am proud to have sought the help of Congress in the past for nations who were so disorganized by war and anarchy that self-help was impossible. But even these appropriations were but a tithe of that which was coincidentally mobilized from the public charity of the United States and foreign countries. There is no such paralysis in the United States, and I am confident that our people have the resources, the initiative, the courage, the stamina and kindliness of spirit to meet this situation in the way they have met their problems over generations.

I will accredit to those who advocate Federal charity a natural anxiety for the people of their States. I am willing to pledge myself that, if the time should ever come that the voluntary agencies of the country together with the local and State governments are unable to find resources with which to prevent hunger and suffering in my country, I will ask the aid of every resource of the Federal Government because I would no more see starvation amongst our countrymen than would any Senator or Congressman. I have the faith in the American people that such a day will not come.

The American people are doing their job today. They should be given a chance to show whether they wish to preserve the principles of individual and local responsibility and mutual self-help before they embark on what I believe is a disastrous system. I feel sure they will succeed if given the opportunity.

The whole business situation would be greatly strengthened by the prompt completion of the necessary legislation of this session of Congress and thereby the unemployment problem would be lessened, the drought area indirectly benefited, and the resources of self-help in the country strengthened.

SOURCE: Public Papers of the Presidents of the United States: Herbert Hoover 1931 (Washington, D.C., 1976), pp. 54–58.

UNIT 21

FDR and the Depression

UNIT SUMMARY

In Unit 21 we look at the Great Depression and the Roosevelt administration's efforts to reverse its effects with the New Deal.

ASSIGNMENT

1. Before viewing Program 21, read this unit, and in *A People and a Nation* read Chapter 25.

2. View Program 21, "FDR and the Depression."

3. Visit the Web site <http://www.learner.org/biographyofamerica>. Explore the exercises for Program 21.

LEARNING OBJECTIVES

Upon completing this unit, students should be able to:

1. Discuss the impact of the Great Depression upon the American people and the economy.

2. Examine FDR's rise from adversity, to New York's governorship, to the presidency.

3. Describe the New Deal programs and their success in addressing the problems of the Depression.

4. Discuss the critics of the New Deal and their impact on national policy.

5. Assess the broad-based coalition of FDR supporters and the reasons for the political realignment within the Democratic Party.

PROGRAM GUIDE

The Great Depression is the greatest economic crisis in the nation's history. The traditional response to a business collapse calls for watching and waiting for signs of recovery. President Herbert Hoover follows this approach, and despair spreads in the early years of the Depression. A sense of hopelessness overwhelms the American public; suicides, abandonment, and starvation are commonplace. The song, *Brother Can You Spare a Dime*, epitomizes the desperation of the Hoover years.

In 1932, Franklin Delano Roosevelt offers Americans a "New Deal," and his confidence and optimism during the presidential campaign electrify the public. Professor Brinkley's profile of Roosevelt reveals the character of the man and the presidency, as FDR and the First Lady, Eleanor Roosevelt, advance the cause of reform during the nation's greatest challenge.

A flurry of legislation passes through Congress in FDR's First 100 Days, addressing the worst effects of the Depression. Relief, reform, and recovery become the watchwords of the New Deal. The administration establishes a multitude of new government programs, administered by so-called "alphabet agencies," to provide relief for the common man. The First Lady travels throughout the country and reports back to the president on the magnitude of the Depression.

FDR's critics come from both the right and the left of the political spectrum. Despite the criticisms, his programs change the role of government, and the nation will never be the same. Still, the New Deal does not end the Depression. It is the massive military expenditures of WWII that finally put the nation back to work.

HISTORICAL OVERVIEW

World War I veterans marched on the nation's capital in the summer of 1932. They came to petition Congress for an early disbursement of a service bonus. It was the third year of the Depression and conditions had pushed Americans to desperate measures. The Army's use of force to dislodge the Bonus Marchers from Washington infuriated the public. In their anger and despair, they elected Franklin Delano Roosevelt president that November. FDR would lead the nation in a new direction.

The stock market crashed on October 29, 1929, inflicting tremendous suffering on the American people. Twelve million people had lost their jobs by the end of Hoover's presidency in 1933. Farmers, tormented by foreclosures in the twenties and dust storms during the Depression, migrated west in search of jobs. California turned out to be an elusive Eden where the "Okies," as migrants from Oklahoma were called, were unwelcome. While families lived on the edge of starvation, suicide, abandonment, domestic abuse increased dramatically, and a new class of homeless became one more grim feature of the Depression. Shantytowns, or "Hoovervilles," as they came to be called, were erected in cities across the nation. The magnitude of the economic calamity is grim when expressed statistically:

- The Gross National Product fell twenty-five percent

- Construction declined by seventy-five percent

- Consumer spending fell by 300 percent

- Inventories rose by 400 percent

- Income levels fell twenty-five percent

Despite all evidence to the contrary, President Hoover maintained that the Depression required no radical measures. He took the traditional approach of waiting and watching for signs of recovery. That recovery failed to happen during his presidency, and although many Americans resigned themselves to the hardships of those years, they wanted solutions. Franklin D. Roosevelt offered them new ideas, optimism, and proven leadership in a time, as he called it, of national emergency.

President Roosevelt knew adversity first hand, having contracted polio in 1923 and becoming permanently disabled. He refused to accept an end to his political dreams, however. New Yorkers elected Roosevelt governor during the Depression, and as governor he experimented with senior pensions, unemployment benefits, and public works projects. His record as a progressive reformer earned him respect within the ranks of the Democratic Party, which nominated him for the presidency in 1932. The candidate promised a "new deal for the common man," and although his promises were vague, Roosevelt exuded confidence and possessed enormous charm and charisma. He was elected with 57 percent of the popular vote; Hoover won only six states.

The new president had assembled a team of advisors he called the "Brain Trust," who promoted ideas and assisted in the formulation of policy. Public relations took on a new meaning with the hiring of the first White House press secretary and the inauguration of "fireside chats," in which the president spoke directly and regularly with the public, rallying citizens to his administration's initiatives. Eleanor Roosevelt, who possessed exceptional political skills, traveled around the country to see for herself the plight of Americans. Mrs. Roosevelt's concern for the downtrodden helped the president to shape the direction of the New Deal.

In his inauguration speech, the president declared that "the only thing we have to fear is fear itself." The administration put into practice the ideas of the English economist John Maynard Keynes, who said that recovery was not guaranteed and that national governments needed to deficit spend to reverse spiraling declines. Relief, reform, and recovery became the watchwords of the New Deal. Relief programs sought to put Americans back to work, and reform initiatives encouraged and imposed regulations upon industry; together these initiatives would lead to recovery. Once in office, FDR declared a banking holiday and set about to reorganize the ailing economy. The public responded by depositing millions into their savings accounts.

Alphabet agencies (so-called because they were known by their initials) were another feature of the New Deal. They were created to arrest further economic decline and, at first, the new initiatives seemed to work. A nine-state conservation project called the Tennessee Valley Authority (TVA) developed the hydroelectric potential of the Tennessee River valley. Farmers received assistance from the Agricultural Adjustment Act (AAA) designed to stop foreclosures, extend loans, and help with other relief measures. With the National Industrial Recovery Act, the government came to recognize the rights of workers to organize and collectively bargain. The NIRA also established industrial codes in an effort to reform business practices. A Security Exchange Commission (SEC) was created to oversee the stock market. FDR's approach revolutionized the role of government in regulating the economy.

Dissenters cursed and criticized the administration for what they perceived as a lackluster economic performance. A Catholic priest, Father Charles Coughlin, took to the radio to blast the administration's monetary policies. Coughlin's anti-Semitism revealed the latent fears and prejudices that the public harbored towards Jews. Dr. Francis E. Townsend, a public health officer who had been thrown out of work at age 67 with only $100 in savings, promoted a government pensions program that would later lead to the Social Security Act. Townsend clubs appeared across the country to pressure the administration to take action on this issue vital to retired Americans. In California the muckraker and socialist Upton Sinclair launched his Democratic candidacy for governor in 1934. He sought Roosevelt's support while promoting an agenda of cooperatives, currency reform, higher taxes for the wealthy, and a pension program for seniors. His candidacy went down to defeat, but it sent shock waves through the ranks of the privileged classes. The president endured a serious attack from within his own party from the populist Huey Long, a senator from Louisiana. Long's "Share Our Wealth" campaign attacked FDR for deficiencies real and imagined. By mid-1935 Long's movement claimed 7 million members, but his campaign ended when he was assassinated in September 1935. One effect of these challengers' attacks was a series of new initiatives in the year preceding the 1936 presidential elections.

The New Deal led to a new democratic coalition. Southerners remained staunch Democrats, joined now by workers, who believed they had a friend in the White House; Roosevelt came to depend upon their vote. Farmers benefited from a host of programs and they, too, became strong supporters of the New Deal. The largest realignment of supporters, however, came from African Americans, who no longer identified with the party of Lincoln. Although they benefited from New Deal programs, the president was no champion of civil rights. His programs depended upon the support of the southerners who controlled all the key committees. It was the First Lady who championed the cause for racial equality. Lynchings continued in the South and racial unrest exploded in New York, Detroit, and other northern cities. Blacks threatened to march on the nation's capital in 1941 unless the president halted the discrimination in hiring within the defense industry.

The New Deal brought national changes that remain with us today. Americans now look to the national government to guarantee prosperity. Keynes's approach remains a permanent feature of our economy, with programs like farm subsidies, defense spending, and regulatory agencies like the Federal Reserve, and Social Security has a permanent place in the national budget. The coalition that FDR forged in the thirties remains part of the Democrats' power base today.

MAP EXERCISE

Refer to the following map and figure in Chapter 25 of *A People and a Nation* to answer the questions listed below.

- The Tennessee Valley Authority (p. 706)
- The Economy Before and After the New Deal, 1929–1941 (p. 708)

1. Which states benefited from the projects of the Tennessee Valley Authority? What types of projects did the government provide in these states?

2. The statistical graphs reveal interesting trends during the Roosevelt presidency. In which areas did the economy improve and why? Can any serious deficiencies be noted?

PEOPLE, EVENTS, AND CONCEPTS

Identify and explain the historical significance of each item.

Franklin Delano Roosevelt

Identification

Significance

Dust Bowl

Identification

Significance

Black Tuesday

Identification

Significance

Dorothea Lange

Identification

Significance

Scottsboro case

Identification

Significance

migrant mothers

Identification

Significance

Eleanor Roosevelt

Identification

Significance

Memorial Day Massacre

Identification

Significance

fireside chats

Identification

Significance

Charles Edward Coughlin

Identification

Significance

Great Plains

Identification

Significance

Frances Perkins

Identification

Significance

Hoovervilles

Identification

Significance

Black Cabinet

Identification

Significance

Huey Long

Identification

Significance

Salvation Army shelters

Identification

Significance

Marion Anderson

Identification

Significance

Tennessee Valley Authority

Identification

Significance

alphabet soup agencies

Identification

Significance

ESSAY QUESTIONS

1. Throughout the 1920's the economy was less healthy than many believed. What were its weaknesses? Contrast the approaches Hoover and Roosevelt took to treating the nation's economic woes.

2. Some historians claim that the New Deal was revolutionary. How did the national government's role change under FDR's leadership?

3. The New Deal's slogan was "relief, reform, and recovery." Which policies reflect the administration's approach to these goals? How successful were they?

4. Evaluate the successes of the New Deal and its shortcomings. How do you explain the continuation of the Depression through World War II?

5. Before FDR, African Americans voted, when they could, for Republicans. What was it about Roosevelt's policies that caused their realignment with the Democrats?

MULTIPLE-CHOICE QUESTIONS

1. Herbert Hoover initially believed that the Great Depression would end if
   a. the national government gave financial aid to banks and businesses.
   b. the American people helped themselves and their neighbors.
   c. the government provided relief directly to the people.
   d. none of the above
2. The veterans' Bonus March on Washington, D.C., in 1932 demanded
   a. the removal of troops from Europe.
   b. lower tariffs to encourage business.
   c. their bonuses from WWI.
   d. an end to the government's laissez-faire policies.
3. Who was a champion of the poor and minorities?
   a. Frances Perkins
   b. John L. Lewis
   c. Harold Ickes
   d. Eleanor Roosevelt
4. In 1935, the Social Security Act was passed to do all of the following except
   a. provide unemployment checks.
   b. provide for citizens' old age.
   c. give universal health care.
   d. aid people with disabilities.
5. President Roosevelt's first order of business upon becoming president was to
   a. restore confidence in the banking industry.
   b. encourage farmers to produce more food.
   c. revise the Hawley-Smoot tariff.
   d. balance the national budget.
6. Southern natural resources were developed by
   a. the Public Works Administration.
   b. the Tennessee Valley Authority.
   c. the Works Progress Administration.
   d. the Social Security Administration.
7. President Roosevelt's most serious political challenger was the maverick
   a. Upton Sinclair.
   b. Father Charles Coughlin.
   c. Huey Long.
   d. Dr. Francis Townsend.
8. The New Deal programs
   a. successfully ended the Depression.
   b. were of little help to the poor.
   c. created the largest deficits since the Civil War.
   d. failed to end the Depression.

Answers

| 1. b | 3. d | 5. a | 7. c |
| 2. c | 4. c | 6. b | 8. d |

PRIMARY SOURCE DOCUMENTS

The accounts of actual participants are useful for understanding the motives and thoughts of historical characters.

1. *Inaugural Address (1933)* Franklin D. Roosevelt

On March 4, 1933, at the depths of the worst economic depression in American history, Franklin D. Roosevelt was inaugurated as president. He had soundly defeated his predecessor, Herbert Hoover, in the 1932 election. Clearly, most of the nation held Hoover and the Republican Party's laissez-faire policies responsible for the Great Depression, which saw unemployment rates rise above 30%. In the election, Roosevelt had not offered much in the way of specific proposals for dealing with the crisis other than a promise to balance the federal budget. His inaugural address presented few new details beyond a commitment to vigorous action by the federal government itself. But with that very promise Roosevelt gave the American public hope, an assurance that their government would do something, and that, as the title of Roosevelt's campaign song proclaimed, "happy days are here again."

Questions to Consider

- Why does Roosevelt use military allusions in his address?
- Does Roosevelt suggest any radical alterations in American politics or society?

I am certain that my fellow Americans expect that on my induction into the Presidency I will address them with a candor and a decision which the present situation of our Nation impels. This is preeminently the time to speak the truth, the whole truth, frankly and boldly. Nor need we shrink from honestly facing conditions in our country to-day. This great Nation will endure as it has endured, will revive and will prosper. So, first of all, let me assert my firm belief that the only thing we have to fear is fear itself—nameless, unreasoning, unjustified terror which paralyzes needed efforts to convert retreat into advance. In every dark hour of our national life a leadership of frankness and vigor has met with that understanding and support of the people themselves which is essential to victory. I am convinced that you will again give that support to leadership in these critical days.

In such a spirit on my part and on yours we face our common difficulties. They concern, thank God, only material things. Values have shrunken to fantastic levels; taxes have risen; our ability to pay has fallen; government of all kinds is faced by serious curtailment of income; the means of exchange are frozen in the currents of trade; the withered leaves of industrial enterprise lie on every side; farmers find no markets for their produce; the savings of many years in thousands of families are gone.

More important, a host of unemployed citizens face the grim problem of existence, and an equally great number toil with little return. Only a foolish optimist can deny the dark realities of the moment.

Yet our distress comes from no failure of substance. We are stricken by no plague of locusts. Compared with the perils which our forefathers conquered because they believed and were not afraid, we have still much to be thankful for. Nature still offers her bounty and human efforts have multiplied it. Plenty is at our doorstep, but a generous use of it languishes in the very sight of the supply. Primarily this is because the rulers of the exchange of mankind's goods have failed, through their own stubbornness and their own incompetence, have admitted their failure, and abdicated. Practices of the unscrupulous money changers stand indicted in the court of public opinion, rejected by the hearts and minds of men.

True they have tried, but their efforts have been cast in the pattern of an outworn tradition. Faced by failure of credit they have proposed only the lending of more money. Stripped of the lure of profit by which to induce our people to follow their false leadership, they have resorted to exhortations, pleading tearfully for restored confidence. They know only the rules of a generation of self-seekers. They have no vision, and when there is no vision the people perish.

The money changers have fled from their high seats in the temple of our civilization. We may now restore that temple to the ancient truths. The measure of the restoration lies in the extent to which we apply social values more noble than mere monetary profit.

Happiness lies not in the mere possession of money; it lies in the joy of achievement, in the thrill of creative effort. The joy and moral stimulation of work no longer must be forgotten in the mad chase of evanescent profits. These dark days will be worth all they cost us if they teach us that our true destiny is not to be ministered unto but to minister to ourselves and to our fellow men.

Recognition of the falsity of material wealth as the standard of success goes hand in hand with the abandonment of the false belief that public office and high political position are to be valued only by the standards of pride of place and personal profit; and there must be an end to a conduct in banking and in business which too often has given to a sacred trust the likeness of callous and selfish wrongdoing. Small wonder that confidence languishes, for it thrives only on honesty, on honor, on the sacredness of obligations, on faithful protection, on unselfish performance; without them it can not live.

Restoration calls, however, not for changes in ethics alone. This Nation asks for action, and action now.

Our greatest primary task is to put people to work. This is no unsolvable problem if we face it wisely and courageously. It can be accomplished in part by direct recruiting by the Government itself, treating the task as we would treat the emergency of a war, but at the same time, through this employment, accomplishing greatly needed projects to stimulate and reorganize the use of our natural resources.

Hand in hand with this we must frankly recognize the overbalance of population in our industrial centers and, by engaging on a national scale in a redistribution, endeavor to provide a better use of the land for those best fitted for the land. The task can be helped by definite efforts to raise the values of agricultural products and with this the power to purchase the output of our cities. It can be helped by preventing realistically the tragedy of the growing loss through foreclosure of our small homes and our farms. It can be helped by insistence that the Federal, State, and local governments act forthwith on the demand that their cost be drastically reduced. It can be helped by the unifying of relief activities which to-day are often scattered, uneconomical, and unequal. It can be helped by national planning for and supervision of all forms of transportation and of communications and other utilities which have a definitely public character. There are many ways in which it can be helped, but it can never be helped merely by talking about it. We must act and act quickly.

Finally, in our progress toward a resumption of work we require two safeguards against a return of the evils of the old order; there must be a strict supervision of all banking and credits and investments; there must be an end to speculation with other people's money, and there must be provision for an adequate but sound currency.

These are the lines of attack. I shall presently urge upon a new Congress in special session detailed measures for their fulfillment, and I shall seek the immediate assistance of the several States.

Through this program of action we address ourselves to putting our own national house in order and making income balance outgo. Our international trade relations, though vastly important, are in point of time and necessity secondary to the establishment of a sound national economy. I favor as a practical policy the putting of first things first. I shall spare no effort to restore world trade by international economic readjustment, but the emergency at home can not wait on that accomplishment.

The basic thought that guides these specific means of national recovery is not narrowly nationalistic. It is the insistence, as a first consideration, upon the interdependence of the various elements in all parts of the United States—a recognition of the old and permanently important manifestation of the American spirit of the pioneer. It is the way to recovery. It is the immediate way. It is the strongest assurance that the recovery will endure.

In the field of world policy I would dedicate this Nation to the policy of the good neighbor—the neighbor who resolutely respects himself and, because he does so, respects the rights of others—the neighbor who respects his obligations and respects the sanctity of his agreements in and with a world of neighbors.

If I read the temper of our people correctly, we now realize as we have never realized before our interdependence on each other; that we can not merely take but we must give as well; that if we are to go forward, we must move as a trained and loyal army willing to sacrifice for the good of a common discipline, because without such discipline no progress is made, no leadership becomes effective. We are, I know, ready and willing to submit our lives and property to such discipline, because it makes possible a leadership which aims at a larger good. This I propose to offer, pledging that the larger purposes will bind upon us all as a sacred obligation with a unity of duty hitherto evoked only in time of armed strife.

With this pledge taken, I assume unhesitatingly the leadership of this great army of our people dedicated to a disciplined attack upon our common problems.

Action in this image and to this end is feasible under the form of government which we have inherited from our ancestors. Our Constitution is so simple and practical that it is possible always to meet extraordinary needs by changes in emphasis and arrangement without loss of essential form. That is why our constitutional system has proved itself the most superbly enduring political mechanism the modern world has produced. It has met every stress of vast expansion of territory, of foreign wars, of bitter internal strife, of world relations.

It is to be hoped that the normal balance of executive and legislative authority may be wholly adequate to meet the unprecedented task before us. But it may be that an unprecedented demand and need for undelayed action may call for temporary departure from that normal balance of public procedure.

I am prepared under my constitutional duty to recommend the measures that a stricken nation in the midst of a stricken world may require. These measures, or such other measures as the Congress may build out of its experience and wisdom, I shall seek, within my constitutional authority, to bring to speedy adoption.

But in the event that the Congress shall fail to take one of these two courses, and in the event that the national emergency is still critical, I shall not evade the clear course of duty that will then confront me. I shall ask the Congress for the one remaining instrument to meet the crisis—broad Executive power to wage a war against the emergency, as great as the power that would be given to me if we were in fact invaded by a foreign foe.

For the trust reposed in me I will return the courage and the devotion that befit the time. I can do no less.

We face the arduous days that lie before us in the warm courage of the national unity; with the clear consciousness of seeking old and precious moral values; with the clean satisfaction that comes from the stern performance of duty by old and young alike. We aim at the assurance of a rounded and permanent national life.

We do not distrust the future of essential democracy. The people of the United States have not failed. In their need they have registered a mandate that they want direct, vigorous action. They have asked for discipline and direction under leadership. They have made me the present instrument of their wishes. In the spirit of the gift I take it.

In this dedication of a Nation we humbly ask the blessing of God. May He protect each and every one of us. May He guide me in the days to come.

SOURCE: Inaugural Addresses of the Presidents of the United States (Washington, D.C., 1961), pp. 235–239.

2. *Share Our Wealth (1935)* Huey P. Long

No member of Congress in the 1930s was as controversial as Senator Huey P. Long of Louisiana. To his many enemies, he was a potential American dictator. To his supporters, Long alone defended the common man against an avaricious business elite. Elected governor of Louisiana in 1928, Long dominated that state in a way rarely seen in the United States. Despite his ruthless tactics and absolute control of Louisiana's politics, he won the affection of the poor through a series of public works projects which improved the lives of thousands of people. In 1932 Long was elected to the Senate, where he quickly became a national figure by attacking both parties for their failure to deal with the Depression. Organizing the Share Our Wealth Society with the slogan "every man a king," Long planned an independent run for the presidency in 1936. But the "Kingfish," as he liked to be called, was gunned down in the Louisiana capitol by a political opponent in 1935.

Questions to Consider

- What exactly does Long want to do?

- Would it have been possible or legal?

- How does Long's program differ from Roosevelt's New Deal?

It is impossible for the United States to preserve itself as a republic or as a democracy when 600 families own more of this Nation's wealth—in fact, twice as much—as all the balance of the people put together. Ninety-six percent of our people live below the poverty line, while 4 percent own 87 percent of the wealth. America can have enough for all to live in comfort and still permit millionaires to own more than they can ever spend and to have more than they can ever use; but America cannot allow the multimillionaires and the billionaires, a mere handful of them, to own everything unless we are willing to inflict starvation upon 125,000,000 people....

...God's law commanded that the wealth of the country should be redistributed ever so often, so that none should become too rich and none should become too poor; it commanded that debts should be canceled and released ever so often, so that the human race would not be loaded with a burden which it could never pay....

It took the genius of labor and the lives of all Americans to produce the wealth of this land. If any man, or 100 men, wind up with all that has been produced by 120,000,000 people, that does not mean that those 100 men produced the wealth of the country; it means that those 100 men stole, directly or indirectly, what 125,000,000 people produced....

Here is the whole sum and substance of the share-our-wealth movement:

1. Every family to be furnished by the Government a homestead allowance, free of debt, of not less than one-third the average family wealth of the country, which means, at the lowest, that every family shall have the reasonable comforts of life up to a value of from $5,000 to $6,000. No person to have a fortune of more than 100 to 300 times the average family fortune, which means that the limit to fortunes is between $1,500,000 and $5,000,000, with annual capital levy taxes imposed on all above $1,000,000.

2. The yearly income of every family shall be not less than one-third of the average family income, which means that, according to the estimates of the statisticians of the United States

Government and Wall Street, no family's annual income would be less than from $2,000 to $2,500. No yearly income shall be allowed to any person larger than from 100 to 300 times the size of the average family income, which means that no person would be allowed to earn in any year more than from $600,000 to $1,800,000, all to be subject to present income-tax laws.

3. To limit or regulate the hours of work to such an extent as to prevent overproduction; the most modern and efficient machinery would be encouraged, so that as much would be produced as possible so as to satisfy all demands of the people, but to also allow the maximum time to the workers for recreation, convenience, education, and luxuries of life.

4. An old-age pension to the persons over 60.

5. To balance agricultural production with what can be consumed according to the laws of God, which includes the preserving and storage of surplus commodities to be paid for and held by the Government for the emergencies when such are needed....

6. To pay the veterans of our wars what we owe them and to care for their disabled.

7. Education and training for all children to be equal in opportunity in all schools, colleges, universities, and other institutions for training in the professions and vocations of life; to be regulated on the capacity of children to learn, and not on the ability of parents to pay the costs. Training for life's work to be as much universal and thorough for all walks in life as has been the training in the arts of killing.

8. The raising of revenue and taxes for the support of this program to come from the reduction of swollen fortunes from the top, as well as for the support of public works to give employment whenever there may be any slackening necessary in private enterprise.

I now ask those who read this circular to help us at once in this work of giving life and happiness to our people—not a starvation dole upon which someone may live in misery from week to week. Before this miserable system of wreckage has destroyed the life germ of respect and culture in our American people let us save what was here, merely by having none too poor and none too rich. The theory of the Share Our Wealth Society is to have enough for all, but not to have one with so much that less than enough remains for the balance of the people....

Let everyone who feels he wishes to help in our work start right out and go ahead.... The reward and compensation is the salvation of humanity. Fear no opposition. "He who falls in this fight falls in the radiance of the future!"

SOURCE: *Congressional Record*, May 23, 1935, 1st Session, vol. 74, pt. 7, pp. 8040–8043.

3. *Socialist Party Platform (1932)* Socialist Party

Opponents of Franklin Roosevelt called him a Socialist. Actual Socialists condemned him as a defender of the capitalist order. In the 1932 election the Socialist Party offered a platform that, if enacted, would have changed American society in several fundamental ways. Roosevelt won an overwhelming victory, but the Socialist candidate, Norman Thomas, received 885,000 votes—an impressive showing for a minor party.

Questions to Consider

*   What, according to the Socialists, is wrong with the United States?
*   Is there any similarity between the Socialist platform and Roosevelt's New Deal?

We are facing a breakdown of the capitalist system…. Unemployment and poverty are inevitable products of the present system. Under capitalism the few own our industries. The many do the work. The wage earners and farmers are compelled to give a large part of the product of their labor to the few. The many in the factories, mines, shops, offices, and on the farms obtain but a scanty income and are able to buy back only a part of the goods that can be produced in such abundance by our mass industries….

The Socialist Party is to-day the one democratic party of the workers whose program would remove the causes of class struggles, class antagonisms, and social evils inherent in the capitalist system.

It proposes to transfer the principal industries of the country from private ownership and autocratic, cruelly inefficient management to social ownership and democratic control…. It proposes the following measures:

…A Federal appropriation of $5,000,000,000 for immediate relief for those in need, to supplement State and local appropriations.

…A Federal appropriation of $5,000,000,000 for public works and roads, reforestation, slum clearance, and decent homes for the workers, by Federal Government, States, and cities….

…The 6-hour day and the 5-day week without a reduction of wages….

…A compulsory system of unemployment compensation with adequate benefits, based on contributions by the Government and by employers.

…Old-age pensions for men and women 60 years of age and over.

…Health and maternity insurance.

…Improved systems of workmen's compensation and accident insurance.

…The abolition of child labor.

…Government aid to farmers and small-home owners to protect them against mortgage foreclosures and a moratorium on sales for nonpayment of taxes by destitute farmers and unemployed workers.

…Adequate minimum wage laws….

…Increased Federal and State subsidies to road building and educational and social services for rural communities….

…Proportional representation.

…Direct election of the President and Vice President.

…The initiative and referendum….

…Abolition of the power of the Supreme Court to pass upon the constitutionality of legislation enacted by Congress….

…Federal legislation to enforce the first amendment to the Constitution so as to guarantee freedom of speech, press, and assembly, and to penalize officials who interfere with the civil rights of citizens.

…The abolition of injunctions in labor disputes, the outlawing of "yellow-dog" contracts and the passing of laws enforcing the rights of workers to organize into unions….

…Legislation protecting aliens from being excluded from this country or from citizenship or from being deported on account of their political, social, or economic beliefs, or on account of activities engaged in by them which are not illegal for citizens….

The enforcement of constitutional guarantees of economic, political, and legal equality for the Negro.

The enactment and enforcement of drastic antilynching laws.

SOURCE: *The Congressional Record,* July 6, 1932, 72nd Congress, 1st Session, vol. 75, pt. 13, pp. 14702–14703.

UNIT 22

World War II: Total War

UNIT SUMMARY

In Unit 22 we look at the events that led to the United States' entry into WWII and American involvement in the war at home and overseas.

ASSIGNMENT

1. Before viewing Program 22, read this unit, and in *A People and a Nation* read Chapters 26 and 27.

2. View Program 22, "World War II: Total War."

3. Visit the Web site <http://www.learner.org/biographyofamerica>. Explore the exercises for Program 22.

LEARNING OBJECTIVES

Upon completing this unit, students should be able to:

1. Evaluate the deterioration of the post-WWI European peace and the continent's descent into war.

2. Discuss isolationism as a diplomatic policy and the steps President Roosevelt took to shift the nation away from neutrality.

3. Discuss the deterioration in U.S.- Japanese relations before Pearl Harbor and the wartime strategies the United States used to defeat Japan.

4. Discuss the relationship between the Allies in formulating military strategy and the nature of their differences at the wartime conferences at Teheran, Yalta, and Potsdam.

5. Discuss the war's impact on American culture and society.

PROGRAM GUIDE

World War II is a total war of unprecedented carnage: a majority of the 55 million dead are civilians. The United States remains isolated at the war's outset, but Pearl Harbor leads the country into the war. Ultimately the American economy overwhelms its enemies and buries them in the rubble of their cities. Ironically, the worst destruction is saved for the war's last days: the atomic bombs dropped on Hiroshima and Nagasaki. Professor Miller takes a personal look at World War II and its effects on those who fought, died, and survived this horrible conflict, including members of the Miller family.

The Japanese attack on Pearl Harbor almost destroys America's Pacific fleet in 1941, but it rallies the American people to the cause. While men fight and die overseas, women play pivotal roles in the war effort at home. Blacks, women, and other Americans migrate across the nation and find jobs in west coast factories and shipyards. In San Francisco, Henry Kaiser's mass-produced, prefabricated Liberty Ships allow the United States to carry the war overseas. Innovations in airplane technology prove indispensible to the war effort, but it is the ground campaigns that ultimately lead to an Allied victory.

HISTORICAL OVERVIEW

The United States entered World War II after the Japanese bombed Pearl Harbor on December 7, 1941. In truth, the nation had already been assisting the British and Soviets against the Nazis and the Chinese against Japan through the Lend-Lease program and diplomatic initiatives like the Atlantic Charter. A Congressional declaration of war the day after Pearl Harbor made it official, ending years of isolationism and rescuing the American people from the depths of the Great Depression.

Although the United States declared war against Japan first, the Allies employed a "Hitler first" strategy against the European fascists. By 1943 Nazi successes had been reversed, and Great Britain and the United States prepared to invade Normandy as the Soviets rolled into eastern Europe. Hitler's thousand-year Reich came to an end within a year of Operation Overlord, or D-Day. In victory, the Allies liberated the Jews from death camps, uncovering the evil character of Nazism. Six months later, the war against Japan ended with the dropping of atomic bombs on Hiroshima and Nagasaki.

Hitler's ravings in *Mein Kampf* established the blueprint for Germany's future empire. The humiliation of World War I would be reversed, he wrote, the nation's borders would be reincorporated into the Reich, and the communist menace in the east would be destroyed. Poland, recreated in the aftermath of Versailles, would disappear under Nazi domination. Hitler's invasion of Poland in September of 1939 was therefore no surprise. Fascist aggression had proceeded unchecked up to this point: the Nazis had helped the dictator General Francisco Franco to power in Spain; Benito Mussolini, the Italian dicatator, had invaded Ethiopia in 1935 without opposition; the Japanese empire had expanded into Manchuria in 1931, and in 1937 had butchered thousands of innocent civilians in the Rape of Nanking. The democracies stood silent in the wake of all these events, and although President Roosevelt warned the nation of the dangers of fascism in his 1937 Quarantine speech, the isolationists stood steadfast against intervention.

Although France and England declared war on Germany after the Polish invasion, neither country took action. Hitler seized the initiative and by the summer of 1940 had captured most of western Europe, including France, and turned his attention to Great Britain. England resisted Nazi efforts to defeat them in the Battle of Britain, while debate raged in the United States between the proponents of neutrality and those who proclaimed that assisting Britain amounted to defending America. The United States stood ready to help, said FDR, as "the arsenal of democracy," by sending war goods to its friends. The Lend-Lease program sent $50 billion of supplies to Britain and her allies to continue the fight against the Germans. In August 1941, FDR and Britain's Prime Minister Winston Churchill signed the Atlantic Charter, which clearly defined their alliance. The Allies vowed to make a world safe for democracy, a world where nations respected the right of self-determination and supported international law.

But, finally, it was the Japanese attack on Pearl Harbor that pushed the United States to fully join the war effort. The United States viewed Japanese expansion into Asia and the Pacific with grave concern. Since the start of the twentieth century, the two nations had sought to stymie the other's initiatives in the region. By 1941 the two nations' imperialist objectives in the Pacific Basin had placed them on a collision course. The Japanese invasion of Manchuria in 1931 warranted a strong protest, but the Hoover Administration took no action. Although President Roosevelt warned of the "virus of militarism" in his 1937 Quarantine speech, isolationist passions continued to dominate across the nation. In late 1940 Washington began to cut off supplies of oil, steel, and other goods that fueled the Japanese war machine. Tensions escalated in the summer of 1941, as the State Department tried to force an end to the occupation of China by freezing Japanese assets and blocking shipments of necessary supplies, forcing the Japanese to either capitulate or resist. They chose to resist. The perfidy of Pearl Harbor was, as FDR said, "a day that would live in infamy," and the isolationists were silenced as Congress declared war on Japan.

Wartime mobilization put the nation back to work. While industry quickly produced the necessary war materials, conscription swelled the ranks of the military. Men shipped out for duty and women took essential jobs as plumbers, electricians, and riveters. Washington directed the overall war effort with an eye on building an overwhelming force in arms. Albert Speer, Germany's industrial czar, feared that America's emphasis on sheer quantity would overwhelm Germany's emphasis on high-quality production. Henry Kaiser's 2,710 Liberty Ships, which carried the bulk of war materials to all combat theaters, confirmed Speer's worst fears as America's enormous productive capacities buried the Third Reich.

World War II altered America's social fabric and tested the nation's commitment to democratic values at home. African Americans, who faced immense barriers in a land dedicated to segregation, moved to California, Washington, and other western states to find work in the war industries. Discrimination remained entrenched, however, and black workers threatened a march on Washington in 1940 against the administration's failure to enforce fair employment practice laws. The threat of this march—and the cry, "What Will Berlin Say?"—encouraged FDR to issue an executive order prohibiting racial discrimination in the War Department. Blacks kept up the pressure with their call for a double victory: victory against fascism abroad and racism at home. The bombing of Pearl Harbor provoked a new governmental transgression against democratic values, however. Executive Order 9066, in early 1942, required Japanese Americans to report to relocation camps.

Allied conferences hammered out plans for winning the war. While the Soviets beat Hitler's army back from Moscow and Stalingrad in 1942–43, the United States, Britain, and their allies forced the Germans out of North Africa. In June 1944, with overwhelming force and a massive military build-up, Churchill and Roosevelt launched D-Day, the Invasion of Normandy. The massive invasion forced the Germans to retreat through France to Germany, and pressed by the Soviets from the east, the Nazis surrendered in May 1945.

In the Pacific, American forces advanced relentlessly toward Japan. After defeating the Japanese Imperial Navy in the battles of the Coral Sea and Midway in the late spring of 1942, the United States settled into an island-hopping campaign across the western Pacific. The liberation of the Philippines and the capturing of Okinawa on the heels of V-E day in Europe left only mainland Japan to conquer. An invasion was bound to be a costly affair, but a new weapon, the atomic bomb, could avoid a bloody invasion and save American lives. President Truman gave the order and two bombs were dropped over a three-day period. The utter destruction of Hiroshima and Nagasaki convinced the Japanese to capitulate. World War II ended on June 2, 1945, with Japan's formal surrender.

Throughout the war, the alliance had remained intact, but it showed signs of strain in 1944, and by the Potsdam conference in June 1945 the alliance had clearly served its purpose. It had been an alliance of mutual enemies, the communists and the capitalists, in a war against a shared enemy, Adolf Hitler and the Germans. After the war, while Winston Churchill warned the world of an impending "iron curtain" of communism in eastern Europe, U.S. foreign policy shifted significantly over protecting the territorial integrity of Greece and Turkey against incursions by the USSR. The early stages of the Cold War had begun.

MAP EXERCISE

Refer to the following maps in Chapters 26 and 27 of *A People and a Nation* to answer the questions listed below.

- Japanese Expansion Before Pearl Harbor (p. 747)

- The Pacific War (p. 764)

- The German Advance, 1939–1942 (p. 749)

- The Allies on the Offensive in Europe, 1942–1945 (p. 762)

1. How far did the Japanese empire extend before Pearl Harbor? What do the maps reveal about America's strategy in defeating Japan?

2. How far did the Nazis advance in the years 1940–42? Where were the pivotal battles fought?

3. Where were the Allied campaigns fought between 1941–45? How did the two-front war affect Germany?

PEOPLE, EVENTS, AND CONCEPTS

Identify and explain the historical significance of each item.

Adolf Hitler

Identification

Significance

Pearl Harbor

Identification

Significance

Benito Mussolini

Identification

Significance

Hiroshima

Identification

Significance

"arsenal of democracy"

Identification

Significance

Ernie Pyle

Identification

Significance

Philippines

Identification

Significance

WASP

Identification

Significance

Blitzkrieg

Identification

Significance

Dresden

Identification

Significance

double victory

Identification

Significance

Nanking

Identification

Significance

Winston Churchill

Identification

Significance

Omaha Beach

Identification

Significance

D-Day

Identification

Significance

Battle of the Bulge

Identification

Significance

Liberty Ships

Identification

Significance

Auschwitz

Identification

Significance

"The Good War"

Identification

Significance

Gen. Douglas MacArthur

Identification

Significance

WACs and WAVEs

Identification

Significance

Josef Stalin

Identification

Significance

ESSAY QUESTIONS

1. Although Americans were opposed to fascist aggressions in Europe and Asia, they remained steadfastly opposed to intervention in World War II until Pearl Harbor. Why did the nation pursue an isolationist policy, even passing Neutrality Acts to affirm that position?

2. How did President Roosevelt move the nation away from its isolationism after 1939? Did U.S. isolationism affect Japan's decision to attack the United States? Was U.S. involvement in WWII inevitable?

3. What was the overall strategy of the Big Three in World War II? How did the alliance unravel, over which issues, and why?

4. How did the war change America? In your answer, explore the war's impact on race relations, the economy, and foreign policy.

MULTIPLE-CHOICE QUESTIONS

1. Which of the following occurred in Munich in 1938?
   a. Germany and Japan agreed to attack the U.S.
   b. Germany and England agreed to attack Russia.
   c. England and France agreed to Hitler's demands on Czechoslovakia.
   d. England and France agreed to let Germany re-occupy the Rhineland.
2. Hitler's non-aggression pact with Russia led to
   a. Germany's attack on Poland.
   b. Germany and England's signing a similar pact.
   c. France and England signing a similar agreement.
   d. none of the above
3. The threat of a march on Washington in 1941 led FDR to issue an executive order
   a. desegregating the armed forces.
   b. forbidding the further introduction of *braceros*.
   c. prohibiting racial discrimination in the defense industries.
   d. sending the Japanese to intern camps.
4. The Battle of Midway
   a. was fought to secure Australia.
   b. led to the defeat of the Japanese in China.
   c. was the turning point in the Pacific war.
   d. forced the Japanese evacuation of the Philippines.
5. Operation Overlord was the code name for
   a. the invasion of Sicily.
   b. an Allied landing in North Africa.
   c. D-Day operations in Normandy.
   d. the secret atomic weapons program.
6. The atomic bomb dropped on Hiroshima and Nagasaki
   a. was meant to shorten the war.
   b. was the brainchild of Albert Einstein.
   c. allowed the emperor of Japan to keep his throne.
   d. was never tested before it was used on Japan.
7. According to Stalin, the Allied agreement at Teheran
   a. established a second front.
   b. arranged for the Soviets to enter the war in Asia immediately.
   c. was his final meeting with Churchill and Roosevelt.
   d. called for Japan's immediate and unconditional surrender.
8. During World War II, African Americans did all of the following except
   a. move north and west seeking jobs.
   b. rally behind the Double Victory.
   c. fight in integrated units.
   d. threaten a march on Washington.

Answers

1. c	3. c	5. c	7. a
2. a	4. c	6. a	8. c

PRIMARY SOURCE DOCUMENTS

The accounts of actual participants are useful for understanding the motives and thoughts of historical characters.

1. *Day of Infamy (1941)* Franklin D. Roosevelt

At noon on December 8, 1941, the day after the Japanese attack on Pearl Harbor, President Franklin D. Roosevelt appeared before both Houses of Congress, the Supreme Court, and his cabinet. In a short but powerful speech, Roosevelt called on Congress to declare war on Japan. With only a lone dissent, Congress approved such a declaration. The following day, Germany and Italy declared war on the United States.

Questions to Consider

- Does Roosevelt offer any explanation for the Japanese attack?

- Did the United States have any alternative to a declaration of war?

Yesterday, December 7, 1941—a date which will live in infamy—the United States of America was suddenly and deliberately attacked by naval and air forces of the Empire of Japan.

The United States was at peace with that nation and, at the solicitation of Japan, was still in conversation with its Government and its Emperor looking toward the maintenance of peace in the Pacific. Indeed, 1 hour after Japanese air squadrons had commenced bombing in Oahu, the Japanese Ambassador to the United States and his colleague delivered to the Secretary of State a formal reply to a recent American message. While this reply stated that it seemed useless to continue the existing diplomatic negotiations, it contained no threat or hint of war or armed attack.

It will be recorded that the distance of Hawaii from Japan makes it obvious that the attack was deliberately planned many days or even weeks ago. During the intervening time the Japanese Government has deliberately sought to deceive the United States by false statements and expressions of hope for continued peace.

The attack yesterday on the Hawaiian Islands has caused severe damage to American naval and military forces. Very many American lives have been lost. In addition American ships have been reported torpedoed on the high seas between San Francisco and Honolulu.

Yesterday the Japanese Government also launched an attack against Malaya.

Last night Japanese forces attacked Hong Kong.

Last night Japanese forces attacked Guam.

Last night Japanese forces attacked the Philippine Islands.

Last night the Japanese attacked Wake Island.

This morning the Japanese attacked Midway Island.

Japan has, therefore, undertaken a surprise offensive extending throughout the Pacific area. The facts of yesterday speak for themselves. The people of the United States have already formed their opinions and well understand the implications to the very life and safety of our Nation.

As Commander in Chief of the Army and Navy I have directed that all measures be taken for our defense.

Always will we remember the character of the onslaught against us.

No matter how long it may take us to overcome this premeditated invasion, the American people, in their righteous might, will win through to absolute victory.

I believe I interpret the will of the Congress and of the people when I assert that we will not only defend ourselves to the uttermost but will make very certain that this form of treachery shall never endanger us again.

Hostilities exist. There is no blinking at the fact that our people, our territory, and our interests are in grave danger.

With confidence in our armed forces—with the unbounded determination of our people—we will gain the inevitable triumph—so help us God.

I ask that the Congress declare that since the unprovoked and dastardly attack by Japan on Sunday, December 7, a state of war has existed between the United States and the Japanese Empire.

SOURCE: *Congressional Record*, 77th Congress, 1st session (1941), vol. 87, pt. 9, pp. 9519–9520.

2. *Four Freedoms (1941)* Franklin D. Roosevelt

When President Franklin D. Roosevelt delivered his annual State of the Union speech to Congress on January 6, 1941, the war in Europe was entering its second year. Over the previous few months Roosevelt and Prime Minister Winston Churchill had worked out the details of "lend-lease," a program intended to supply Britain with munitions and ships. In the following speech Roosevelt hoped to increase public support for his pro-British policies by clarifying what was at stake for America in the European conflict. Though U.S. entry to the war was nearly a year away, Roosevelt's "Four Freedoms" can be taken as a public expression of future war aims.

Questions to Consider

• Were Roosevelt's critics fair in charging him with sneaking the United States into World War II?

• Why should the United States be "the arsenal of democracy," as Roosevelt called it in an earlier speech?

Address of the President of the United States

…I address you, the Members of the Seventy-seventh Congress, at a moment unprecedented in the history of the Union. I use the word "unprecedented," because at no previous time has American security been as seriously threatened from without as it is today….

Every realist knows that the democratic way of life is at this moment being directly assailed in every part of the world—assailed either by arms or by secret spreading of poisonous propaganda by those who seek to destroy unity and promote discord in nations still at peace.

During 16 months this assault has blotted out the whole pattern of democratic life in an appalling number of independent nations, great and small. The assailants are still on the march, threatening other nations, great and small.

Therefore, as your President, performing my constitutional duty to "give to the Congress information of the state of the Union," I find it necessary to report that the future and the safety of our country and of our democracy are overwhelmingly involved in events far beyond our borders.

Armed defense of democratic existence is now being gallantly waged in four continents. If that defense fails, all the population and all the resources of Europe, Asia, Africa, and Australasia will be dominated by the conquerors. The total of those populations and their resources greatly exceeds the sum total of the population and resources of the whole of the Western Hemisphere—many times over.

In times like these it is immature—and incidentally untrue—for anybody to brag that an unprepared America, single-handed, and with one hand tied behind its back, can hold off the whole world.

No realistic American can expect from a dictator's peace international generosity, or return of true independence, or world disarmament, or freedom of expression, or freedom of religion—or even good business.

Such a peace would bring no security for us or for our neighbors....

As a Nation we may take pride in the fact that we are soft-hearted; but we cannot afford to be soft-headed....

Therefore, the immediate need is a swift and driving increase in our armament production....

I also ask this Congress for authority and for funds sufficient to manufacture additional munitions and war supplies of many kinds, to be turned over to those nations which are now in actual war with aggressor nations.

Our most useful and immediate role is to act as an arsenal for them as well as for ourselves. They do not need manpower. They do need billions of dollars' worth of the weapons of defense....

I recommend that we make it possible for those nations to continue to obtain war materials in the United States, fitting their orders into our own program. Nearly all of their matériel would, if the time ever came, be useful for our own defense....

In fulfillment of this purpose we will not be intimidated by the threats of dictators that they will regard as a breach of international law and as an act of war our aid to the democracies which dare to resist their aggression. Such aid is not an act of war, even if a dictator should unilaterally proclaim it so to be.

When the dictators are ready to make war upon us, they will not wait for an act of war on our part. They did not wait for Norway or Belgium or the Netherlands to commit an act of war.

Their only interest is in a new one-way international law, which lacks mutuality in its observance and, therefore, becomes an instrument of oppression....

In the future days, which we seek to make secure, we look forward to a world founded upon four essential human freedoms.

The first is freedom of speech and expression everywhere in the world.

The second is freedom of every person to worship God in his own way everywhere in the world.

The third is freedom from want, which, translated into world terms, means economic understandings which will secure to every nation a healthy peacetime life for its inhabitants everywhere in the world.

The fourth is freedom from fear—which, translated into world terms, means a world-wide reduction of armaments to such a point and in such a thorough fashion that no nation will be in a position to commit an act of physical aggression against any neighbor—anywhere in the world.

That is no vision of a distant millennium. It is a definite basis for a kind of world attainable in our own time and generation. That kind of world is the very antithesis of the so-called new order of tyranny which the dictators seek to create with the crash of a bomb.

To that new order we oppose the greater conception—the moral order. A good society is able to face schemes of world domination and foreign revolutions alike without fear....

SOURCE: *Congressional Record,* 77th Congress, 1st session (1941), vol. 87, pt. 1, pp. 44–47.

3. *Effects of the Atomic Bombs (1945)* **The United States Strategic Bombing Survey**

Few actions of the United States government remain as controversial as those that terminated World War II. On August 6, 1945, a single atomic bomb was dropped on the Japanese city of Hiroshima. Three days later a second bomb was detonated at Nagasaki. No one at the time knew exactly what this new form of weaponry would accomplish, which was reason enough for several prominent American scientists to oppose its use. Within days it was obvious to the world that the United States possessed the most awesome and destructive technology imaginable. In 1944 a joint Army-Navy group, the United States Strategic Bombing Survey, had been organized to study the effect of the air war on the military, economic, and political structures of Germany and Japan. Their report on Hiroshima and Nagasaki enormously influenced both government policy and popular perceptions of the power of atomic bombs.

Questions to Consider

•   What lessons were learned from these atomic attacks?

•   Was the United States justified in its use of these bombs?

A single atomic bomb, the first weapon of its type ever used against a target, exploded over the city of Hiroshima at 0815 on the morning of 6 August 1945. Most of the industrial workers had already reported to work, but many workers were enroute and nearly all the school children and some industrial employees were at work in the open on the program of building removal to provide firebreaks and disperse valuables to the country.... Because of the lack of warning and the populace's indifference to small groups of planes, the explosion came as an almost complete surprise, and the people had not taken shelter. Many were caught in the open, and most of the rest in flimsily constructed homes or commercial establishments.

...Hiroshima was uniformly and extensively devastated. Practically the entire densely or moderately built-up portion of the city was leveled by blast and swept by fire. A "fire-storm" ...developed in Hiroshima: fires springing up almost simultaneously over the wide flat area around the center of the city drew in air from all directions.... The "fire-wind" attained a maximum velocity of 30 to 40 miles per hour 2 to 3 hours after the explosion. The "fire-wind" and the symmetry of the built-up center of the city gave a roughly circular shape to the 4.4 square miles which were almost completely burned out....

At Nagasaki, the scale of destruction was greater than at Hiroshima, though the actual area destroyed was smaller because of the terrain and the point of fall of the bomb. The Nagasaki Prefectural Report describes vividly the impress of the bomb on the city and its inhabitants:

Within a radius of 1 kilometer from ground zero, men and animals died almost instantaneously from the tremendous blast pressure and heat; houses and other structures were smashed, crushed and scattered; and fires broke out. The strong complex steel members of the structures of the Mitsubishi Steel Works were bent and twisted like jelly and the roofs of the reinforced concrete National Schools were crumpled and collapsed, indicating a force beyond imagination. Trees of all sizes lost their branches or were uprooted or broken off at the trunk....

...The most striking result of the atomic bombs was the great number of casualties. The exact number of dead and injured will never be known because of the confusion after the explosions. Persons unaccounted for might have been burned beyond recognition in the falling buildings, disposed of in one of the mass cremations of the first week of recovery, or driven out of the city to die or recover without any record remaining.... The Survey believes the dead at Hiroshima to have been between 70,000 and 80,000, with an equal number injured; at Nagasaki over 35,000 dead and somewhat more than that injured....

Most of the immediate casualties did not differ from those caused by incendiary or high-explosive raids. The outstanding difference was the presence of radiation effects, which became unmistakable about a week after the bombing....

The seriousness of these radiation effects may be measured by the fact that 95 percent of the traced survivors of the immediate explosion who were within 3,000 feet suffered from radiation disease....

A plausible estimate of the importance of the various causes of death would range as follows:
Flash burns, 20 to 30 percent.
Other injuries, 50 to 60 percent.
Radiation sickness, 15 to 20 percent....

...The flash of the explosion, which was extremely brief, emitted radiant heat travelling at the speed of light. Flash burns thus followed the explosion instantaneously....

Survivors in the two cities stated that people who were in the open directly under the explosion of the bomb were so severely burned that the skin was charred dark brown or black and that they died within a few minutes or hours....

Because of the brief duration of the flash wave and the shielding effects of almost any objects—leaves and clothing as well as buildings—there were many interesting cases of protection. The radiant heat came in a direct line like light, so that the area burned corresponded to this directed exposure. Persons whose sides were toward the explosion often showed definite burns of both sides of the back while the hollow of the back escaped. People in buildings or houses were apparently burned only if directly exposed through the windows. The most striking instance was that of a man writing before a window. His hands were seriously burned but his exposed face and neck suffered only slight burns due to the angle of entry of the radiant heat through the window....

Unfortunately, no exact definition of the killing power of radiation can yet be given, nor a satisfactory account of the sort and thickness of concrete or earth that will shield people.... In the meanwhile the awesome lethal effects of the atomic bomb and the insidious additional peril of the gamma rays speak for themselves.

There is reason to believe that if the effects of blast and fire had been entirely absent from the bombing, the number of deaths among people within a radius of one-half mile from ground zero would have been almost as great.... Instead of being killed outright as were most of these victims, they would have survived for a few days or even 3 or 4 weeks, only to die eventually of radiation disease....

SOURCE: The United States Strategic Bombing Survey, *The Effects of the Atomic Bombs on Hiroshima and Nagasaki* (Washington, D.C., 1946), pp. 3, 11–17, 19.

UNIT 23

The Fifties: From War to Normalcy

UNIT SUMMARY

In Unit 23 we look at America at the beginning of the nuclear age. We explore how returning war veterans sought to create new lives for themselves in the era of the Cold War, civil rights, and rock 'n' roll.

ASSIGNMENT

1. Before viewing Program 23, read this unit, and in *A People and a Nation* read Chapters 28 and 29.

2. View Program 23, "The Fifties: From War to Normalcy."

3. Visit the Web site <http://www.learner.org/biographyofamerica>.
    Explore the exercises for Program 23.

LEARNING OBJECTIVES

Upon completing this unit, students should be able to:

1. Discuss the origins of the Cold War and its impact on foreign and domestic policy.

2. Describe the mood of the nation following the war and discuss the development of the post-war economy.

3. Discuss President Truman's efforts to continue FDR's New Deal policies.

4. Evaluate the reasons for the "red scare" in domestic politics and discuss the casualties of that era.

5. Examine the strength of the civil rights movement after WWII and the significance of events following the Supreme Court's *Brown v. Board of Education* decision.

6. Discuss the Eisenhower years as an age of consensus and conformity.

PROGRAM GUIDE

After the Nazis are defeated, the United States turns the fury of its military machine upon the Japanese. Professor Miller describes the war's bitter end in the Pacific, where fighting is fierce and the loss of life staggering. More Americans are killed on Okinawa than were killed on D-Day. Japanese soldiers resist unto death, adhering to the ancient warrior code of the bushido. The United States uses airpower to break down Japanese resistance, but ultimately, two atomic bombs end the war.

After the war, soldiers return home to build new lives. The GI Bill allows millions of vets to buy homes and go to college. The economy booms after the war, and the nation enjoys unperiled prosperity. An expanding middle class embraces consumerism while largely ignoring the social issues of the day.

Life in the fifties is comfortable for many, but beneath the surface tensions simmer. Rock 'n' roll becomes a part of teen culture, and alienation is on the rise. Cold War fears and civil rights demonstrations in the wake of the *Brown v. Board of Education* decision signal that times are changing.

HISTORICAL OVERVIEW

Two atomic bombs in three days ended the war in Japan. The United States emerged from WWII victorious over the forces of fascism, but another menace to world peace loomed: communism. Soviet strength had grown to formidable proportions during the war and now the superpowers, the United States and the Soviet Union, began a struggle for world dominance that would last more than forty years.

Although the United States, in 1945, had the world's only nuclear weapons, the Soviet Union quickly mobilized its scientific community to respond in kind, and in 1949, the Soviets detonated an atomic bomb.

The nuclear age meant a radical departure for American diplomacy as the United States moved away from its policy of non-intervention and neutrality towards Europe to one of activism and intervention. While the Truman Doctrine promised military and economic aid to Greece and Turkey to ward off communism, the Marshall Plan promised billions to rebuild Europe. Winston Churchill's warning of an Iron Curtain falling across Eastern Europe was taken seriously in the West. When Soviet leader Josef Stalin moved to cut off Western access to the jointly occupied city of Berlin, the United States ordered a massive airlift of food, fuel, and other supplies to keep the city alive. After the Soviets backed down, Western Europe joined America in a new military alliance: NATO. One of NATO's aims was to halt the expansion of communism beyond the Soviet's satellite community. In Asia, the United States took active steps to stem the threat of communism. While America pushed Japan to develop along democratic lines, it sent aid to France in its war against Vietnamese nationalists. The Communist Mao Tse-Tung's victory in China worried policy makers that countries throughout the region would fall like dominoes, and President Truman committed the nation to a crusade to halt the communists in southeast Asia.

At home, World War II had ended the Great Depression, but with peace came doubts about the future of the economy. The nation's efforts towards reconversion led to problems. Workers wanted to enjoy their earnings and resented continued wartime restrictions and the rising prices of peacetime. Wages lagged behind and labor demonstrated its strength by taking to the picket line. Exasperated by the labor unrest, Congress passed the Taft-Hartley Act (over Truman's veto), a measure to curtail the union movement's strength. The post-war years were a time of open warfare between the president and Congress over domestic matters, as the executive and legislative branches collided over the direction of the post-war economy. Truman's Fair Deal initiatives sought to advance social policies associated with the New Deal, but Congress balked at new expenditures for social programs.

Civil rights campaigns continued after WWII. Long before the war, the NAACP legal defense team had won an impressive series of victories in the Supreme Court over issues like interstate transportation, voting, higher education, and housing. President Truman joined the campaign to end racial segregation in his 1948 State of the Union Address, calling for government action against discrimination. Truman, the NAACP, and the black community launched an aggressive campaign for racial equality, and in 1949 Truman ordered the desegregation of the military. In 1954, the Supreme

Court decision in *Brown v. Board of Education* declared an end to segregated schools. The following years in Montgomery, Little Rock, and Greensboro made it clear that African Americans were not going to be held back from sharing in the American dream.

President Truman presided over a tumultuous period in American history. His leadership in the area of desegregation led to open rebellion in the ranks of the Democratic Party. Southern Democrats formed the Dixiecrats (States Rights Democratic Party) in the 1948 election, in opposition to Truman's pro-civil rights stance. Truman won the election in a surprise upset over Republican challenger Thomas Dewey, but the president faced a hostile Congress. In the debacle of the Korean War, the public soured towards Truman and he chose not to seek re-election in 1952.

The American public now turned to a tested and beloved hero for president in 1952: General Dwight D. Eisenhower. "Ike" promised to end the war in Korea and end the country's drift toward "creeping socialism." After his victory over Adlai Stevenson, whom he defeated again in 1956, the president went to Korea and an armistice soon followed. The new administration took an aggressive diplomatic posture against the communists. While Ike expanded America's nuclear arsenal, Secretary of State John Foster Dulles promoted a policy of brinksmanship in the Cold War. The United States threatened massive retaliation against its enemies and promised to roll back any communist advances. Clandestine operations initiated by the Central Intelligence Agency committed the nation to campaigns around the globe. The CIA moved to destabilize unfriendly regimes in countries like Iran, Guatemala, Vietnam, Egypt, and Cuba. These actions raised questions about the nation's commitment to the principle of self-determination, but destroying communism was seen as primary to America's global interests.

Eisenhower presided over a public eager to enjoy the material comforts of consumerism. Veterans took advantage of benefits offered by the GI Bill, and the middle class expanded in the fifties. Americans settled down into the comforts of suburbia and had children at a unprecedented rate. The baby boom generation fueled the booming economy as many parents spoiled their children with toys, clothes, and lavish attention. Despite the best intentions of the adults, some youngsters would reach adolescence in the sixties feeling alienated, ungrateful, and unenamored of their elders' values.

MAP EXERCISE

Refer to the following maps in Chapter 29 of *A People and a Nation* to answer the questions listed below.

- Divided Europe (p. 830)

- The Rise of the Third World: Newly Independent Nations Since 1943 (p. 844)

1. The United States and Soviets each had their own post-war allies, and victory over the European fascists did not bring world peace. Which nations joined the United States in the NATO alliance and which joined the Soviets in the Warsaw pact? Which events increased tensions between the superpowers? How significant were economic and military affairs in escalating the Cold War?

2. World War II forced the imperial powers to let go of their empires. Where did the United States and its imperialist allies resist independence movements? Where did this lead to direct military involvement?

PEOPLE, EVENTS, AND CONCEPTS

Identify and explain the historical significance of each item.

Ernie Pyle

Identification

Significance

Okinawa

Identification

Significance

death by mass production

Identification

Significance

sunbelt

Identification

Significance

way of Bushido

Identification

Significance

H-bomb

Identification

Significance

baby boom

Identification

Significance

Philip Morrison

Identification

Significance

George Kennan

Identification

Significance

throwaway society

Identification

Significance

G.I. Bill

Identification

Significance

Silent Spring

Identification

Significance

Beale Street

Identification

Significance

Elvis Presley

Identification

Significance

godless communism

Identification

Significance

Dwight D. Eisenhower

Identification

Significance

Levittown, New York

Identification

Significance

Montgomery, Alabama

Identification

Significance

transistor radios

Identification

Significance

Rosa Parks

Identification

Significance

Fair Deal

Identification

Significance

McCarthyism

Identification

Significance

redbaiting

Identification

Significance

ESSAY QUESTIONS

1. How would the following events influence the Cold War?

   - Wartime diplomacy and the question of Poland

   - President Truman's policy of containment

   - Soviet support for communist regimes in Asia

2. Why did McCarthyism take hold following WWII? Was there ever a real threat to democratic institutions in the United States?

3. What was the impact of the post-war boom on suburbia and on the families that relocated there from urban centers?

4. Why did the United States move against North Korea? What were President Truman's goals for the Korean peninsula? Should General MacArthur have been allowed to continue in command of the troops?

5. Compare and contrast Truman's and Eisenhower's approaches to:

   - the Cold War

   - the economy

   - civil rights

6. What role did the NAACP play in the events leading up to the *Brown* decision? Why did the Supreme Court vote to reverse the *Plessy* decision?

7. How important was the leadership of Dr. Martin Luther King, Jr., to the civil rights struggle? What unique characteristics did he bring to the movement?

MULTIPLE-CHOICE QUESTIONS

1. Americans liked Dwight D. Eisenhower's
   a. caution, moderation, and traditionalism.
   b. pursuit of a balanced budget and reduced taxes.
   c. record as a war hero.
   d. all of the above

2. The economic boom after WWII and into the sixties resulted from all of the following except
   a. the rising middle class and its purchasing power.
   b. lower energy costs.
   c. the rising productivity of the work force.
   d. the equitable redistribution of wealth.

3. Congress passed the Taft-Hartley Act in an effort to curtail the power of
   a. African Americans.
   b. President Truman.
   c. the labor movement.
   d. monopolies like General Motors.

4. The expansion of suburbia after WWII led to
   a. the baby boom.
   b. increased integration of schools.
   c. an increase in inner city poverty.
   d. a fall in urban crime rates.

5. Cold War tensions can be traced to disagreements after the war in
   a. Third World nationalist movements.
   b. Asian and Pacific nations.
   c. Europe.
   d. Africa and the Middle East.

6. The Truman Doctrine redirected United States foreign policy away from neutrality in
   a. communist China and North Korea.
   b. Greece and Turkey.
   c. Iran and Egypt.
   d. Poland.

7. President Truman supported efforts to weed out communists within the U.S. government through
   a. the Taft-Hartley Act.
   b. the Smith Act.
   c. the House on Un-American Activities Committee.
   d. the Loyalty Review Board.

8. The Supreme Court advanced the cause of civil rights because
   a. presidents Roosevelt and Eisenhower had ordered desegregation.
   b. Congress had failed to take action.
   c. the courts were dominated with liberal jurists.
   d. only the Court had the authority to legislate such matters.

Answers

1. d	3. c	5. c	7. d
2. d	4. c	6. b	8. b

PRIMARY SOURCE DOCUMENTS

The accounts of actual participants are useful for understanding the motives and thoughts of historical characters.

1.   *The Communist Menace (1947)* **J. Edgar Hoover**

As the first director of the Federal Bureau of Investigation, J. Edgar Hoover devoted almost as much energy to pursuing Communists as to apprehending criminals. Hoover had been instrumental in the first "Red scare" in 1919, only to be disappointed by the nation's lack of sustained concern for this crusade. In the immediate aftermath of World War II, Hoover again sought to make the United States aware of the danger it faced from the Communists. In 1947 he found the perfect forum for this warning, the notorious House Un-American Activities Committee (HUAC), whose most prominent member, Richard M. Nixon of California, was launching a national career based on his opposition to the Communist menace. Hoover appeared before HUAC on March 26, 1947.

Questions to Consider

- •   Given the small number of Communists in the United States, why was Hoover so fearful?
- •   Was there any reality to this Cold War fear of foreign subversion?

My feelings concerning the Communist Party of the United States are well known. I have not hesitated over the years to express my concern and apprehension. As a consequence its professional smear brigades have conducted a relentless assault against the FBI.... I do not mind such attacks. What has been disillusioning is the manner in which they have been able to enlist support often from apparently well-meaning but thoroughly duped persons....

The great god of the American Communists, Comrade Lenin—whose writings are their Bible—in various speeches and writings urged the use of deceit and trickery and his converts live by his injunction....

The Communist movement in the United States… stands for the destruction of free enterprise; and it stands for the creation of a "Soviet of the United States" and ultimate world revolution.

…The preamble of the latest constitution of the Communist Party of the United States, filled with Marxian "double talk," proclaims that the party "educates the working class, in the course of its day-to-day struggles, for its historic mission, the establishment of socialism."

The phrase "historic mission" has a sinister meaning. To the uninformed person it bespeaks tradition, but to the Communist, using his own words, it is "achieving the dictatorship of the proletariat" ….

The Communist, once he is fully trained and indoctrinated, realizes that he can create his order in the United States only by "bloody revolution."

…The Communist Party line changes from day to day. The one cardinal rule that can always be applied to what the party line is or will be is found in the fundamental principle of Communist teachings that the support of Soviet Russia is the duty of Communists of all countries.

One thing is certain. The American progress which all good citizens seek, such as old-age security, houses for veterans, child assistance and a host of others is being adopted as window dressing by the Communists to conceal their true aims and entrap gullible followers....

The mad march of Red fascism is a cause for concern in America. But the deceit, the trickery, and the lies of the American Communists are catching up with them. Whenever the spotlight of truth is focused upon them they cry, "Red baiting." Now that their aims and objectives are being exposed they are creating a Committee for the Constitutional Rights of Communists, and are feverishly working to build up what they term a quarter-million-dollar defense fund to place ads in papers, to publish pamphlets, to buy radio time. They know that today it is a fight to the finish and that their backs will soon be to the wall....

The numerical strength of the party's enrolled membership is insignificant. But it is well known that there are many actual members who because of their position are not carried on party rolls.... The Daily Worker boasts of 74,000 members on the rolls....

What is important is the claim of the Communists themselves that for every party member there are 10 others ready, willing, and able to do the party[']s work. Herein lies the greatest menace of communism. For these are the people who infiltrate and corrupt various spheres of American life. So rather than the size of the Communist Party the way to weigh its true importance is by testing its influence, its ability to infiltrate.

The size of the party is relatively unimportant because of the enthusiasm and iron-clad discipline under which they operate. In this connection, it might be of interest to observe that in 1917 when the Communists overthrew the Russian Government there was one Communist for every 2,277 persons in Russia. In the United States today there is one Communist for every 1,814 persons in the country....

Identifying undercover Communists, fellow travelers, and sympathizers: The burden of proof is placed upon those who consistently follow the ever-changing, twisting party line. Fellow travelers and sympathizers can deny party membership but they can never escape the undeniable fact that they have played into the Communist hands, thus furthering the Communist cause by playing the role of innocent, gullible, or willful allies....

SOURCE: Investigation of Un-American Propaganda Activities in the United States, Hearings Before the Committee on Un-American Activities, House of Representatives, 80th Congress, 1st Session (Washington, D.C., 1947), pp. 34.

2. *The Truman Doctrine (1947)* Harry S. Truman

In the aftermath of World War II, Communists attempted to seize power in Greece and Turkey. Those governments, backed by the British, resisted with military force. But in 1947 Great Britain informed the U.S. government that it could no longer maintain the expense of continuing aid to those nations. President Harry Truman personally appeared before a joint session of Congress on March 12, 1947, to request that the United States abandon its historic commitment to nonintervention in Europe during peacetime and extend full aid to Greece and Turkey. Congress approved what has since become known as the "Truman Doctrine" by huge majorities.

Questions to Consider

- Why does Truman frame his request in the context of an international conflict?
- What American interests were involved in the political fate of Greece and Turkey?

The gravity of the situation which confronts the world today necessitates my appearance before a joint session of the Congress.

The foreign policy and the national security of this country are involved....

One of the primary objectives of the foreign policy of the United States is the creation of conditions in which we and other nations will be able to work out a way of life free from coercion. This was a fundamental issue in the war with Germany and Japan. Our victory was won over countries which sought to impose their will, and their way of life, upon other nations.

...We shall not realize our objectives, however, unless we are willing to help free peoples to maintain their free institutions and their national integrity against aggressive movements that seek to impose upon them totalitarian regimes. This is no more than a frank recognition that totalitarian regimes imposed upon free peoples, by direct or indirect aggression, undermine the foundations of international peace and hence the security of the United States.

The peoples of a number of countries of the world have recently had totalitarian regimes forced upon them against their will.... At the present moment in world history nearly every nation must choose between alternative ways of life. The choice is too often not a free one.

One way of life is based upon the will of the majority, and is distinguished by free institutions, representative government, free elections, guarantees of individual liberty, freedom of speech and religion, and freedom from political oppression.

The second way of life is based upon the will of a minority forcibly imposed upon the majority. It relies upon terror and oppression, a controlled press and radio, fixed elections, and the suppression of personal freedoms.

I believe that it must be the policy of the United States to support free peoples who are resisting attempted subjugation by armed minorities or by outside pressures.

I believe that we must assist free peoples to work out their own destinies in their own way.

I believe that our help should be primarily through economic and financial aid which is essential to economic stability and orderly political processes....

It is necessary only to glance at a map to realize that the survival and integrity of the Greek nation are of grave importance in a much wider situation. If Greece should fall under the control of an armed minority, the effect upon its neighbor, Turkey, would be immediate and serious. Confusion and disorder might well spread throughout the entire Middle East.

Moreover, the disappearance of Greece as an independent state would have a profound effect upon those countries in Europe whose peoples are struggling against great difficulties to maintain their freedoms and their independence while they repair the damages of war....

Should we fail to aid Greece and Turkey in this fateful hour, the effect will be far reaching to the West as well as to the East.

We must take immediate and resolute action....

The seeds of totalitarian regimes are nurtured by misery and want. They spread and grow in the evil soil of poverty and strife. They reach their full growth when the hope of a people for a better life has died.

We must keep that hope alive.

The free peoples of the world look to us for support in maintaining their freedom.

If we falter in our leadership, we may endanger the peace of the world—and we shall surely endanger the welfare of this Nation.

Great responsibilities have been placed upon us by the swift movement of events.

I am confident that the Congress will face these responsibilities squarely.

Source: Public Papers of the Presidents of the United States, Harry S. Truman, 1947 (Washington, D.C., 1948), pp. 176, 178–180.

3. *Brown v. Board of Education (1954)* U.S. Supreme Court

Charles Houston, head of the National Association for the Advancement of Colored People's Legal Defense Fund from 1933 until his death in 1950, devoted his life to fighting the Supreme Court's "separate but equal" decision in *Plessy v. Ferguson.* Houston developed the strategy of slowly whittling away at *Plessy* by demonstrating that separate could never be equal. Appreciating the centrality of education in American life, Houston concentrated his efforts there, traveling through the South with his brilliant student, Thurgood Marshall, filming dilapidated black schools and gathering information for his appeals. Marshall took over from Houston in 1950, building on Houston's initial successes. Marshall first argued the case against the Board of Education of Topeka, Kansas, in 1952. With the Court divided over whether to overturn *Plessy,* the justices asked both sides to reargue the case again in the October 1953 term, paying special attention to the intention of the Fourteenth Amendment. The sudden death of Chief Justice Fred Vinson, who had opposed overturning *Plessy,* led to the appointment of a new Chief Justice, the governor of California, Earl Warren. Warren crafted a unanimous decision in favor of putting an end to segregated education by focusing on the question of the harm done to black children, relying on sociological evidence and placing much of the argument in his footnotes. Probably no decision since *Plessy* has had such a long-range impact on the United States.

Questions to Consider

- Why could separate not be equal?
- Is the Court effectively overturning *Plessy v. Ferguson* or simply limiting its reach?
- How does the Court propose to desegregate the nation's schools?

Mr. Chief Justice Warren delivered the opinion of the Court.

…The plaintiffs contend that segregated public schools are not "equal" and cannot be made "equal," and that hence they are deprived of the equal protection of the laws.…

…[T]here are findings below that the Negro and white schools involved have been equalized, or are being equalized, with respect to buildings, curricula, qualifications and salaries of teachers, and other "tangible" factors. Our decision, therefore, cannot turn on merely a comparison of these tangible factors in the Negro and white schools involved in each of the cases. We must look instead to the effect of segregation itself on public education.

In approaching this problem, we cannot turn the clock back to 1868 when the Amendment was adopted, or even to 1896 when *Plessy v. Ferguson* was written. We must consider public education in the light of its full development and its present place in American life throughout the Nation. Only in this way can it be determined if segregation in public schools deprives these plaintiffs of the equal protection of the laws.

Today, education is perhaps the most important function of state and local governments. Compulsory school attendance laws and the great expenditures for education both demonstrate our recognition of the importance of education to our democratic society. It is required in the performance of our most basic public responsibilities…. Today it is a principal instrument in awakening the child to cultural values, in preparing him for later professional training, and in helping him to adjust normally to his environment. In these days, it is doubtful that any child may reasonably be expected to succeed in life if he is denied the opportunity of an education. Such an opportunity, where the state has undertaken to provide it, is a right which must be made available to all on equal terms.

We come then to the question presented: Does segregation of children in public schools solely on the basis of race, even though the physical facilities and other "tangible" factors may be equal, deprive the children of the minority group of equal educational opportunities? We believe that it does.

...To separate [children] from others of similar age and qualifications solely because of their race generates a feeling of inferiority as to their status in the community that may affect their hearts and minds in a way unlikely ever to be undone. The effect of this separation on their educational opportunities was well stated by a finding in the Kansas case by a court which nevertheless felt compelled to rule against the Negro plaintiffs:

Segregation of white and colored children in public schools has a detrimental effect upon the colored children. The impact is greater when it has the sanction of the law; for the policy of separating the races is usually interpreted as denoting the inferiority of the negro group. A sense of inferiority affects the motivation of a child to learn. Segregation with the sanction of law, therefore, has a tendency to [retard] the educational and mental development of negro children and to deprive them of some of the benefits they would receive in a racial[ly] integrated school system.

Whatever may have been the extent of psychological knowledge at the time of *Plessy v. Ferguson* this finding is amply supported by modern authority. Any language in *Plessy v. Ferguson* contrary to this finding is rejected.

We conclude that in the field of public education the doctrine of "separate but equal" has no place. Separate educational facilities are inherently unequal. Therefore, we hold that the plaintiffs and others similarly situated for whom the actions have been brought are, by reason of the segregation complained of, deprived of the equal protection of the laws guaranteed by the Fourteenth Amendment. This disposition makes unnecessary any discussion whether such segregation also violates the Due Process Clause of the Fourteenth Amendment....

SOURCE: 347 *U.S. Reports* (Washington, D.C., 1954), pp. 483–496.

UNIT 24

The Sixties

UNIT SUMMARY

In Unit 24 we look at the turmoil of the nineteen-sixties and its impact upon the American people.

ASSIGNMENT

1. Before viewing Program 24, read this unit, and in *A People and A Nation* read Chapter 30 and Chapter 31, pages 883–906.

2. View Program 24, "The Sixties."

3. Visit the Web site <http://www.learner.org/biographyofamerica>. Explore the exercises for Program 24.

LEARNING OBJECTIVES

Upon completing this unit, students should be able to:

1. Discuss U.S.-Cuban relations in the early sixties and the role of the Soviets in the Cuban Missile Crisis.

2. Discuss the escalation of the war in Vietnam and the war's impact on domestic affairs.

3. Discuss the civil rights movement and the events that led to the Civil Rights and Voting Rights acts.

4. Discuss the crises of 1968 that shocked Americans to open rebellion against the government.

5. Explain how Richard Nixon sought to end the war in Vietnam by changing the dynamics of the Cold War.

PROGRAM GUIDE

The sixties divide the nation. Professor Scharff tells the story of the decade in the events of the civil rights movement, the Vietnam War, and the Watergate scandal. *A Biography of America* takes a close look at the pivotal characters that capture the nation's attention: John F. Kennedy, Lyndon B. Johnson, Stokely Carmichael, Fanny Lou Hamer, and Richard M. Nixon.

Reconstruction ended in 1877, but that unfinished revolution in civil rights again seizes center stage in the nineteen-sixties. Presidential candidate John F. Kennedy makes vague promises to promote the struggle for equality during his 1960 campaign, and he is challenged to fulfill these promises throughout his administration. Freedom Riders are beaten for their efforts to promote civil rights, but they force the president to act. In 1962 Kennedy orders U.S. marshals to protect James Meredith, the first African American to attend the University of Mississippi. After police in

Birmingham, Alabama attack nonviolent civil rights demonstrators, including children, with fire hoses, snarling dogs, and cattle prods, in May 1963, President Kennedy calls for a civil rights bill outlawing discrimination. He does not live to see its passage, however, he is assassinated in November 1963.

JFK's presidency is dominated by the events of the Cold War. After a stunning defeat by Cuban leader Fidel Castro at the Bay of Pigs in April 1961 and the construction of the Berlin Wall by the Soviets, also in 1961, Kennedy is forced to respond somehow to communist aggression. He chooses Vietnam as the acid test of America's resolve. Continuing Eisenhower's commitment, JFK expands U.S. forces in South Vietnam; his successor, Lyndon B. Johnson, commits the nation to full-scale war.

While Johnson sincerely wants to end discrimination and build a Great Society at home, the war derails his lofty objectives. By 1968 America is in full-scale rebellion. Students across the country are either demonstrating for an end to the war or proclaiming free love. The assassinations of Dr. Martin Luther King, Jr., and presidential candidate Robert F. Kennedy that spring divide the nation deeper. In the November elections, Americans turn to the old Cold Warrior Richard Nixon to lead them out of the national nightmare, Vietnam. His promise of peace with honor and the illusion of presidential strength is shattered, however, by the Watergate debacle.

HISTORICAL OVERVIEW

Television changed American politics. Americans watched Kennedy debate Nixon, dogs attack civil rights demonstrators, soldiers die in Vietnam, and national leaders in hotel kitchens, men walk on the moon, and a president resign from office in disgrace—all on live television. The Kennedy-Nixon debates during the 1960 election signaled a new age in politics, one in which the media would exercise greater control over the political process. Kennedy understood the power of television and used it skillfully during the debates and throughout his presidency: his press conferences set a precedent for speaking directly to the public. Television also forced the president to take action, as when violence erupted in Birmingham, Alabama, in June 1963. Kennedy's assassination in November 1963 riveted the nation's attention to their TV sets. Later, TV coverage of the Vietnam war brought the life and death struggles of American soldiers in a faraway land right into American living rooms. Body bags and body counts, search and destroy missions, the VC, all became part of our national lexicon.

The Cold War continued in the sixties. Soviet Premier Nikita Khrushchev promised wars of national liberation against the imperialists. President Kennedy warned the Soviets in turn that the United States would pay any price and bear any burden to safeguard democracy. While the superpowers engaged in an escalating arms race, two conflicts dominated foreign affairs: Cuba and Vietnam. In 1959, Cuba's Fidel Castro seized power in a popular revolution against the U.S.-supported dictatorship of Fulgencio Batista. When Castro refused to continue business as usual, the CIA trained Cuban exiles to attack and depose him. The fiasco that followed at the Bay of Pigs had several consequences. Castro's defiance against the Yankees consolidated his power at home, and Kennedy's lackluster response emboldened Khrushchev to give aid to the Cubans. During the summer of 1961, the Soviets erected the Berlin Wall aimed at stemming the exodus out of East Berlin to the West. Although Kennedy had threatened war over Berlin, he took no action. The Cuban Missile Crisis was next, as Khrushchev attempted to place missiles aimed at the United States on Cuban soil. Nuclear war was narrowly averted, and the United States and the Soviets went on to discuss a nuclear test ban treaty. In Vietnam, where the Kennedy administration had been giving military and economic assistance to Ngo Dinh Diem, popular protests, civil war, and military disillusionment with the Diem regime led to a coup in November 1963. Before he was assassinated in

Dallas, JFK had increased military aid to South Vietnam: 16,000 troops and $1 million per day. His successor, Lyndon Johnson, widened the war and U.S. involvement.

The sixties were a critical period in the civil rights movement. Demonstrations exploded across the South at the beginning of the decade, as civil rights organizations practiced passive resistance and took non-violent action against Jim Crow segregation. Dr. Martin Luther King, Jr., called upon people of good will everywhere to attack racism. Saying that immoral, unjust, and undemocratic laws had no place in American society, King asked Americans to demonstrate to reverse the tide of discrimination. In the first half of the decade, direct action campaigns inspired the sit-ins, Freedom Rides, integration campaigns, the March on Washington, the Mississippi Freedom Summer, and the Voting Rights March.

Washington responded with momentous measures: the 1964 Civil Rights Act and the 1965 Voting Rights Act. President Johnson seemed committed to the cause; declaring an unconditional war against poverty, he said that America was in the process of building a Great Society. The boldness and expansive character of Johnson's progressivism compared with FDR's New Deal. Despite his good intentions, however, the war in Vietnam and protests against it at home derailed LBJ's efforts. Ultimately, the war ended his presidency.

LBJ had promised American voters in the 1964 campaign that he would not send American boys to die in Vietnam; he depicted his opponent, Barry Goldwater, as a warmongering madman. After an incident in the Gulf of Tonkin that summer, however, LBJ escalated the war. What followed was an endless stream of troop deployments, government funding, and outright lies to the American public. The Tet Offensive in 1968 jolted Americans, raising questions at last about the winnability of the war and making clear the grim reality of the conflict. As TV captured the war's horrors, trusted TV commentator Walter Cronkite called for the withdrawal of U.S. forces. Eugene McCarthy entered the presidential campaign as a peace candidate, and LBJ stunned the nation by announcing his decision not to run for reelection. The violence was not confined to Vietnam, however. That spring Dr. King and Robert F. Kennedy, who had joined the race for the Democratic nomination, fell victims to assassins' bullets. 1968 was a year of senseless violence.

The Republicans nominated Richard Nixon in 1968. He promised law and order and an end "with honor" to the war in Vietnam. Nixon knew that America's "silent majority"—his term for the average law-abiding citizen—wanted an end to the protests, rebellions, and acts of violence plaguing the nation. He won in a close contest with LBJ's vice president, Hubert Humphrey, and he soon withdrew some U.S. troops, announcing a policy of "Vietnamization": turning the fighting over to the Vietnamese. However, the secret bombing of Cambodia, a neutral country, in 1970 widened the war. Protests at home increased; at Kent State University in Ohio, the National Guard killed four student protesters.

The American economy meanwhile suffered from declining production, especially in the auto industry, and from inflationary pressures caused by the war. The expanded war in southeast Asia and economic stagflation at home hurt the Nixon administration, and as the nation prepared for another presidential election, in 1972, President Nixon took a bold step to end the Cold War: he went to Beijing and Moscow. Nixon sought to exploit the rift between the two communist giants to end the Vietnam War. Both trips were elaborately staged and televised, and assisted by a rumor (planted by his aides) that "peace is at hand," Nixon was reelected to a second term. Despite the lopsided victory in November and his foreign policy successes, Nixon's 1972 campaign was the beginning of the Watergate scandal, which would bring down his presidency.

Richard Nixon committed the worst political mistake of his long career when he ordered the cover-up of the Watergate burglary. During the 1972 campaign, CREEP (the Committee to Reelect the President), under the direction of Nixon aide John Mitchell, authorized the bugging of the Democratic National Committee headquarters in the Watergate building. At first the arrest of burglars at the DNC offices captured little attention, but the dogged pursuit of answers by reporters

Carl Bernstein and Bob Woodward of the *Washington Post* helped to expose the scandal. Although the president did not order or know about the crime beforehand, he ordered the cover-up afterward and obstructed the congressional investigation that followed. His denial of the events, the cover-up, and the lying to Congress destroyed his presidency. Nixon's resignation in August 1974 brought to a close the long, turbulent era of the sixties.

The sixties were years of vast changes in the United States. The civil rights movement made large strides in race relations, but that struggle continues into the new century. The war in Vietnam remains a dark chapter in our nation's past. Perhaps the greatest challenge facing the country, however, is this: the problem of restoring the trust in political leaders that was lost in the sixties. The credibility of the government and of the nation's leader himself was the biggest casualty of what JFK optimistically called the New Frontier.

MAP EXERCISE

Refer to the following maps in Chapters 30 and 31 of *A People and a Nation* to answer the questions listed below.

- Race Riots, 1965–1968 (p. 865)

- Southeast Asia and the Vietnam War (p. 892)

1. Americans have traditionally tended to see race relations as a Southern concern. What does the map reveal about racial unrest in the sixties? Where have recent events of racial violence occurred, and what does this suggest about race in America?

2. What does the map tell us about U.S. involvement in southeast Asia between 1964 and 1975? Was the U.S. involved only in Vietnam? What does the map tell us about the way the war ended?

PEOPLE, EVENTS, AND CONCEPTS

Identify and explain the historical significance of each item.

Greensboro, North Carolina

Identification

Significance

bus boycott

Identification

Significance

Dr. Martin Luther King, Jr.

Identification

Significance

Little Rock, Arkansas

Identification

Significance

Montgomery, Alabama

Identification

Significance

SNCC and CORE

Identification

Significance

Freedom Rides

Identification

Significance

Bay of Pigs

Identification

Significance

Great Society

Identification

Significance

Fidel Castro

Identification

Significance

Birmingham, Alabama

Identification

Significance

March on Washington

Identification

Significance

Fannie Lou Hamer

Identification

Significance

Black Power

Identification

Significance

Stokely Carmichael

Identification

Significance

Gulf of Tonkin

Identification

Significance

Ho Chi Minh

Identification

Significance

Dienbienphu

Identification

Significance

domino theory

Identification

Significance

Cambodia

Identification

Significance

Vietcong

Identification

Significance

Woodward and Bernstein

Identification

Significance

Watergate complex

Identification

Significance

credibility gap

Identification

Significance

ESSAY QUESTIONS

1. How did the civil rights movement gain momentum in the early 1960s? What specific events helped convince politicians that action on civil rights was long overdue?

2. John F. Kennedy inspired genuine idealism in Americans. Why do you think Americans were so receptive to his message to "ask not what your country can do for you; ask what you can do for your country"?

3. Although Richard Nixon did not order the break-in of the Democratic National Committee headquarters, subsequent events forced his resignation. What led to the articles of impeachment and to Nixon's demise? Did the president violate his oath of office? Explain your answer.

MULTIPLE-CHOICE QUESTIONS

1. The Kennedy Administration's first challenge in foreign affairs occurred
   a. in the Middle East over the Suez Crisis.
   b. with the escalating losses in Vietnam.
   c. when Cuban exiles were routed at the Bay of Pigs.
   d. when the Soviets constructed a wall around Berlin.
2. Television's most significant and longest lasting change was in the way
   a. political campaigns distorted and marginalized substantive issues.
   b. the Vietnam War was covered in the nightly news broadcasts.
   c. civil rights demonstrations were publicized.
   d. advertisements were designed to appeal to a younger audience.
3. The United States' early support in the Vietnam conflict can be traced to
   a. helping France against Ho Chi Minh.
   b. sending military assistance to the regime of Ngo Dinh Diem.
   c. providing economic assistance to Ho Chi Minh.
   d. sending bombers to defend the French at Dienbienphu.
4. John Kennedy made the main issue of his campaign in 1960
   a. the need to build up our nuclear arsenal.
   b. the importance of ending the communist experiment in Cuba.
   c. the danger that the United States had fallen behind the Soviets in power and prestige.
   d. the failure of all Americans to achieve full equality.
5. Lyndon Johnson enjoyed greater success in legislative achievements than Kennedy because of
   a. JFK's unpopular positions on civil rights.
   b. Johnson's ability to speak plainly to the American public.
   c. the Republicans' greater willingness to work with Johnson.
   d. the Democrats' landslide victory in 1964, which gave them control of Congress.
6. The Civil Rights Act of 1964 was crafted to secure
   a. an end to segregation in public schools.
   b. voting safeguards for African Americans.
   c. an end to discrimination.
   d. more black representation in Congress.
7. The antiwar candidates that forced LBJ out of the race in 1968 were
   a. Richard Nixon and Ronald Reagan.
   b. Hubert Humphrey and John Lindsay.
   c. Robert Kennedy and Eugene McCarthy.
   d. George Wallace and Curtis LeMay.
8. Opposition to Nixon's policy decisions in Vietnam in 1970 began with
   a. the continued U.S. bombing of Haiphong Harbor.
   b. Nixon's sending bombers and troops into Cambodia.
   c. Nixon's policy of Vietnamization.
   d. the president's decision to go to Beijing and Moscow.

Answers

1. c	3. a	5. d	7. c
2. a	4. c	6. c	8. b

PRIMARY SOURCE DOCUMENTS

The accounts of actual participants are useful for understanding the motives and thoughts of historical characters.

1. *Farewell Address (1961)* Dwight D. Eisenhower

The leader of the Allied forces in Europe during World War II and Republican president of the United States during eight bitter years of Cold War, Dwight D. Eisenhower surprised many people with his farewell address to the nation. The combination of the defense needs imposed on the United States by the Cold War and remarkable advances in technology was giving excessive power and influence to the military and its allies in the armaments industry. Though an unusual messenger for this warning, Eisenhower, as a Republican and military leader, certainly knew the operation of the system he described. Eisenhower delivered this televised speech from the Oval Office on January 17, 1961.

Questions to Consider

- Has any part of Eisenhower's warning come true?
- What preventative steps did Eisenhower recommend?

Three days from now, after half a century in the service of our country, I shall lay down the responsibilities of office as, in traditional and solemn ceremony, the authority of the Presidency is vested in my successor.

This evening I come to you with a message of leave-taking and farewell, and to share a few final thoughts with you, my countrymen....

Our people expect their President and the Congress to find essential agreement on issues of great moment, the wise resolution of which will better shape the future of the Nation.

My own relations with the Congress, which began on a remote and tenuous basis when, long ago, a member of the Senate appointed me to West Point, have since ranged to the intimate during the war and immediate post-war period, and, finally, to the mutually interdependent during these past eight years.

In this final relationship, the Congress and the Administration have, on most vital issues, cooperated well, to serve the national good rather than mere partisanship, and so have assured that the business of the Nation should go forward. So, my official relationship with the Congress ends in a feeling, on my part, of gratitude that we have been able to do so much together.

We now stand ten years past the midpoint of a century that has witnessed four major wars among great nations. Three of these involved our own country. Despite these holocausts America is today the strongest, the most influential and most productive nation in the world. Understandably proud of this pre-eminence, we yet realize that America's leadership and prestige depend, not merely upon our unmatched material progress, riches and military strength, but on how we use our power in the interests of world peace and human betterment.

Throughout America's adventure in free government, our basic purposes have been to keep the peace; to foster progress in human achievement; and to enhance liberty, dignity and integrity among people and among nations. To strive for less would be unworthy of a free and religious people. Any failure traceable to arrogance, or our lack of comprehension or readiness to sacrifice would inflict upon us grievous hurt both at home and abroad.

Progress toward these noble goals is persistently threatened by the conflict now engulfing the world. It commands our whole attention, absorbs our very beings. We face a hostile ideology—global in scope, atheistic in character, ruthless in purpose, and insidious in method. Unhappily the danger it poses promises to be of indefinite duration. To meet it successfully, there is called for, not so much the emotional and transitory sacrifices of crisis, but rather those which enable us to carry forward steadily, surely, and without complaint the burdens of a prolonged and complex struggle—with liberty the stake. Only thus shall we remain, despite every provocation, on our charted course toward permanent peace and human betterment.

Crises there will continue to be. In meeting them, whether foreign or domestic, great or small, there is a recurring temptation to feel that some spectacular and costly action could become the miraculous solution to all current difficulties. A huge increase in newer elements of our defense; development of unrealistic programs to cure every ill in agriculture; a dramatic expansion in basic and applied research—these and many other possibilities, each possibly promising in itself, may be suggested as the only way to the road we wish to travel.

But each proposal must be weighed in the light of a broader consideration: the need to maintain balance in and among national programs.... Good judgment seeks balance and progress; lack of it eventually finds imbalance and frustration.

The record of many decades stands as proof that our people and their government have, in the main, understood these truths and have responded to them well, in the face of stress and threat. But threats, new in kind or degree, constantly arise. I mention two only.

A vital element in keeping the peace is our military establishment. Our arms must be mighty, ready for instant action, so that no potential aggressor may be tempted to risk his own destruction.

Our military organization today bears little relation to that known by any of my predecessors in peacetime, or indeed by the fighting men of World War II or Korea.

Until the latest of our world conflicts, the United States had no armaments industry. American makers of plowshares could, with time and as required, make swords as well. But now we can no longer risk emergency improvisation of national defense; we have been compelled to create a permanent armaments industry of vast proportions. Added to this, three and a half million men and women are directly engaged in the defense establishment. We annually spend on military security more than the net income of all United States corporations.

This conjunction of an immense military establishment and a large arms industry is new in the American experience. The total influence—economic, political, even spiritual—is felt in every city, every State house, every office of the Federal government. We recognize the imperative need for this development. Yet we must not fail to comprehend its grave implications. Our toil, resources and livelihood are all involved; so is the very structure of our society.

In the councils of government, we must guard against the acquisition of unwarranted influence, whether sought or unsought, by the military-industrial complex. The potential for the disastrous rise of misplaced power exists and will persist.

We must never let the weight of this combination endanger our liberties or democratic processes. We should take nothing for granted. Only an alert and knowledgeable citizenry can compel the proper meshing of the huge industrial and military machinery of defense with our peaceful methods and goals, so that security and liberty may prosper together.

Akin to, and largely responsible for the sweeping changes in our industrial-military posture, has been the technological revolution during recent decades.

In this revolution, research has become central; it also becomes more formalized, complex, and costly. A steadily increasing share is conducted for, by, or at the direction of, the Federal government.

Today, the solitary inventor, tinkering in his shop, has been overshadowed by task forces of scientists in laboratories and testing fields. In the same fashion, the free university, historically the fountainhead of free ideas and scientific discovery, has experienced a revolution in the conduct of research. Partly because of the huge costs involved, a government contract becomes virtually a substitute for intellectual curiosity. For every old blackboard there are now hundreds of new electronic computers.

The prospect of domination of the nation's scholars by Federal employment, project allocations, and the power of money is ever present—and is gravely to be regarded.

Yet, in holding scientific research and discovery in respect, as we should, we must also be alert to the equal and opposite danger that public policy could itself become the captive of a scientific-technological elite.

It is the task of statesmanship to mold, to balance, and to integrate these and other forces, new and old, within the principles of our democratic system—ever aiming toward the supreme goals of our free society.

Another factor in maintaining balance involves the element of time. As we peer into society's future, we—you and I, and our government—must avoid the impulse to live only for today, plundering, for our own ease and convenience, the precious resources of tomorrow. We cannot mortgage the material assets of our grandchildren without risking the loss also of their political and spiritual heritage. We want democracy to survive for all generations to come, not to become the insolvent phantom of tomorrow.

Down the long lane of the history yet to be written America knows that this world of ours, ever growing smaller, must avoid becoming a community of dreadful fear and hate, and be, instead, a proud confederation of mutual trust and respect.

Such a confederation must be one of equals. The weakest must come to the conference table with the same confidence as do we, protected as we are by our moral, economic, and military strength. That table, though scarred by many past frustrations, cannot be abandoned for the certain agony of the battlefield.

Disarmament, with mutual honor and confidence, is a continuing imperative. Together we must learn how to compose differences, not with arms, but with intellect and decent purpose. Because this need is so sharp and apparent I confess that I lay down my official responsibilities in this field with a definite sense of disappointment. As one who has witnessed the horror and the lingering sadness of war—as one who knows that another war could utterly destroy this civilization which has been so slowly and painfully built over thousands of years—I wish I could say tonight that a lasting peace is in sight.

Happily, I can say that war has been avoided. Steady progress toward our ultimate goal has been made. But, so much remains to be done....

To all the peoples of the world, I once more give expression to America's prayerful and continuing aspiration:

We pray that peoples of all faiths, all races, all nations, may have their great human needs satisfied; that those now denied opportunity shall come to enjoy it to the full; that all who yearn for freedom may experience its spiritual blessings; that those who have freedom will understand also, its heavy responsibilities; that all who are insensitive to the needs of others will learn charity; that the scourges of poverty, disease and ignorance will be made to disappear from the earth, and that, in the goodness of time, all peoples will come to live together in a peace guaranteed by the binding force of mutual respect and love.

SOURCE: Public Papers of the Presidents of the United States: Dwight D. Eisenhower, 1960–1961 (Washington, D.C., 1962), pp. 1035–1040.

2.   *Inaugural Address (1961)* **John F. Kennedy**

John F. Kennedy was the youngest man ever elected to the presidency. For many Americans, Kennedy's narrow victory symbolized the dawning of a new era in the history of the United States. Kennedy spoke to that image in his inaugural address, stating that "a new generation" had taken responsibility for America's future. Kennedy's speech promised hope for the world, backed by the awesome power of the United States. Both the hope and power would seem meaningless within a few short years.

Questions to Consider

- What does Kennedy mean by insisting that people should "ask what you can do for your country"?

- Is this speech an idealistic call for peace or another example of Cold War militarism?

Mr. Chief Justice, President Eisenhower, Vice President Nixon, President Truman, reverend clergy, fellow citizens, we observe today not a victory of party, but a celebration of freedom—symbolizing an end, as well as a beginning—signifying renewal, as well as change. For I have sworn before you and Almighty God the same solemn oath our forebears prescribed nearly a century and three quarters ago.

The world is very different now. For man holds in his mortal hands the power to abolish all forms of human poverty and all forms of human life. And yet the same revolutionary beliefs for which our forebears fought are still at issue around the globe—the belief that the rights of man come not from the generosity of the state, but from the hand of God.

We dare not forget today that we are the heirs of that first revolution. Let the word go forth from this time and place, to friend and foe alike, that the torch has been passed to a new generation of Americans—born in this century, tempered by war, disciplined by a hard and bitter peace, proud of our ancient heritage—and unwilling to witness or permit the slow undoing of those human rights to which this Nation has always been committed, and to which we are committed today at home and around the world.

Let every nation know, whether it wishes us well or ill, that we shall pay any price, bear any burden, meet any hardship, support any friend, oppose any foe, in order to assure the survival and the success of liberty.

This much we pledge—and more.

To those old allies whose cultural and spiritual origins we share, we pledge the loyalty of faithful friends. United, there is little we cannot do in a host of cooperative ventures. Divided, there is little we can do—for we dare not meet a powerful challenge at odds and split asunder.

To those new States whom we welcome to the ranks of the free, we pledge our words that one form of colonial control shall not have passed away merely to be replaced by a far greater iron tyranny. We shall not always expect to find them supporting our view. But we shall always hope to find them strongly supporting their own freedom—and to remember that, in the past, those who foolishly sought power by riding the back of the tiger ended up inside.

To those peoples in the huts and villages across the globe struggling to break the bonds of mass misery, we pledge our best efforts to help them help themselves, for whatever period is required—not because the Communists may be doing it, not because we seek their votes, but because it is right. If a free society cannot help the many who are poor, it cannot save the few who are rich.

To our sister republics south of our border, we offer a special pledge—to convert our good words into good deeds, in a new alliance for progress, to assist free men and free governments in casting off the chains of poverty. But this peaceful revolution of hope cannot become the prey of hostile powers. Let all our neighbors know that we shall join with them to oppose aggression or subversion anywhere in the Americas. And let every other power know that this hemisphere intends to remain the master of its own house.

To that world assembly of sovereign states, the United Nations, our last best hope in an age where the instruments of war have far outpaced the instruments of peace, we renew our pledge of support—to prevent it from becoming merely a forum for invective—to strengthen its shield of the new and the weak—and to enlarge the area in which its writ may run.

Finally, to those nations who would make themselves our adversary, we offer not a pledge but a request: that both sides begin anew the quest for peace, before the dark powers of destruction unleashed by science engulf all humanity in planned or accidental self-destruction.

We dare not tempt them with weakness. For only when our arms are sufficient beyond doubt can we be certain beyond doubt that they will never be employed.

But neither can two great and powerful groups of nations take comfort from our present course—both sides overburdened by the cost of modern weapons, both rightly alarmed by the steady spread of the deadly atom, yet both racing to alter that uncertain balance of terror that stays the hand of mankind's final war.

So let us begin anew—remembering on both sides that civility is not a sign of weakness, and sincerity is always subject to proof. *Let us never negotiate out of fear. But let us never fear to negotiate.*

Let both sides explore what problems unite us instead of laboring those problems which divide us.

Let both sides, for the first time, formulate serious and precise proposals for the inspection and control of arms—and bring the absolute power to destroy other nations under the absolute control of all nations.

Let both sides seek to invoke the wonders of science instead of its terrors. Together let us explore the stars, conquer the deserts, eradicate disease, tap the ocean depths, and encourage the arts and commerce.

Let both sides unite to heed in all corners of the earth the command of Isaiah—to "undo the heavy burdens and to let the oppressed go free."

And if a beachhead of cooperation may push back the jungle of suspicion, let both sides join in creating a new endeavor, not a new balance of power, but a new world of law, where the strong are just and the weak secure and the peace preserved.

All this will not be finished in the first 100 days. Nor will it be finished in the first 1,000 days, nor in the life of this administration, nor even perhaps in our lifetime on this planet. But let us begin.

In your hands, my fellow citizens, more than in mine, will rest the final success or failure of our course. Since this country was founded, each generation of Americans has been summoned to give testimony to its national loyalty. The graves of young Americans who answered the call to service are found around the globe.

Now the trumpet summons us again—not as a call to bear arms, though arms we need; not as a call to battle, though embattled we are; but a call to bear the burden of a long twilight struggle, year in, and year out, "rejoicing in hope, patient in tribulation"—a struggle against the common enemies of man: tyranny, poverty, disease, and war itself.

Can we forge against these enemies a grand and global alliance, North and South, East and West, that can assure a more fruitful life for all mankind? Will you join in that historic effort?

In the long history of the world, only a few generations have been granted the role of defending freedom in its hour of maximum danger. I do not shrink from this responsibility— I welcome it. I do not believe that any of us would exchange places with any other people or any other generation. The energy, the faith, the devotion which we bring to this endeavor will light our country and all who serve it—and the glow from that fire can truly light the world.

And so, my fellow Americans, ask not what your country can do for you: Ask what you can do for your country.

My fellow citizens of the world: Ask not what America will do for you, but what together we can do for the freedom of man.

Finally, whether you are citizens of America or citizens of the world, ask of us the same high standards of strength and sacrifice which we ask of you. With a good conscience our only sure reward, with history the final judge of our deeds, let us go forth to lead the land we love, asking His blessing and His help, but knowing that here on earth God's work must truly be our own.

SOURCE: Inaugural Addresses of the Presidents of the United States (Washington, D.C., 1961), pp. 267–270.

3.   *The Watts Riots (1965)* **The California Governor's Commission On The Los Angeles Riots**

On August 12, 1965, the complacency of white Americans was shattered by a violent outburst of frustration and anger in Los Angeles. Many whites thought that the recent successes in the Civil Rights Movement, exemplified by the passage of the Civil Rights Act, would lead to a lessening of racial animosity. Most leaders were therefore completely unprepared for the riots that broke out, not in the South, but in the West, in liberal California. What had been largely ignored was the long simmering anger of urban African Americans over their poverty, mistreatment by largely white police forces, and confinement to ghettos. In August 12, 1965, amidst repeated tales of police brutality, some of them accurate, a crowd began stoning police cars and passing whites. There followed six days of burning, looting, and shooting, culminating in thirty-four deaths, more than a thousand injuries, the destruction of hundreds of buildings, and nearly four thousand arrests. The following account is drawn from the records of the Los Angeles police and was compiled by the California Governor's Commission on the Los Angeles Riots, chaired by John McCone. Though the Commission felt that a small number of criminals bore responsibility for the riots, they estimated that at least seven thousand people took part in the uprising.

Questions to Consider

   •   Why would angry crowds destroy property in their own communities?

   •   Was the police response appropriate? What could officials have done to avoid the riot?

August 12, 1965

By 12:20 A.M. approximately 50 to 75 youths were on either side of Avalon Blvd. at Imperial Highway, throwing missiles at passing cars and the police used vehicles with red lights and sirens within the riot area perimeter in an effort to disperse the crowd. As they did so, the rock throwing crowd dispersed, only to return as the police left the scene. Some of the older citizens in the area were inquiring, "What are those crazy kids doing?" A number of adult Negroes expressed the opinion that the police should open fire on the rock throwers to stop their activity. The police did not discharge firearms at rioters.

It was estimated that by 12:30 A.M. 70% of the rioters were children and the remainder were young adults and adults. Their major activity was throwing missiles at passing vehicles driven by Caucasians. One rioter stationed himself a block from the intersection of Avalon Blvd. and Imperial Highway, where the major group of rioters was centered, and signaled to this group whenever a vehicle driven by a Caucasian approached the intersection, so that it could be stoned.

Supervisor Kenneth Hahn and his assistant, Mr. Pennington, drove to the riot scene at about 12:35 A.M. and did not observe road blocks or policemen in the area.

Rioters continued to attack vehicles in the vicinity of Imperial Highway and Avalon Blvd. Some spectators described the crowd as having the appearance of a carnival, with persons acting with abandon and some spectators apparently enjoying the activity as if it were a sporting event.

A dozen vehicles were attacked by about 150 rioters, among them the vehicle of Supervisor Hahn and his assistant, whose automobile was struck by bricks and rocks thrown from the crowd near San Pedro St. and Avalon Blvd. The windshield and one window of his car were broken. Glass cut Mr. Hahn's head.

By 1:00 A.M. the rioters appeared to gather into about four groups of 50 to 100 persons each.

Supervisor Hahn made contact with Sheriff's deputies in the field, utilized a citizen's telephone to communicate with the watch commander at Firestone Station and then rode to that station with Sheriff's deputies. Supervisor Hahn urged action by the LAPD and the Sheriff's Department to prepare for additional trouble which might develop, based upon his view of the rioters....

Two cars were set afire by rioters at the intersection of San Pedro Street and Imperial Highway and at 2:00 A.M. the first looted market was observed at 116th St. and Avalon Boulevard....

Several staff members of the Los Angeles County Human Relations Commission went to the disturbed area around midnight of August 11–12. They spoke with persons in the crowd, with youths who were throwing rocks and with police officers. They attempted to get the youth to leave the streets and allow tensions to subside but were unsuccessful. Some of the staff state they observed the uniformed police officers and police cruisers at the police command post were the targets of the crowd. They state they suggested to a police command officer on the scene that the removal of police and police vehicles from the area for the purpose of eliminating the objects of attack would be advisable. They state their suggestions also included that the streets by blocked to prevent through traffic from entering the affected area, but that their suggestions were not immediately accepted. They did notice that the police moved the command post a short time later, although traffic was allowed to continue to move through the affected area and the crowd stoned passing cars. It was noted that only cars driven by Caucasian drivers were victims of the rock throwing....

August 13, 1965

State Assemblyman Mervyn Dymally of Los Angeles, accompanied by Robert Hall, co-chairman of the Non-violent Action Committee, went to the vicinity of Imperial Highway and Avalon Blvd. shortly after midnight on the morning of August 13th for the purpose of assisting in getting people to leave the streets and return to their homes. A group of youths were burning an information center, automobiles were being halted, overturned and burned, two liquor stores were looted, then a doctor's office and a hot-dog stand. Other fires were also started by the rioters and Assemblyman Dymally's requests to the rioters were, to a large measure, ignored....

The fire department attempted to respond to a rubbish fire at Imperial and Central at 12:19 A.M. but its equipment was turned back because rioters would not let firemen proceed and were throwing rocks and bottles at the vehicles. One fireman was hit on the head by a rock thrown by a rioter....

At 1:28 A.M. a church was reported on fire at Imperial Highway and Central Ave. and the fire department dispatched equipment....

At 1:57 A.M. the Los Angeles Sheriff's deputies on perimeter control refused entry into the riot area to fire department units for the safety of the firemen....

At 2:16 A.M. a group of rioters proceeding north on Central Ave., on 120th Street overturned and burned automobiles in the street....

August 14, 1965

...Moneycre Whitmore was shot and killed by police officers at 59th St. and Vermont Ave. while he was allegedly looting (the Coroner's inquest ruled this was a justifiable homicide).

At 12:45 A.M. the National Guard relieved LAPD in the Watts area....

Looters proceeded as far north as 18th St. on Broadway, Avalon Blvd., Main St. and Central Avenue, looting and burning as they proceeded northward from the areas previously struck by the rioters. Arrests in large numbers were being made by the police.

At 12:55 A.M. two suspects drove an automobile at a high speed into a National Guard skirmish line at Avalon Blvd. and Santa Barbara Ave. The vehicle struck and injured a National Guardsman. General Hill was present and observed the incident. He states the action by the driver was an obvious attempt to run down more than one of the Guardsmen, and one was seriously hurt. At that time the National Guardsmen had also been fired on by rioters in other places. Up to this point they were supplied with rifle ammunition but had been ordered not to place the ammunition in their rifles. On witnessing the incident at Avalon Blvd. and Santa Barbara Ave., General Hill personally issued the order that all National Guardsmen were to load their rifles with live ammunition. Bayonets were affixed to rifles....

SOURCE: Governor's Commission on the Los Angeles Riots, *Transcripts, Depositions, Consultants' Reports, and Selected Documents*, Vol. 2, *Chronology* (Sacramento, Ca., 1966), pp. 28–32, 83–86, 168–169.

UNIT 25

Contemporary History

UNIT SUMMARY

In Unit 25 we look at events of the past twenty-five years and the greater meaning of history in the lives of Americans.

ASSIGNMENT

1. Before viewing Program 25, read this unit, and in *A People and a Nation* read Chapter 31 (pages 902–915), Chapter 32, and Chapter 33.

2. View Program 25, "Contemporary History."

3. Visit the Web site <http://www.learner.org/biographyofamerica>. Explore the exercises for Program 25.

LEARNING OBJECTIVES

Upon completing this unit, students should be able to:

1. Analyze the reasons for the declining economy in the 1970s and how the crisis of stagflation forced Americans to reexamine their way of life.

2. Discuss the Iranian hostage crisis and its consequences for the Carter presidency.

3. Evaluate "Reaganomics" and its consequences.

4. Describe Reagan's resurrection of old Cold War theories and the United States' involvement in civil wars in Central America.

5. Assess the Iran-contra affair and its effect on Ronald Reagan's place in history.

6. Discuss the challenges historians face interpreting historical events objectively.

PROGRAM GUIDE

In this program, the entire team of historians considers the meaning of the last quarter of the twentieth century. What is the historian's task? Why is it important to provide events with a historical perspective? Television critic John Leonard adds his insights on TV's impact on the way the public experiences history in the making.

The study of history is essential to our understanding of who we are as a people and what our options are for the future. History is constantly being revised. For many, the past twenty-five years are a blur, but the historian's task is to make sense of those years. The political process has marginalized many Americans in the past twenty-five years, a dangerous thing for a democracy. Many people look to our government for solutions to problems, but Americans disagree about what the role of government should be in their lives. Television lures the public into a world of consumerism, with distorted images and the trends of the day. How will people cope with the pace of change in the twenty-first century? History will have more to say about the past few decades in the years to come. Historians will continue to search for meaning in our lives.

HISTORICAL OVERVIEW

While the nation celebrated America's bicentennial, memories of Watergate figured prominently in the November 1976 presidential election. Jimmy Carter took office at a time when Americans were increasingly disillusioned about democracy and the political process. A low voter turnout continued through the eighties and nineties. Ronald Reagan's eight-year presidency promised a revolution in government, but it ended with the largest debt in the nation's history, a mammoth debacle in the savings and loans industry, and the Iran-Contra scandal. His successor, George Bush, led the nation in popular crusades against one-time allies in Panama and Iraq, but the nation chose not to reelect him in 1992. Bill Clinton presided over an era of unparalleled prosperity, but the legacy of that economic boom is far from clear. Today the nation has entered a new century, perhaps more prosperous, but unsure about the future and somewhat oblivious to the past. How do we make sense of these recent events and the larger meaning of the twentieth century?

Jimmy Carter promised that he would never lie to us, but telling the truth did not get him reelected in 1980. During that election year campaign, Ronald Reagan asked Americans one question: were they better off in 1980 than they were in 1976? Carter had tried to wean the nation from its over-dependence on foreign oil, to protect the environment, and to bring fiscal responsibility to Washington, but stagflation, skyrocketing interest rates, and the Iranian hostage crisis allowed Reagan to exploit national anxieties. Throughout the campaign, Reagan promised a "New Morning in America." Reagan would "make America great again." His solution to the problems plaguing the nation was to build up national defense and return to a laissez-faire economy. Slogans and appeals to patriotism dominated the Reagan rhetoric, and despite Carter's efforts to rally the public around a comprehensive energy program and a human rights policy abroad, the faltering economy and the Iranian crisis ended his presidency.

President Reagan heightened the public's contempt for government in his Inaugural Address with his announcement that government was not the solution to the nation's problems but was itself the problem. The Reagan administration moved quickly to implement its program of supply-side economics and a massive military buildup. Congress and the public supported the massive tax cuts, the borrowing, the rising debt, and the military's expansion. The Reagan Revolution swept across the nation as a new conservative program promised prosperity. It was not painless: the worst recession since the Depression ensued in 1981–82. But despite growing unemployment and income equality, the economy began to recover in 1984 (the Pentagon budget created a robust job market), just in time for Reagan to be reelected. Poverty and homelessness emerged as serious problems with the Reagan spending cuts, but some Americans grew less compassionate for people Reagan had identified as lazy welfare cheats.

A Cold War chill returned to international affairs during the Reagan years. The Iranian crisis, Soviet intervention in Afghanistan, and revolutions in Central America inspired the military buildup. The president's "evil empire" scenario—in which the Soviet Union was a malevolent force, willing to commit any crime to achieve a communist world—justified the huge expenditure of national resources to assist "freedom fighters," or anticommunist movements, around the globe. America returned to a fifties policy of brinkmanship with an unprecedented escalation in the arms race.

Reagan's Strategic Defense Initiative, or "Star Wars," as his critics lampooned it, promised to intercept Soviet missiles before they reached U.S. airspace. For several years, diplomatic initiatives with the Soviets collapsed (although, in 1987, the United States and the Soviets signed an arms control treaty). Meanwhile, the administration supported Iraq's Saddam Hussein in his war against Soviet-backed Iran and funded insurgent "freedom fighters" in Afghanistan. The administration also faced its worst scandal in the realm of foreign affairs: Iran-Contra. When Congress outlawed further assistance to the contras, rebels attempting to overthrow the Nicaraguan government, Reagan authorized the secret sale of weapons to Iran. Money from the sale, which the administration initially disavowed, was illegally diverted to the Nicaraguan rebels. The scandal, which Reagan denied knowing anything about, led to cries of impeachment.

Although the Reagan presidency survived a stock market collapse and the Savings and Loan debacle in October 1987, the cost to the American taxpayer for the massive military spending and the S & L crisis was several trillions of dollars. In 1988 George Bush, Reagan's vice president, defeated the Democratic challenger Michael Dukakis. But President Bush was unable to keep a campaign promise not to raise taxes in the wake of massive deficits, and although his popularity rose during the Gulf War, Americans elected a new leader to navigate the stormy economic times inherited from the Reagan Revolution.

Bill Clinton, born in 1946, was the first baby boomer president. Opponents committed themselves to destroying his presidency long before Clinton took office. The president demonstrated a remarkable resilience, however, and outlasted his detractors. While Clinton suffered the indignity of possible impeachment, the American public was less concerned about his indiscretions and more concerned about the economy, currently enjoying the longest expansion in American history. What will the future say about the Clinton administration's monetary, trade, and economic legacies? *Globalization* has been the buzzword of the Clinton years, years that saw the North America Free Trade Agreement (NAFTA) and the World Trade Organization send jobs overseas, years in which the carrot of "most favored nation" status was dangled before the Chinese, years when the experiment with laissez-faire capitalism in Russsia advanced but failed to bring democratic change. At home, economic consolidation progressed at an unparalleled pace, despite the past history of anti-trust legislation designed to regulate predatory capitalism. Indeed, the history of the Clinton administration remains to be written.

One task of the historian is to interpret and provide perspective. History is constantly in need of revision. Certainly the struggle for independence and the Civil War were defining events in American history. How we interpret those events is significant. Our biases, our education, and the crucible of the times in which we came of age influence each historian's interpretations. Interpretations of events therefore vary and sometimes clash. But analyses help students sort through the vicissitudes of the past and form opinions based upon a range of perspectives. We all share in the hope that students will find the study of history compelling.

MAP EXERCISE

Refer to the following maps and figures in Chapters 31 and 32 of *A People and a Nation* to answer the questions listed below.

- The United States in the Caribbean and Central America (p. 909)

- The Continued Shift to the Sunbelt in the 1970s and 1980s (p. 927)

- While the Rich Got Richer in the 1980s, the Poor Got Poorer (p. 937)

1. The United States has intervened many times in the Caribbean and Central America. Where has the nation intervened militarily in last fifty years and why?

2.   The nation's population has shifted west over the past fifty years. This sunbelt phenomenon has had its greatest impact on which states? Where has the negative shift in population occurred and why?

3.   The income gap between rich and poor Americans has grown wider in these economic boom times. What accounts for the gap? What does it mean for the nation?

PEOPLE, EVENTS, AND CONCEPTS

Identify and explain the historical significance of each item.

Bill Gates

Identification

Significance

Age of Greenspan

Identification

Significance

George Bush

Identification

Significance

Newt Gingrich

Identification

Significance

third world cities

Identification

Significance

communications revolution

Identification

Significance

Bill Clinton

Identification

Significance

Internet

Identification

Significance

Michael Eisner

Identification

Significance

Camp David

Identification

Significance

historical record

Identification

Significance

oral histories

Identification

Significance

Nicaragua

Identification

Significance

New Federalism

Identification

Significance

Ronald Reagan

Identification

Significance

Afghanistan

Identification

Significance

voodoo economics

Identification

Significance

Saddam Hussein

Identification

Significance

Iraq and Iran

Identification

Significance

ESSAY QUESTIONS

1. Jimmy Carter attempted to bring honesty and decency to the office of the president and was initially very popular. However, his approval rating fell below Nixon's, and not because he was deceitful or abused his power. How do you explain his declining popularity? To what extent did events, foreign and domestic, spin out of his control?

2. Why did Ronald Reagan return the United States to a Cold War posture in foreign affairs after the efforts of another Republican, Richard Nixon, to thaw relations between old enemies? Was Reagan a success in diplomatic affairs?

3. The United States has been involved in various conflicts around the globe since the end of the Cold War. Discuss why the United States took action in the following areas and American success in meeting the stated objectives in Panama, the Persian Gulf, and Yugoslavia.

4. What will be the legacy of Clinton's presidency? Do you think President Clinton's image will survive the scandals of his administration? Explain.

MULTIPLE-CHOICE QUESTIONS

1. The economic decline of the seventies can be explained in terms of
   a. declining productivity and inflation.
   b. deregulation.
   c. spiraling wage increases.
   d. protectionism.
2. The first woman nominated to run for the vice presidency was
   a. Phyllis Schlafly.
   b. Geraldine Ferraro.
   c. Sally Ride.
   d. Sandra Day O'Connor.

3. President Carter's political demise resulted from the foreign policy crisis over
   a. revolutions in El Salvador and Nicaragua.
   b. transfer of the Panama Canal to the Panamanians.
   c. the Olympic boycott by the Soviets.
   d. the seizure of Americans by Iranian students.
4. The Reagan Revolution could claim a new constituency of activists among
   a. conservatives.
   b. fundamentalist Christians.
   c. voters from the sunbelt states.
   d. "new democrats."
5. A woman's right to choose is protected by the Supreme Court's decision on
   a. Miranda v. Arizona.
   b. Roe v. Wade.
   c. Engle v. Vitale.
   d. Plessy v. Ferguson.
6. Ronald Reagan promised to shrink the size of government by
   a. cutting health care and Social Security benefits.
   b. trimming the Pentagon's budget.
   c. reducing the federal budget and cutting taxes.
   d. ending all entitlement programs.
7. The end of the Cold War came symbolically with the
   a. pro-democracy movement in Red China.
   b. fall of the Berlin Wall.
   c. Gulf War.
   d. Camp David Accords.
8. President Clinton's administration has been successful at home in the realm of
   a. gay rights in the military.
   b. campaign finance reform.
   c. improved race relations.
   d. deficit reduction measures.

Answers

| 1. a | 3. d | 5. b | 7. b |
| 2. b | 4. b | 6. c | 8. d |

PRIMARY SOURCE DOCUMENTS

The accounts of actual participants are useful for understanding the motives and thoughts of historical characters.

1. *The Strategic Defense Initiative (1983)* Ronald Reagan

In the following speech of March 23, 1983, President Ronald Reagan stunned the nation by proposing that the United States could prevent war by building space weapons capable of shooting down hostile missiles. That such technology did not yet exist did not bother a president famous for his complete confidence in American ingenuity. Reagan's science advisors assured him that with the proper financial support the arms industry could certainly create a foolproof system capable of targeting and destroying enemy missiles in midflight. The White House labeled this program the Strategic Defense Initiative, or S.D.I. The public quickly renamed it "Star Wars," after a popular series of movies. Congress appropriated the billions of dollars required to begin production, continuing to fund the program over the next twelve years despite doubts of its utility.

Questions to Consider

- Why does Reagan feel that current defense systems are inadequate?

- Wouldn't other nations, such as the Soviet Union, perceive S.D.I. as a threat to their security?

―――――――――――

The subject I want to discuss with you, peace and national security, is both timely and important. Timely, because I've reached a decision which offers a new hope for our children in the 21st century, a decision I'll tell you about in a few minutes. And important because there's a very big decision that you must make for yourselves. This subject involves the most basic duty that any President and any people share, the duty to protect and strengthen the peace....

The defense policy of the United States is based on a simple premise: The United States does not start fights. We will never be an aggressor. We maintain our strength in order to deter and defend against aggression—to preserve freedom and peace.

Since the dawn of the atomic age, we've sought to reduce the risk of war by maintaining a strong deterrent and by seeking genuine arms control. "Deterrence" means simply this: making sure any adversary who thinks about attacking the United States, or our allies, or our vital interests, concludes that the risks to him outweigh any potential gains. Once he

understands that, he won't attack. We maintain the peace through our strength; weakness only invites aggression.

This strategy of deterrence has not changed. It still works. But what it takes to maintain deterrence has changed. It took one kind of military force to deter an attack when we had far more nuclear weapons than any other power; it takes another kind now that the Soviets, for example, have enough accurate and powerful nuclear weapons to destroy virtually all of our missiles on the ground. Now, this is not to say that the Soviet Union is planning to make war on us. Nor do I believe a war is inevitable—quite the contrary. But what must be recognized is that our security is based on being prepared to meet all threats....

For 20 years the Soviet Union has been accumulating enormous military might. They didn't stop when their forces exceeded all requirements of a legitimate defensive capability. And they haven't stopped now. During the past decade and a half, the Soviets have built up a massive arsenal of new strategic nuclear weapons—weapons that can strike directly at the United States....

There was a time when we were able to offset superior Soviet numbers with higher quality, but today they are building weapons as sophisticated and modern as our own....

Every item in our defense program—our ships, our tanks, our planes, our funds for training and spare parts—is intended for one all-important purpose: to keep the peace. Unfortunately, a decade of neglecting our military forces had called into question our ability to do that.

When I took office in January 1981, I was appalled by what I found: American planes that couldn't fly and American ships that couldn't sail for lack of spare parts and trained personnel and insufficient fuel and ammunition for essential training....

...I've become more and more deeply convinced that the human spirit must be capable of rising above dealing with other nations and human beings by threatening their existence.

Feeling this way, I believe we must thoroughly examine every opportunity for reducing tensions and for introducing greater stability into the strategic calculus on both sides….

…Let me share with you a vision of the future which offers hope. It is that we embark on a program to counter the awesome Soviet missile threat with measures that are defensive. Let us turn to the very strengths in technology that spawned our great industrial base and that have given us the quality of life we enjoy today….

I know this is a formidable, technical task, one that may not be accomplished before the end of this century. Yet, current technology has attained a level of sophistication where it's reasonable for us to begin this effort. It will take years, probably decades of effort on many fronts. There will be failures and setbacks, just as there will be successes and breakthroughs. And as we proceed, we must remain constant in preserving the nuclear deterrent and maintaining a solid capability for flexible response. But isn't it worth every investment necessary to free the world from the threat of nuclear war? We know it is….

I clearly recognize that defensive systems have limitations and raise certain problems and ambiguities. If paired with offensive systems, they can be viewed as fostering an aggressive policy, and no one wants that. But with these considerations firmly in mind, I call upon the scientific community in our country, those who gave us nuclear weapons, to turn their great talents now to the cause of mankind and world peace, to give us the means of rendering these nuclear weapons impotent and obsolete.

Tonight, consistent with our obligations of the ABM treaty and recognizing the need for closer consultation with our allies, I'm taking an important first step. I am directing a comprehensive and intensive effort to define a long-term research and development program to begin to achieve our ultimate goal of eliminating the threat posed by strategic nuclear missiles…. We seek neither military superiority nor political advantage. Our only purpose— one all people share—is to search for ways to reduce the danger of nuclear war….

SOURCE: The Public Papers of the Presidents of the United States: Ronald Reagan, 1983, Book 1 (Washington, D.C., 1984), pp. 437–440, 442–443.

2. *The Gulf War (1990)* George Bush

On August 2, 1990, the Iraqi army invaded Kuwait. Iraq's dictator, Saddam Hussein, immediately announced the annexation of Kuwait. Over the next month the United States and its former Cold War opponent, the USSR, attempted to persuade Hussein to withdraw from Kuwait. The United States sent troops to Saudi Arabia within a week to protect that country from a possible Iraqi assault. On September 11, 1990, President George Bush appeared before a joint session of Congress to explain his policies on the Persian Gulf while calling for a balanced budget. On January 16, 1991, the United States and its allies launched a massive air attack on Iraq; on February 23 allied troops invaded Iraq. The ground war lasted only four days, leaving Hussein in power but no longer in possession of Kuwait.

Questions to Consider

- Why was it necessary for the United States to respond militarily to Iraq's invasion of Kuwait?

- What relationship existed between the conflict in the Persian Gulf and a balanced budget?

- Was it possible to balance the budget while increasing military expenditures?

We gather tonight, witness to events in the Persian Gulf as significant as they are tragic. In the early morning hours of August 2d, following negotiations and promises by Iraq's dictator Saddam Hussein not to use force, a powerful Iraqi army invaded its trusting and much weaker neighbor, Kuwait. Within 3 days, 120,000 Iraqi troops with 850 tanks had poured into Kuwait and moved south to threaten Saudi Arabia. It was then that I decided to act to check that aggression.

At this moment, our brave servicemen and women stand watch in that distant desert and on distant seas, side by side with the forces of more than 20 other nations. They are some of the finest men and women of the United States of America. And they're doing one terrific job....

A soldier, Private First Class Wade Merritt of Knoxville, Tennessee, now stationed in Saudi Arabia, wrote his parents of his worries, his love of family, and his hope for peace. But Wade also wrote, "I am proud of my country and its firm stance against inhumane aggression. I am proud of my army and its men. I am proud to serve my country." Well, let me just say, Wade, America is proud of you and is grateful to every soldier, sailor, marine, and airman serving the cause of peace in the Persian Gulf. I also want to thank the Chairman of the Joint Chiefs of Staff, General Powell; the Chiefs here tonight; our commander in the Persian Gulf, General Schwartzkopf; and the men and women of the Department of Defense. What a magnificent job you all are doing. And thank you very, very much from a grateful people. I wish I could say that their work is done. But we all know it's not.

So, if there ever was a time to put country before self and patriotism before party, the time is now.... So, tonight I want to talk to you about what's at stake—what we must do together to defend civilized values around the world and maintain our economic strength at home.

Our objectives in the Persian Gulf are clear, our goals defined and familiar: Iraq must withdraw from Kuwait completely, immediately, and without condition. Kuwait's legitimate government must be restored. The security and stability of the Persian Gulf must be assured. And American citizens abroad must be protected. These goals are not ours alone. They've been endorsed by the United Nations Security Council five times in as many weeks. Most countries share our concern for principle. And many have a stake in the stability of the Persian Gulf. This is not, as Saddam Hussein would have it, the United States against Iraq. It is Iraq against the world.

As you know, I've just returned from a very productive meeting with Soviet President Gorbachev. And I am pleased that we are working together to build a new relationship. In Helsinki, our joint statement affirmed to the world our shared resolve to counter Iraq's threat to peace. Let me quote: "We are united in the belief that Iraq's aggression must not be tolerated. No peaceful international order is possible if larger states can devour their smaller neighbors." Clearly, no longer can a dictator count on East-West confrontation to stymie concerted United Nations action against aggression. A new partnership of nations has begun.

We stand today at a unique and extraordinary moment. The crisis in the Persian Gulf, as grave as it is, also offers a rare opportunity to move toward an historic period of cooperation. Out of these troubled times, our fifth objective—a new world order—can emerge: a new era—freer from the threat of terror, stronger in the pursuit of justice, and more secure in the quest for peace. An era in which the nations of the world, East and West, North and South, can prosper and live in harmony. A hundred generations have searched for this elusive path to peace, while a thousand wars raged across the span of human endeavor. Today that new world is struggling to be born, a world quite different from the one we've known. A world where the rule of law supplants the rule of the jungle. A world in which nations recognize the shared responsibility for freedom and justice. A world where the strong respect the rights of the weak. This is the vision that I shared with President Gorbachev in Helsinki. He and other leaders from Europe, the Gulf, and around the world understand that how we manage this crisis today could shape the future for generations to come.

The test we face is great, and so are the stakes. This is the first assault on the new world that we seek, the first test of our mettle. Had we not responded to this first provocation with clarity of purpose, if we do not continue to demonstrate our determination, it would be a signal to actual and potential despots around the world. America and the world must defend common vital interests—and we will. America and the world must support the rule of law—and we will. America and the world must stand up to aggression—and we will. And one thing more: In the pursuit of these goals America will not be intimidated.

Vital issues of principle are at stake. Saddam Hussein is literally trying to wipe a country off the face of the Earth. We do not exaggerate. Nor do we exaggerate when we say Saddam Hussein will fail. Vital economic interests are at risk as well. Iraq itself controls some 10 percent of the world's proven oil reserves. Iraq plus Kuwait controls twice that. An Iraq permitted to swallow Kuwait would have the economic and military power, as well as the arrogance, to intimidate and coerce its neighbors—neighbors who control the lion's share of the world's remaining oil reserves. We cannot permit a resource so vital to be dominated by one so ruthless. And we won't.

Recent events have surely proven that there is no substitute for American leadership. In the face of tyranny, let no one doubt American credibility and reliability. Let no one doubt our staying power. We will stand by our friends. One way or another, the leader of Iraq must learn this fundamental truth. From the outset, acting hand in hand with others, we've sought to fashion the broadest possible international response to Iraq's aggression. The level of world cooperation and condemnation of Iraq is unprecedented. Armed forces from countries spanning four continents are there at the request of King Fahd of Saudi Arabia to deter and, if need be, to defend against attack. Moslems and non-Moslems, Arabs and non-Arabs, soldiers from many nations stand shoulder to shoulder, resolute against Saddam Hussein's ambitions.

We can now point to five United Nations Security Council resolutions that condemn Iraq's aggression. They call for Iraq's immediate and unconditional withdrawal, the restoration of Kuwait's legitimate government, and categorically reject Iraq's cynical and self-serving attempt to annex Kuwait. Finally, the United Nations has demanded the release of all foreign nationals held hostage against their will and in contravention of international law. It is a mockery of human decency to call these people "guests." They are hostages, and the whole world knows it....

We're now in sight of a United Nations that performs as envisioned by its founders. We owe much to the outstanding leadership of Secretary-General Javier Perez de Cuellar. The United Nations is backing up its words with action. The Security Council has imposed mandatory economic sanctions on Iraq, designed to force Iraq to relinquish the spoils of its illegal conquest. The Security Council has also taken the decisive step of authorizing the use of all means necessary to ensure compliance with these sanctions. Together with our friends and allies, ships of the United States Navy are today patrolling Mideast waters. They've already intercepted more than 700 ships to enforce the sanctions. Three regional leaders I spoke with just yesterday told me that these sanctions are working. Iraq is feeling the heat. We continue to hope that Iraq's leaders will recalculate just what their aggression has cost them. They are cut off from world trade, unable to sell their oil. And only a tiny fraction of goods gets through.

The communiqué with President Gorbachev made mention of what happens when the embargo is so effective that children of Iraq literally need milk or the sick truly need medicine. Then, under strict international supervision that guarantees the proper destination, then food will be permitted.

At home, the material cost of our leadership can be steep. That's why Secretary of State Baker and Treasury Secretary Brady have met with many world leaders to underscore that the burden of this collective effort must be shared. We are prepared to do our share and more to help carry that load; we insist that others do their share as well.

The response of most of our friends and allies has been good. To help defray costs, the leaders of Saudi Arabia, Kuwait, and the UAE—the United Arab Emirates—have pledged to provide our deployed troops with all the food and fuel they need. Generous assistance will also be provided to stalwart front-line nations, such as Turkey and Egypt....

There's an energy-related cost to be borne as well. Oil-producing nations are already replacing lost Iraqi and Kuwaiti output. More than half of what was lost has been made up. And we're getting superb cooperation. If producers, including the United States, continue steps to expand oil and gas production, we can stabilize prices and guarantee against hardship. Additionally, we and several of our allies always have the option to extract oil from our strategic petroleum reserves if conditions warrant. As I've pointed out before, conservation efforts are essential to keep our energy needs as low as possible. And we must then take advantage of our energy sources across the board: coal, natural gas, hydro, and nuclear. Our failure to do these things has made us more dependent on foreign oil than ever before. Finally, let no one even contemplate profiteering from this crisis. We will not have it.

I cannot predict just how long it will take to convince Iraq to withdraw from Kuwait. Sanctions will take time to have their full intended effect. We will continue to review all options with our allies, but let it be clear: we will not let this aggression stand.

Our interest, our involvement in the Gulf is not transitory. It predated Saddam Hussein's aggression and will survive it. Long after all our troops come home—and we all hope it's soon, very soon—there will be a lasting role for the United States in assisting the nations of the Persian Gulf. Our role then: to deter future aggression. Our role is to help our friends in their own self-defense. And something else: to curb the proliferation of chemical, biological, ballistic missile and, above all, nuclear technologies.

Let me also make clear that the United States has no quarrel with the Iraqi people. Our quarrel is with Iraq's dictator and with his aggression. Iraq will not be permitted to annex Kuwait. That's not a threat, that's not a boast, that's just the way it's going to be.

Our ability to function effectively as a great power abroad depends on how we conduct ourselves at home. Our economy, our Armed Forces, our energy dependence, and our cohesion all determine whether we can help our friends and stand up to our foes. For America to lead, America must remain strong and vital. Our world leadership and domestic strength are mutual and reinforcing; a woven piece, strongly bound as Old Glory. To revitalize our leadership, our leadership capacity, we must address our budget deficit—not after election day, or next year, but now.

Higher oil prices slow our growth, and higher defense costs would only make our fiscal deficit problem worse. That deficit was already greater than it should have been—a projected $232 billion for the coming year. It must—it will—be reduced.

To my friends in Congress, together we must act this very month—before the next fiscal year begins on October 1st—to get America's economic house in order. The Gulf situation helps us realize we are more economically vulnerable than we ever should be. Americans must never again enter any crisis, economic or military, with an excessive dependence on foreign oil and an excessive burden of Federal debt....

…Congress should, this month, enact a prudent multiyear defense program, one that reflects not only the improvement in East-West relations but our broader responsibilities to deal with the continuing risks of outlaw action and regional conflict. Even with our obligations in the Gulf, a sound defense budget can have some reduction in real terms; and we're prepared to accept that. But to go beyond such levels, where cutting defense would threaten our vital margin of safety, is something I will never accept. The world is still dangerous. And surely, that is now clear. Stability's not secure. American interests are far reaching. Interdependence has increased. The consequences of regional instability can be global. This is no time to risk America's capacity to protect her vital interests….

…Congress should, this month, enact a 5-year program to reduce the projected debt and deficits by $500 billion—that's by half a trillion dollars. And if, with the Congress, we can develop a satisfactory program by the end of the month, we can avoid the ax of sequester— deep across-the-board cuts that would threaten our military capacity and risk substantial domestic disruption. I want to be able to tell the American people that we have truly solved the deficit problem. And for me to do that, a budget agreement must meet these tests: It must include the measures I've recommended to increase economic growth and reduce dependence on foreign oil. It must be fair. All should contribute, but the burden should not be excessive for any one group of programs or people. It must address the growth of government's hidden liabilities. It must reform the budget process and, further, it must be real….

Once again, Americans have stepped forward to share a tearful goodbye with their families before leaving for a strange and distant shore. At this very moment, they serve together with Arabs, Europeans, Asians, and Africans in defense of principle and the dream of a new world order. That's why they sweat and toil in the sand and the heat and the sun. If they can come together under such adversity, if old adversaries like the Soviet Union and the United States can work in common cause, then surely we who are so fortunate to be in this great Chamber—Democrats, Republicans, liberals, conservatives—can come together to fulfill our responsibilities here….

SOURCE: Public Papers of the Presidents of the United States: George Bush, 1990 (Washington, D.C., 1991), 2:1218–1222.

3. *Events in Waco (1993)* **House Judiciary Committee**

In February 1993, agents of the Bureau of Alcohol, Tobacco and Firearms (BAFT) attempted to arrest David Koresh, the leader of a religious cult known as the Branch Davidians, on charges of possessing illegal weapons. The Branch Davidians opened fire, killing four of the agents and suffering six deaths themselves. Thus began a seven-week standoff between law enforcement officials and members of the cult. On April 19 the new attorney general, Janet Reno, ordered an immediate attack on the Branch Davidian compound. In the ensuing battle, the entire compound was set aflame and eighty people died, including twenty-four children. For many Americans, especially on the political right, the events in Waco became a symbol of government excess and violence. On April 23, 1993, the House Judiciary Committee began an investigation of the Waco encounter. While critical of some details of the Justice Department's handling of the Branch Davidians, the committee charged no one with a crime or even negligence.

Questions to Consider

*   Why did Attorney General Reno decide to proceed with the attack on the compound?
*   What were some of the larger issues addressed here?

•   Did the government use excessive force in effecting these arrests?

━━━━━━━━━━━━━━━━

Statement of Hon. Janet Reno, Attorney General of the United States

…This is one of the hardest decisions that anybody could ever be asked to make. We deliberated long and carefully before reaching a decision. Nothing we do now can change the suffering felt by the families of the ATF agents or the families of those who perished in the compound; but as you have pointed out so eloquently, we must do everything we can to learn from these events about what we can do in the future to prevent people like David Koresh, or people motivated by other thoughts from causing such a senseless, horrible loss of human life….

Weapons used by the Branch Davidians included .50-caliber rifles having an effective range of 3,000 yards, a distance from the Capitol to the White House….

After the [first] shootout, the remaining ATF agents established a protective perimeter around the compound…. ATF officials then requested that the FBI dispatch its Hostage Rescue Team, which we refer to as HRT.

On February 28, 1993, agents of the Federal Bureau of Investigation, including the HRT, arrived on the scene. The FBI found an armed fortress compound consisting of approximately 70 acres located on Route 7 near Waco.

I took office on March 12, 1993…. I was advised that the primary goal of the FBI's Hostage Rescue Team was to negotiate with Koresh to secure the release of the children and the surrender and prosecution of all those who participated in the murder and assault of the Federal agents without further violence or injury to anyone concerned. I concurred that we must try to negotiate to avoid further bloodshed to the extent that we could.

As this situation evolved, the FBI had consistently rejected a direct assault on the compound because of the danger of heavy casualties to the agents and to the children and because of the layout which prevented a surprise assault. I was told, as I was briefed, that the FBI had a trained negotiator on the scene and that they had, and during the course of these deliberations, continued to consult with behavioral experts and others who had knowledge of the cult to determine how best to proceed to negotiate with Koresh.

From the start, the negotiation tactics focused on restricting the activities of those inside the compound and of depriving them of a comfortable environment so as to bring the matter to a conclusion without further violence.

Those inside the compound were advised of the FBI's rules of engagement. Under those rules, the agents conveyed the information that they would not use deadly force against any person except when necessary in self-defense or defense of another, or when they had reason to believe that they or another were in danger of death or grievous bodily harm.

The FBI installed lights to illuminate the compound at night and loudspeakers to ensure they could communicate with all members of the compound at once rather than to rely solely on a single telephone line available to speak to Koresh and those he permitted to talk on the phone. They also used loudspeakers to disrupt their sleep. They cut off their electricity and they sought to restrict communications of those within the compound just to the hostage negotiators.

Additionally, they sent in letters from family members and made other good-faith efforts designed to encourage surrender by those who wished to leave the compound. In particular—and I asked about this during the course of our deliberations—they made repeated efforts to secure the release of the children.

In further efforts to encourage the negotiating process, attorneys representing Koresh and Steve Schneider were allowed to enter the compound or communicate by telephone with them on several occasions. Throughout this 51-day process, Koresh continued to assert that he and others inside would at some point surrender. However, the FBI advised that at no point did he keep his word on any of his promises.

Despite all efforts, the negotiators concluded that negotiations were at a standstill and that they had not been able to negotiate a single item with Koresh. Although 21 children and 14 adults had been allowed to leave the compound between February 28 and March 23, 1993, those persons who left the compound did so because Koresh affirmatively wanted them out as they were not fully committed to his cause; they were a drain on his efforts in internal discipline and resources; or he viewed them as potential spokespersons to the media.

During the week of April 5, the FBI advised me that they were developing a plan for the possible use of tear gas in an effort to increase the pressure on those in the compound to surrender. Thereafter, I had a series of meetings with the FBI to discuss the emerging proposal.

The threshold question I asked was whether the gas would cause permanent injury to the children. I did not even want to consider the matter further if we could not be certain about this factor. The FBI assured me that the gas would not cause permanent injury....

Then the primary question I asked again and again during the ensuing discussion was: "Why now? Why not wait?" I asked about their food and water supply and was told that it could last at least a year or more.... We explored but could not develop a feasible method for cutting off their water supply.... I became convinced that short of allowing David Koresh to go free, he was not coming out voluntarily.

Given that unacceptable result, in light of the fact that he was such a dangerous criminal, allowing the status quo to remain was not going to lead to an ultimate peaceful resolution and eliminate any risk to the safety of the innocent children in the compound, the public at large or the Government agents at the scene. On the contrary, the passage of time only increased the likelihood of incidents and possible injuries and attendant injuries and harm....

I advised the President on the Sunday before the operation of my decision to authorize the FBI's use of tear gas at the compound, and he said he would support my decision.

I believed that we were dealing with a situation that would not resolve itself by mere acquiescence to the standoff. Negotiations had proven to be fruitless; and despite our best efforts, we could not secure the release of the children.... It was my call, and I made it the best way I know how....

I think as a footnote to this, one of the things we didn't count on was that when—and I think one of the things that we will have to review and look at and understand is, why the gas didn't cause more discomfort immediately....

Mr. [John] *Conyers* [of Michigan]. ...Madam Attorney General, I am extremely disappointed in the decisions that have been made out of the Department of Justice, the Federal Bureau of Investigation, and the Bureau of Alcohol, Tobacco and Firearms.

In Philadelphia, we had a mayor that bombed people out of an eviction. In Jonestown, we lost the life of my colleague, Congressman Ryan,...because of a miscalculation about cult people. We had Patty Hearst and the Symbionese Liberation Army. We had Wounded Knee with the Indians.

Now, when in God's name is the law enforcement at the Federal level going to understand that these are very sensitive events that you cannot put barbed wire, guns, FBI, Secret Service around them, send in sound 24 hours a day and night and then wonder why they do something unstable?

The root cause of this problem was that it was considered a military operation, and it wasn't. This is a profound disgrace to law enforcement in the United States of America, and you did the right thing by offering to resign....

Now, there is no longer any reason why the Bureau of Alcohol, Tobacco and Firearms cannot be folded into the Federal Bureau of Investigation, and if there is some reason for continuing ATF, I would like to hear it today, and I will be introducing legislation to that point very, very shortly.

And now I would like you to know that there is at least one Member in the Congress that is not going to rationalize the death of two dozen children that were not cultists, they were not nuts, they were not criminals. They happened to be the children of people and they were innocently trapped in there. The decision that was jointly made by these agencies bears extreme criticism.

And it is not President Clinton's fault. He is taking your advice. He is taking Judge Sessions' advice. He is taking Mr. Higgins' advice.

...Doesn't anybody have any historical recollection in Federal law enforcement about how to deal with these kinds of people?...

Ms. Reno. I have not tried to rationalize the death of children, Congressman. I feel more strongly about it than you will ever know. But I have neither tried to rationalize the death of four ATF agents, and I will not walk away from a compound where ATF agents have been killed by people who knew they were agents and leave them unsurrounded.

...Congressman, I will not engage in recrimination. I will look to the future to try to learn everything I can from this situation to avoid tragedies such as this in the future.

Mr. Conyers. Are you concluded?

Ms. Reno. I am not concluded if you have further questions of me, sir.

Mr. Conyers. Well, I consider that a nonresponsive answer.

Ms. Reno. You did not ask me a question, sir. You asked me if I had any comments.

Mr. Conyers. And I consider those nonresponsive comments.

Ms. Reno. Do you have a question of me, sir?

Mr. Conyers. I have more questions of you than I will ever get time to ask you in this committee.

Ms. Reno. I will answer any questions, and I will come to your office....

SOURCE: Events Surrounding the Branch Davidian Cult Standoff in Waco, Texas: Hearing Before the Committee on the Judiciary, House of Representatives, 103d Congress, 1st Session, Serial No. 95, (Washington, D.C., 1995), pp. 13–15, 17, 20, 25–26.

UNIT 26

The Redemptive Imagination

UNIT SUMMARY

In Unit 26 we look at the role of storytelling as a force in shaping historical writing.

ASSIGNMENTS

1. Before viewing Program 26, read this unit.

2. View Program 26, "The Redemptive Imagination."

3. Visit the Web site <http://www.learner.org/biographyofamerica>. Explore the exercises for Program 26.

LEARNING OBJECTIVES

Upon completing this unit, students should be able to:

1. Discuss the historian's role in bringing a subject to life.

2. Assess the ways novelists supplement the work of historians in their fictional accounts of actual events.

3. Consider whether history is a "crippled discipline" and explain this view.

PROGRAM GUIDE

Good historical writing embodies the craft of the storyteller. Historians use the power of our collective memory to write tales of the past. Professor Miller is joined by novelists Charles Johnson, Arthur Golden, and Esmeralda Santiago to discuss the intersection of history and story.

What is history? Professor Miller calls it "a crippled discipline," because, he says, historians can never get at the whole truth—records are lost, libraries burn. Nevertheless, the study of history gives people a sense of who they are, a link to their cultural sense of being. History places humans in touch with their past, and history is relevant to their future. Esmeralda Santiago, who wrote *America's Dream,* assures us that the struggles of immigrants are real: their lives are "not just a bunch of data and statistics." Charles Johnson, author of *Middle Passage*, encourages historians not to abandon storytelling. The stories writers tell reveal the deeper meaning of history, he says, by showing empathy with the subject. *A Biography of America* concludes with reflections by author Kurt Vonnegut on the power of the human imagination.

HISTORICAL OVERVIEW

The struggle for equality and freedom fills the pages of America's story. Historians must constantly revisit the struggle of American women, indigenous peoples, immigrants, Latinos, Asians, and blacks. The Spirit of 1776 proclaimed that humans are "endowed by their Creator with certain unalienable rights; that among these are life, liberty and the pursuit of happiness… and whenever any form of government becomes destructive to these ends, it is the right of the people to alter or abolish it… to effect their safety and happiness." Americans' efforts to achieve these ideals are the material historians use to make the story of the United States relevant to the people.

The struggle of African Americans for equality is a narrative that spans almost four hundred years of our national history. Blacks have sacrificed their lives in every war this nation has fought, and they have led the struggle to redeem America's soul. Authors like Alex Haley, Toni Morrison, Zora Neale Hurston, and others tell the story of that struggle. Their craft storytelling brings the history of our nation to life.

Good storytelling can shake a nation to its very foundation. President Lincoln told Harriet Beecher Stowe that her account of slavery in her novel *Uncle Tom's Cabin* had caused the Civil War. Lincoln deliberately exaggerated, but the book did force northerners to consider the evils of slavery, many for the first time. This is the power of empathy, and it captured the imagination of an entire nation.

How significant was the novelist's contribution to that defining moment in United States history? More than one hundred years after Gettysburg, Michael Shaara wrote *The Killer Angels*. It inspired several historians to a fresh interpretation of the Civil War. Filmmaker Ken Burns, who created the PBS series The Civil War, wrote that Shaara's book changed my life…I had never visited Gettysburg, knew almost nothing about that battle before I read the book, but here it all came alive…I wept. No book, novel or nonfiction, had ever done that to me before." It was the Gettysburg battle that offered what Lincoln described as a fresh start for "a new birth of freedom—and that government of the people, by the people, for the people, shall not perish from earth." Abraham Lincoln, too, knew how to turn a good phrase and tell a good story.

More than 200,000 people descended on the nation's capitol in 1963 for the historic March on Washington for Jobs and Freedom. Equality would remain elusive for millions of citizens, but on that day Americans listened to a dreamer who spoke of redemption. Dr. Martin Luther King, Jr., concluded his speech with a powerful description of his dream for the nation's future:

> "I say to you today my friends—so even though we face the difficulties of today and tomorrow, I still have a dream. It is a dream deeply rooted in the American dream. I have a dream that one day this nation will rise up and live out the true meaning of its creed: "We hold these truths to be self-evident, that all men are created equal."…I have a dream that my four little children will one day live in a nation where they will not be judged by the color of their skin but by the content of their character…I have a dream today…I have a dream that one day every valley shall be exalted, and every hill and mountain shall be made low, the rough places will be made plain, and the crooked places will be made straight, and the glory of the Lord shall be revealed and all flesh shall see it together…This will be the day, this will be the day when all of God's children will be able to sing with new meaning "My country 'tis of thee, sweet land of liberty, of thee I sing. Land where my father's died, land of the the Pilgrim's pride, from every mountainside, let freedom ring!"…Let freedom ring. And when this happens, and when we allow freedom ring—when we let it ring from every village and every hamlet, from every state and every city, we will be able to speed up that day when all of God's children—black men and white men, Jew and Gentiles, Protestants and Catholics—will be able to join hands and sing in the words of the old Negro spiritual: "Free at last! Free at last! Thank God Almighty, we are free at last!"

On the night of Dr. King's death, presidential candidate Robert Kennedy spoke to a crowd of shocked supporters. King had dedicated his life to love and to justice for his fellowman and died for his efforts, Kennedy said. "Let us dedicate ourselves to what the Greeks wrote so many years ago: to tame the savageness of man and to make gentle the life of this world. Let us dedicate ourselves to that, and say a prayer for our country, and for our people."

The United States has just entered a new century. The eloquent words of Dr. King and Robert Kennedy remind the nation that our work remains unfinished.

This program examines the historian's craft and the importance of good storytelling in capturing history. Kurt Vonnegut ends our series with thoughts on the human imagination. The wisest histories of every sort, he says, speak of the human imagination. "Our artists have again and again done what so many mothers have asked their gifted children, or even ordinary children, to do if they can: Make this a better world than it was before you got here." Perhaps the best that history can do for the human race is tell us who we are, where we have been, and where we can go, if we are willing to use the history of our imaginations and dream.

ESSAY QUESTIONS

1. What is the task of the historian in the classroom? What does the historian's craft reveal about the nature of history?

2. Imagine that the local school board is considering eliminating history from the curriculum. Your essay will try to persuade the board one way or the other. What position will you argue and why?

3. Name the three events, in your opinion, in United States history that most fundamentally reveal the nation's paramount struggle for equality. Explain your choices.

4. Do you agree that the study of history is essential to our humanity? Why or why not?

5. Is history a "crippled discipline"? How important is it to know *all* the truth of an event? Do you think the expression is a criticism or a warning? Explain.

PRIMARY SOURCE DOCUMENTS

The accounts of the actual participants are useful for understanding the motives and thoughts of historical characters.

1. *Declaration of Independence (1776)* **Thomas Jefferson**

Written by Thomas Jefferson, the Declaration marked the official separation of the thirteen colonies from the British Empire. Jefferson sought to justify America's actions to the world in his brief listing of Britain's crimes. Most of Jefferson's contemporaries focused on this list of grievances, but the Declaration's general political statements would cause a great deal of trouble for established elites as different groups struggled to extend its promise of freedom and equality to themselves. In the nineteenth century, leading conservatives from Rufus Choate to Stephen Douglas mocked and derided Jefferson's language, but Abraham Lincoln succeeded in convincing most Americans that the Declaration deserved to be considered one of the founding documents of this nation.

Questions to Consider

- What were the crimes of George III, and does he merit all the blame?

- Does the language of the Declaration still have resonance?

In Congress July 4, 1776
The Unanimous Declaration of the Thirteen United States of America

When in the Course of human events, it becomes necessary for one people to dissolve the political bands which have connected them with another, and to assume among the Powers of the earth, the separate and equal station to which the Laws of Nature and of Nature's God entitle them, a decent respect to the opinions of mankind requires that they should declare the causes which impel them to the separation.

We hold these truths to be self-evident, that all men are created equal, that they are endowed by their Creator with certain unalienable rights, that among these are Life, Liberty and the pursuit of Happiness. That to secure these rights, Governments are instituted among Men, deriving their just powers from the consent of the governed. That whenever any form of Government becomes destructive to these ends, it is the Right of the People to alter or to abolish it, and to institute a new Government, laying its foundation on such principles and organizing its powers in such form, as to them shall seem most likely to effect their Safety and Happiness. Prudence, indeed, will dictate that Governments long established should not be changed for light and transient causes; and accordingly all experience hath shown that mankind are more disposed to suffer, while evils are sufferable, than to right themselves by abolishing the forms to which they are accustomed. But when a long train of abuses and usurpations, pursuing invariably the same Object evinces a design to reduce them under absolute Despotism, it is their right, it is their duty, to throw off such Government, and to provide new Guards for their future security.—Such has been the patient sufferance of these Colonies; and such is now the necessity which constrains them to alter their former Systems of Government. The history of the present King of Great Britain is a history of repeated injuries and usurpations, all having in direct object the establishment of an absolute Tyranny over these States. To prove this, let Facts be submitted to a candid world:

He has refused his Assent to Laws, the most wholesome and necessary for the public good.

He has forbidden his Governors to pass Laws of immediate and pressing importance, unless suspended in their operation till his Assent should be obtained; and when so suspended, he has utterly neglected to attend to them.

He has refused to pass other Laws for the accommodation of large districts of people, unless those people would relinquish the right of Representation in the Legislature, a right inestimable to them and formidable to tyrants only.

He has called together legislative bodies at places unusual, uncomfortable, and distant from the depository of their Public Records, for the sole purpose of fatiguing them into compliance with his measures.

He has dissolved Representative Houses repeatedly, for opposing with manly firmness his invasions on the rights of the people.

He has refused for a long time, after such dissolutions, to cause others to be elected; whereby the Legislative Powers, incapable of Annihilation, have returned to the People at large for their exercise; the State remaining in the mean time exposed to all the dangers of invasion from without, and convulsions within.

He has endeavored to prevent the population of these States; for that purpose obstructing the Laws of Naturalization of Foreigners; refusing to pass others to encourage their migration hither, and raising the conditions of new Appropriations of Lands.

He has obstructed the Administration of Justice, by refusing his Assent to Laws for establishing Judiciary Powers.

He has made Judges dependent on his Will alone, for the tenure of their offices, and the amount and payment of their salaries.

He has erected a multitude of New Offices, and sent hither swarms of Officers to harass our People, and eat out their substance.

He has kept among us, in times of peace, Standing Armies without the Consent of our legislature.

He has affected to render the Military independent of and superior to the Civil Power.

He has combined with others to subject us to a jurisdiction foreign to our constitution, and unacknowledged by our laws; giving his Assent to their acts of pretended legislation:

For quartering large bodies of armed troops among us:

For protecting them, by mock Trial, from Punishment for any Murders which they should commit on the Inhabitants of these States:

For cutting off our Trade with all parts of the world:

For imposing taxes on us without our Consent:

For depriving us in many cases, of the benefits of Trial by Jury:

For transporting us beyond Seas to be tried for pretended offenses:

For abolishing the free System of English laws in a neighboring Province, establishing therein an Arbitrary government, and enlarging its Boundaries so as to render it at once an example and fit instrument for introducing the same absolute rule into these Colonies:

For taking away our Charters, abolishing our most valuable Laws, and altering fundamentally the Forms of our Governments:

For suspending our own Legislature, and declaring themselves invested with Power to legislate for us in all cases whatsoever.

He has abdicated Government here, by declaring us out of his Protection and waging War against us.

He has plundered our seas, ravaged our Coasts, burnt our towns, and destroyed the lives of our people.

He is at this time transporting large armies of foreign mercenaries to complete the works of death, desolation and tyranny, already begun with circumstances of Cruelty and perfidy scarcely paralleled in the most barbarous ages, and totally unworthy the Head of a civilized nation.

He has constrained our fellow Citizens taken Captive on the high Seas to bear Arms against their Country, to become the executioners of their friends and Brethren, or to fall themselves by their Hands.

He has excited domestic insurrections amongst us, and has endeavored to bring on the inhabitants of our frontiers, the merciless Indian Savages, whose known rule of warfare, is undistinguished destruction of all ages, sexes and conditions.

In every stage of these Oppressions We have Petitioned for Redress in the most humble terms: Our repeated Petitions have been answered only by repeated injury. A Prince, whose character is thus marked by every act which may define a Tyrant, is unfit to be the ruler of a free People.

Nor have We been wanting in attention to our British brethren. We have warned them from time to time of attempts by their legislature to extend an unwarrantable jurisdiction over us. We have reminded them of the circumstances of our emigration and settlement here. We have appealed to their native justice and magnanimity, and we have conjured them by the ties of our common kindred to disavow these usurpations, which, would inevitably interrupt our connections and correspondence. They too have been deaf to the voice of justice and consanguinity. We must, therefore, acquiesce in the necessity, which denounces our Separation, and hold them, as we hold the rest of mankind, Enemies in War, in Peace Friends.

We, therefore, the Representatives of the United States of America, in General Congress Assembled, appealing to the Supreme Judge of the world for the rectitude of our intentions, do, in the Name, and by the Authority of the good People of these Colonies, solemnly publish and declare, That these United Colonies are, and of Right ought to be, Free and Independent States; that they are Absolved from all Allegiance to the British Crown, and that all political connection between them and the State of Great Britain is, and ought to be, totally dissolved; and that as Free and Independent States, they have full Power to levy War, conclude Peace, contract Alliances, establish Commerce, and to do all other Acts and Things which Independent States may of right do. And for the support of this Declaration, with a firm reliance on the Protection of Divine Providence, we mutually pledge to each other our Lives, our Fortunes and our sacred Honor.

John Hancock

SOURCE: Charles C. Tansill, ed., *Documents Illustrative of the Formation of the Union of the American States* (Washington, D.C., 1927), pp. 22–25.

2. *The Gettysburg Address (1863)* Abraham Lincoln

Justly celebrated as one of the greatest—and briefest—speeches in American history, Lincoln's Gettysburg Address was delivered at the commemoration of the battlefield cemetery. After the bloody Union triumph at Gettysburg, a special national commission sought to make a memorial of the battlefield. On November 19, 1863, Edward Everett, the prominent former governor and senator from Massachusetts, spoke for two hours on the soldiers' sacrifices and the cause of the Union. He was followed by President Lincoln, who finished his speech before many in the crowd of 15,000 were even aware that he had begun. Everett correctly perceived that his own speech would be forgotten, while Lincoln's would attain immortality.

Questions to Consider

- Why, according to Lincoln, are Americans fighting one another?
- What duty lies before those still alive?

Fourscore and seven years ago our fathers brought forth on this continent a new nation, conceived in liberty, and dedicated to the proposition that all men are created equal.

Now we are engaged in a great civil war, testing whether that nation, or any nation so conceived and so dedicated, can long endure. We are met on a great battle-field of that war. We have come to dedicate a portion of that field as a final resting-place for those who here gave their lives that that nation might live. It is altogether fitting and proper that we should do this.

But, in a larger sense, we cannot dedicate—we cannot consecrate—we cannot hallow—this ground. The brave men, living and dead, who struggled here, have consecrated it far above our poor power to add or detract. The world will little note nor long remember what we say here, but it can never forget what they did here. It is for us, the living, rather, to be dedicated here to the unfinished work which they who fought here have thus far so nobly advanced. It is rather for us to be here dedicated to the great task remaining before us—that from these honored dead we take increased devotion to that cause for which they gave the last full measure of devotion; that we here highly resolve that these dead shall not have died in vain; that this nation, under God, shall have a new birth of freedom; and that government of the people, by the people, for the people, shall not perish from the earth.

SOURCE: John G. Nicolay and John Hay, eds., *Complete Works of Abraham Lincoln* (New York, 1905), 9: pp. 209–210.